Screwing Mother Nature for Profit

"The challenges and crises facing the world today are signs that the planet is in the midst of an incredible evolutionary upheaval. In *Screwing Mother Nature for Profit*, Elaine Smitha provides a compendium of research, personal experiences and insights as to how we arrived at our current crossroads. This work invites readers to move beyond misperceived limitations so that we may create a more positive and viable future."

> **Bruce H. Lipton**, *Ph.D., cell biologist and bestselling author of*
> The Biology of Belief: Unleashing the Power of Consciousness, Matter and Miracles *and co-author of* Spontaneous Evolution: Our Positive Future (And A Way To Get There From Here)

"I found this book a truly clear and revealing statement of what Corporations are doing to the environment, and what they would keep doing unless there is a rapid growth in society's sense of responsibility."

> **Ervin Laszlo**, *Ph.D., author of 85 books, founder/president of Club of Budapest, the World Wisdom Council and General Evolution Research think-tanks, WorldShift Network, a fellow of the World Academy of Arts and Sciences.*

"Our scientific paradigm is shifting from the primacy of consciousness... we are not separate from our environment. All serious social thinkers should be inspired to read her book."

> **Amit Goswami**, *Ph.D., theoretical nuclear physicist and author of* The Self-Aware Universe, God is not Dead, *and* Creative Evolution. *Included in the film* What The Bleep Do We Know!

"Elaine Smitha questions the viability of our current economic model to investigate an integration of biology and business...a new system that can help guide the evolution of humankind, where quality of life triumphs."

> **Bruce LaRue**, *Ph.D., president of Applied Development Services, co-author of* Leading Organisations from the Inside Out

"This is a book about our time, for our time, and for those to whom it matters!"

Eldon Taylor, *Ph.D., co-founder of Progressive Awareness Research, Inc.*

"Smitha's book offers a veritable treasure trove of new ideas for corporate leaders."

Larry Lange, *author, speaker and business journalist including reporting for* CNET, CMP Media *and* Forbes

"Magnificently, Elaine Smitha envisions a time when the entrepreneurial spirit of private enterprise is cultivated from the principles of New Biology. With application of this cellular theory, our businesses may be viewed as living organisms that are capable of quantum change. Thought-provoking, enlightening and entertaining."

Jayme Hirashiki, *president, Ziquin Educational Group LLC*

"Elaine Smitha's book is an impassioned yet well-reasoned book that cries for a redefinition of the concept of a 'corporation'. The concept must and should include wider considerations beyond maximizing shareholder value in strictly monetary terms. It is a call for incorporating a longer term and wider view of what 'shareholder value' means; value that incorporates responsibility for the shareholders' other vested interests that corporations affect almost always adversely. Not to be restrictive in her prescriptions she puts equal emphasis on the responsibilities that shareholders must in turn execute…toward their own same broader vested interests; hopefully to secure a future worth having, not only for us but also for generations to come. The book is a good read. I recommend it."

Sesh Velamoor, *trustee, Foundation for the Future*

About the Author

Elaine Smitha is the perfect person to advance a unique approach to business as a living system. As author of the self-healing handbook *If You Make the Rules, How Come You're Not Boss? Minding Your Body's Business* (Hampton Roads, 2003), with foreword by Bruce H. Lipton, Ph.D., Smitha proposes that the biological imperative to sustain life on Planet Earth is the same for sustainable growth in business and personal performance.

Internationally recognized as a "rare media personality", Smitha is creator, producer and host of the cutting-edge television show *Evolving Ideas©*, reaching a million households weekly in local and syndicated markets, including PAX TV. Since 2005, Smitha's weekly interviews are heard on Dr. Gary Null's Progressive Radio Network on the Internet. Amit Goswami, Ervin Laszlo, Richard Bach, Bruce Lipton, Richard Bach, Deepak Chopra, Larry Dossey, Fred Alan Wolf and Jack Canfield are among the guests who have appeared on her show.

Smitha is a multi-talented professional speaker for businesses, universities, colleges and prestigious organizations, including the World Future Society, the Creative Problem Solving Institute and the International Conference on Global Security, Safety & Sustainability held at the University of East London. She affiliated with the National Speakers Association, the Golden Voice and International Platform Speakers in 1983, and since 2008 she has been on the advisory board of Ziquin Inc. In 1993, she founded the Webworks lecture series to bring authors and researchers in progressive fields to public awareness.

In four decades as a businesswoman, communicator, artist and educator, Smitha has taught at every level of the education ladder, from first grade to college. As a craftsman, she exhibited and sold her original handcrafted designs at Elaine Smitha Fine Jewelry on Balboa Island in Newport Beach, California. She is also a private pilot.

Articles by or about Elaine Smitha have appeared in *Kosmos*, the *Los Angeles Times*, the Tacoma *News Tribune*, *Orange County Daily Pilot*, the *Orange County Register*, *Orange County Illustrated*, *New Times* and *The Olympian*. Smitha is listed in *Who's Who in American Art* and *World Who's Who of Women*. She lives in Olympia, Washington.

Also by Elaine Smitha

IF YOU MAKE THE RULES, HOW COME YOU'RE NOT BOSS?
Minding Your Body's Business

SCREWING MOTHER NATURE FOR PROFIT

HOW CORPORATIONS BETRAY OUR TRUST – AND WHY THE 'NEW BIOLOGY' OFFERS AN ETHICAL AND SUSTAINABLE FUTURE

ELAINE SMITHA

WATKINS PUBLISHING

LONDON

This edition first published in the UK and USA 2011 by
Watkins Publishing, Sixth Floor, Castle House,
75–76 Wells Street, London W1T 3QH

Design and typography copyright © Watkins Publishing 2011
Text copyright © Elaine Smitha 2011

1 3 5 7 9 10 8 6 4 2

Designed and typeset by Mark Bracey
Printed and bound in China

British Library Cataloguing-in-Publication Data Available
Library of Congress Cataloging-in-Publication Data Available

ISBN: 978-1-78028-018-9
www.watkinspublishing.co.uk

Distributed in the USA and Canada by Sterling Publishing Co., Inc.
387 Park Avenue South, New York, NY 10016-8810

For information about custom editions, special sales, premium and
corporate purchases, please contact Sterling Special Sales
Department at 800-805-5489 or specialsales@sterlingpub.com

Acknowledgements

Without the Timberland Library Reference Librarians, especially Judy Sherrill and Rosemary Connor at the Lacey, Washington branch, the research process for this book could have been more tedious. Their dedicated interest and tenacity to delve deep and wide in catalogues and inventories assisted in unveiling truths and certainly deserve my praise.

Larry Lange, New York author, journalist, musician and composer, who made himself available for early-morning phone calls to discuss strategies, whose reassurance supported me in the development of this book, and who continues to cheer me on, is the kind of friend everyone needs in their corner. I appreciate the input from early readers who were brave enough to read my rough beginnings: Jeanette Susor, Karyn Lindberg, Linda Bremer, especially Susan Einhorn for her insights and astute organizational suggestions.

To Randy Rogers for his kind computer assistance in developing my idea for this book's graphical cover and for his computer savvy when things didn't quite work right.

To Robert Mueller and Jeff Rische in the development of the book's title, suffering through the many variations as a feedback loop, but whose sense of humor was always welcome. Janet Zibell's suggestions and feedback of the cover design helped assuage the uncertainty, as well.

To David Zibell for his skill, kindness and generosity in making sure I had reliable transportation and in so many other ways supporting my efforts and cheering me on. I cannot thank you enough.

To my longtime friend Pavel Mikolowski, who took me under his wing to recommend my work to Susan Mears, Literary Agent, who from the start could see the potential in this book and encouraged me in so many ways, Thank you, Thank you.

It has been a pleasure to work with publisher Michael Mann, as well as Penny Stopa, of Watkins Publishing. Anne Barthel, editor, who took time to laugh with me when words got tangled in meaning and assured me that the process was a learning experience for her as well. She is the best.

Contents

Foreword

One of the ancient tribes in North America, the Hopi, is still culturally intact, with its oral tradition and ceremonial cycle dating back thousands of years. Many other tribes make pilgrimages to Hopi to talk to the elders about the past and the future. Elaine Smitha, too, references the Hopi in this important book. There is a reason many of us draw upon the Hopi as we ponder what to do to get corporations and the economy in sync with nature's ways.

My time with the Hopi started in 1973 when a friend and I left Sausalito, California, around midnight one evening. Driving all night, we got to the south rim of the Grand Canyon the next day around sunset, then drove further east into the Hopi Nation. On a dirt road just outside Old Oraibi, Arizona, we came to a sign that said something like "Warning, white man! Because you cannot obey your own laws, let alone ours, you are hereby prohibited from entering this village." The night was upon us, so we camped along the road. The Milky Way was stellar and we could hear the drumbeat from a ceremony going on in this forbidden village.

The next day, we went to the nearby village of Kyakotsmovi and knocked on the door of Thomas Banyacya's traditional Hopi house. Thomas, I was to learn, was from the Coyote Clan. Coyotes are barkers. His role was one of spreading the word about the Hopi relationship with nature and their message of peace. His wife, Fermina Banyacya, answered the door. I was 23 years old and spellbound by her singsong voice, her beauty, and what she had to say about nature and future and purpose. She invited us in, and to this day she remains a friend. From Fermina, Thomas, and many other Hopi I came to a deeper understanding of what counts in life.

I lived among the Hopi for the next ten years. I learned many lessons from them, including that the laws of nature are final. Natural laws will prevail regardless of man-made laws or governments or the drive for corporate profit. When we disturb the cycles of nature by interfering with the natural elements, changing or destroying species of life, the consequences may be immediate, or they may fall upon our children or our children's children— but we will suffer and pay for our mistakes.

There is a Hopi story that made a deep impression on me, about their key symbol of the Circle and the Cross. The circle represents the cycles of nature and the holism of the planet. The cross within the circle represents our ability to divide and rearrange things: engineering, technology, and the economy. If technology and the economy are within the cycles of nature, then everything is okay. That is what appropriate technology and the green economy are all about.

It was in the 1500s that the Hopi saw the first conquistadores marching up from Mexico. They were anxious to see what was the symbol of these newcomers' society. However, when the Hopi saw the "distinguished visitors" carrying the cross with no circle, there was deep concern. This culture had lost touch with the cycles of nature. The Hopi thought they might be in for a bad time. That turned out to be the case.

Out on Hopi lands, the circle-and-cross image is part of a sandstone petroglyph they call Prophecy Rock. On it are three circles that represent great earthshaking events. Some think they could be *three* tragic world wars. Fortunately for us, there is a line between World War II and World War III that represents an opportunity to chart a better course. We can help bring the cross back within the circle, in which case the future is pictured by healthy corn plants. Otherwise we will experience a chaotic future, pictured by lightning strikes. The window of opportunity is upon us now.

In this book, Elaine Smitha asks us to rethink the nature of businesses and the economy. She asks us to ponder our life's work and make some responsible decisions. Can we rally to the task in time? Can we rally on a scale commensurate with the problem and the urgency? The answer lies in what you can do to shoulder your responsibility, remembering that it is not enough to just care. Remembering, as well, it is not about profiteering, but spreading love—love for Mother Nature and love for her myriad creatures. There is real joy in pursuing what is right for nature and our future. I see how the earth could be in 20, 100, or 500 years and it is beautiful.

Together we can learn from the Hopi and from Elaine Smitha. Together we can become advocates recapturing the power of public governance and harness it to build the green economy in ways Elaine suggests. Together we can become great storytellers, describing the future Elaine writes about so clearly. Together we will fight for a good outcome—doing what we can and must to build a better world.

Randy Hayes, Founder, Rainforest Action Network

CHAPTER ONE

PLANETARY CRISIS
Gambling the Future

Nearly 30 years ago, on a mission to touch the living history of mankind's evolution, I visited Papua New Guinea, a culture more than ten thousand years old, well behind modern civilization. It remains one of the most fascinating of my journeys around the world. True, the men still wore penis gourds for protection from the deep bush environment, as well as "ass grass" cuttings from local shrubbery. Yet to survive in a jungle so dense that planes downed during World War II have yet to be found requires ingenuity, resourcefulness, and a community spirit.

When the war ended, the U.S. abandoned its temporary airfield there, leaving behind all manner of hardware that was quickly reconnoitered by the country's inhabitants for use in their villages. Most useful were huge water drums to catch some of the 150 inches of rainfall each year to store for off-season. Corrugated sheet metal fencing replaced native grass huts with arable thatched roofs which natives replaced every two years. While the metal roofing was waterproof, it made living in the grass huts quite hot and noisy. Roofs, however, were not the only commercial corrupting influence on the virgin landscape by big corporations.

Today, Freeport-McMoRan, a copper and precious metal mining company at work in Papua New Guinea's highland rain forest, "pursues a virtually bottomless store of gold hidden inside."[1] As in all mining processes, extracting the earth's treasures produces waste, and waste needs disposal. It is rather like a dog digging into the ground for a buried goodie: a lot of debris is left in its wake. In this case, limestone sludge is dumped down steep inclines to rivers feeding into lowlands where tribesmen live on the banks, where most lowlanders depend upon fishing as part of their food supply. Where is the consciousness of Freeport management, investors and local government in this scenario? A billion tons of mine waste is being dumped directly into a jungle river system, destroying one of the world's last native environments, without any clear conservation methods put in place. A report made available to *The New York Times* by the Indonesian Environment Ministry makes clear that not only are rivers upstream now "unsuitable for aquatic life," but adjacent wetlands are also polluted.[2]

Cheating on the creator has consequences. With the world's largest reserves of gold, silver and copper still in the ground, Papua New Guinea's virgin landscape will continue to produce for 35 more years. If mining practices remain the same, the land will eventually be unfit for habitation, and one of the last remaining rain forests and primitive Neolithic cultures on the planet will have been destroyed.

It is understandable that some business ventures are risky. Lacking integrity and a cooperative spirit, governments, military and police find ways to coerce companies to cough up more money for protection. On the other hand, Freeport's lack of responsible action in not appropriating funds to handle mine wastes is costing a native environment its habitat. It is unconscionable. Living in a toxic dump caused by business malpractice and condoned by the government is not a model to which any person, business or country should aspire.

Screwing Mother Nature for Profit evolved out of just such seeming incongruities: wars for oil, General Motors killing the electric car, Monsanto and Syngenta genetically altering plant genes so farmers must forever purchase their seeds to survive. It seeks to show where business has gone wrong and show the way back to a path of sustainability and integrity. Above all, *Screwing Mother Nature for Profit* is a wake-up call for humanity to pay attention to what we're doing—to ourselves and to the environment—and to realize that money is merely a tool of exchange, not a life-giving entity. Greenbacks are not found in nature, yet the U.S. financial system, like other countries' monetary mediums of exchange, is based on the supposition that green is gold and you can take it to the bank.

Where for hundreds of years natives lived in the sheltered environment of Mother Earth in the Amazon forest, lush and abundant with wildlife, now corporations pilfer the plants that support all of life. While native peoples of the Amazon rainforest have long used different plants with healing properties to heal themselves, scientists now draw on these plant sources to derive new drugs for AIDS, diabetes, arthritis and Alzheimer's, as well as muscle relaxants, steroids and cancer drugs, of which only 25 percent are possible cures and only 1 percent have been tested. For centuries, the natural environment has supplied remedies for maladies useful to humanity, and today supplies 121 plant-derived prescription drugs.

Forests around the world, once verdant with trees 100 to 200 feet tall, have been leveled. Natives who live off the land are told that they can plant seeds to grow their own food, but only if they use genetically modified seeds supplied by Monsanto and Syngenta, "terminator" seeds that do not replicate themselves beyond one season. In other areas, forests are cleared to build more homes and shopping malls. Native environments are being invaded, not by aliens from outside our solar system, but by big corporations right here on Planet Earth. Magnificent creatures of all kinds are disappearing with the help of poachers paid to capture them. Convinced of the benefit to be reaped from this activity, natives become party to the devastation, only later to realize their folly. Told they can plant seeds to feed their families, they till the soil, but have little success with the GMO seeds they have to buy. Now too late to restore the lush green forest with the natural herbs and medicinal plants they always used to heal themselves, natives have killed themselves while multinational corporations patent those plants, effectively controlling who lives and dies, for any infringement on their patent is punishable by law.

This is the reason for the success of the movie *Avatar*, James Cameron's hit about corporations exploiting the natural environment to increase profits and engaging the military-industrial complex to assist in their efforts. It struck a sensitive chord in the mind of viewers as it charted the exploitation journey in pursuit of the Unobtanium rock, defined by Wikipedia as "any extremely rare, costly or physically impossible material, or less commonly known device needed to fulfill a given design for a given application." Today, that description might even apply to oil.

In Washington State, where I live, nature thrives despite the loss of all the trees that have been cut down to build housing tracts and businesses, to make railroad ties for train tracks, while the excess lies at the waterfront awaiting the barges to haul it away to foreign countries like China, Japan and

Korea. When I returned to Washington State after some years in California, I noticed more trees cut down along highway corridors. I sought out the Highway Department director to ask why. Were they ignorant of the fact that trees bring rain to nourish the land and hold it together, as well as clean the air of pollutants? Further, I said, without the trees, you'll turn the beautiful Pacific Northwest into a desert like Southern California, where I once lived.

It didn't take too many years before the powers that be wised up to the fact that trees indeed are a natural treasure. Now, tree planting all over the Pacific Northwest is going on at a rapid pace. They finally realize that trees are not only beautiful, but beneficial for all the right reasons: trees absorb automobile and truck exhaust fumes to keep the air breathable, bring rain to feed the native environment, and in doing so make city streets and highways into natural treasures. From the redwood forest north into Canada, the lush environment provides a haven for wildlife, while running streams and magnificent views from Mt. Rainier invite humans to connect with the force of Mother Nature and to stand in awe of her beauty.

But corporations have a different view, and while our lush environment is green, it isn't money. The deforestation of the Amazon is cause for considerable alarm for reasons beyond the region: it changes the weather, endangers ecosystems and erodes the natural world of which we are all a part. Trees and their undercover bring rain to feed the land with moisture, and they provide habitats that ensure the continuity of life in its many manifestations.

The drive for money at the expense of Mother Nature is a sad purpose and a sorry model for any business, and it's often a death knell to responsible action. Altering the genetic pattern as in genetically modified seeds that kill the regenerative ability in seeds is poisoning the human organism and its future. Why are birth defects in humans more common now than ever before? Why are creatures that have lived on earth for centuries disappearing? We have only to look to the toxic chemical combos being irresponsibly dumped into our waterways to see the damage. Attempting to control Mother Nature with manmade chemical concoctions is damaging the very life of Life.

You know the story of the Boston Tea Party, in which a boatload of East India Company tea shipped from the British Isles to colonial merchants was dumped overboard in retaliation for taxation by the British parliament, which expected Britain to handsomely profit from the new continent.

Fast-forward through the centuries: attitudes about business success shifted from quality, service and responsibility to the acquisition of great sums of money, in some cases without regard for the impact on the environment or the people upon whose labor companies depend. This tenacious pursuit of wealth, achieved at the expense of workers' families and the natural world with potentially devastating effects, has had the same voracious drive as that of the person who is starving.

The comparison is apt: the growth of business as an institution led to consortiums called corporations gaining the legal status of a "living person" in 1886. How could a piece of legislation written on a sheet of paper possibly be interpreted as creating a living person? The question still confounds the thoughtful individual, who sees the ruling as a manipulated shield designed to favor the wealthy. In any case, according to court documents, there was no argument when the U.S. Supreme Court decided that a private corporation is a person and entitled to the legal rights and protections the Constitution affords to any person under the Fourteenth Amendment.

The Corporation's primer says: spread the gospel of consumerism to every corner of the world to assure continued profitability. As a privileged business entity, it functions seemingly without controls that could be set in place through legislation to constrain its abilities to plunder, while earmarks make loopholes for representatives in government to jump through in order to favor corporations with unfair advantage, such as laws that enable them to evade taxes.

Most every day, news agencies report Corporation's intrusions into the affairs of Mother Nature: corrupting the lifeblood of the environment, aiding and abetting land grabs, polluting the air and water, while our food supply is adversely affected by manmade chemicals and misguided farm and feed practices. Pharmaceutical drugs and specialized health care, while beneficial to some, effectively make the population dependent on doctors for everything from pimples to senility, obviating common sense. The United States is rapidly becoming the sickest country in the world, more addicted to prescription drugs than those sold on the street, while efforts to decriminalize marijuana, which would help reduce the need for prescription drugs, lie fallow in the U.S. Congress. Humans make up only a small part of Mother Nature's vast library of creations, but their institutions presume to exercise legal authority over all of nature and all expressions of life. How in the world did this happen?

My curiosity was piqued when business friends living in Mill Valley, CA, phoned, insisting I see a film titled *The Corporation*. This documentary, based on the book *The Corporation: The Pathological Pursuit of Profit and Power* by Canadian attorney Joel Bakan, went straight to the heart of my inquiry as I viewed it and the trailers several times over the weeks that followed. In it, a chorus of voices—CEOs, whistleblowers, gurus, spies—talked about how the modern business corporation had come to exercise such power over our lives. "Corporations are artificial creations," the activist and historian Howard Zinn said bluntly. "You might say they're monsters trying to devour as much profit as possible at anyone's expense." Michael Moore put it another way: "I think of a whale. A gentle, big fish, which could swallow you in an instant." It was shocking to hear corporate executives in live interviews unabashedly admitting to policies and practices that put the bottom line ahead of any other goal, regardless of the damage they might do to anyone or anything involved.

I sought to understand how Corporation's pernicious attacks on the innate intelligence of Mother Nature, with her gifts of regeneration could possibly be mistaken for legitimate tools of the trade. Some humans insult Mother Nature by thinking she is unaware of the misdeeds perpetrated against her. How silly can we be?

Over the next three years, my journey coursed through many halls of inquiry, turning up facts of irresponsible behavior unbecoming to humans in general and business in particular. It took over my life, absorbed as I was in the mission of discovery. I'd awaken some mornings at 3 a.m., nudged to get up and write about my research, sometimes until noon—some days unable to stop for 12 hours, so important was the issue. The drive for insights and examples charged my engine of intention.

Surely, a few corporations are doing some good in the world, I thought, as I hunted for redeeming values to offset the damage being done by some multinationals whose vision of success is focused solely on the amount of money to be made. Sadly, I came away disappointed as I found one corporation after another vandalizing pristine forests, ravaging sacred lands and exploiting innocent life. Those scarred landscapes sucked of their resources leave voids felt in neighboring communities and beyond. How *do* we live in harmony with each other and with Mother Nature? It's the challenge of the 21st century.

Clearly, the United States as a nation has taken a wrong turn. I suggest that one reason is that the pharmaceutical industry moved the markers, and another is that war and unrelenting fear have gripped the U.S. since September 11, 2001. In addition, globalization is bringing rapid, and often disturbing, change on many fronts. Thanks to the World Trade Organization, resources and labor, once the strength of the U.S. economy, are now farmed out to Third World countries at lower wages to increase corporate profits. As a result, the U.S. is losing its manufacturing sectors and falling behind in technology, while workers' ability to dependably support themselves is becoming problematic. The economic environment's downturn in 2008 and the dramatic shift from high-quality American manufacturing to sweatshops in underdeveloped countries is cause for alarm, especially when we learn that employees are treated as chattels, paid very low wages—some as low as 43 cents an hour—and crammed into squalid living quarters where women become targets for sexual abuse. *The New York Times* reported in 1995 how the U.S. government promoted and U.S. taxpayers financed Free Trade Zones that allowed sweatshops in Central America and the Caribbean to flourish. In China, audits attempt to track the treatment of workers, but many factories keep a double set of books to avoid discovery and pressure workers to lie about conditions.[3]

Globally, meanwhile, multinational companies feed the frenzy with executive pay, stock options, elaborate severance packages, private jets and a plethora of other perks to create an environmental debacle for which greed is largely responsible. The U.S. economy has serious problems, a reflection of troubling times. In 2008, when the price of oil reached record highs and gasoline in the U.S. rose to over $4.00 a gallon, not only were consumers affected, but also related industries and state budgets that rely on gas tax revenue to keep up their roads.

Meanwhile, some corporations thrive at the expense of the public, encumbering the public with easy credit and high interest rates. They bait an attractive trap to lure the hungry to taste the good life espoused in TV shows and movies about the rich and famous, while some lenders and loan sharks unscrupulously stiff borrowers, then pat themselves on the back and laugh all the way to Wall Street.

Intent on increasing market share, and presuming itself infallible, the Corporation pursues its profit goals at the expense of fair practices. Exploitive wars offer other avenues of acquisition, as do corporate takeovers, where people and countries with natural resources struggle for place, identity and survival. The drive to be king of the hill for the status it brings beckons the power-hungry, whose insatiable appetite for wealth is bent on the oppressive control of people, places and things, while the truth remains undigested in the bowels of business to protect stock portfolios. With some corporations' awkward posturing they look more and more like lumbering dinosaurs with bloated bodies and too small brains that see the world through myopic vision while their unwieldy management styles desecrate seas and lands and the air they, too, must breathe. While their heads are in the clouds of lofty glass-walled offices high above the antlike brigade of workers below, they trample everything alive under the weight of their decisions, destroying life, creatures and the very earth upon which they tread.

Naturally, some companies will reinvent themselves to meet 21st-century challenges. For others, greed and competitive stomping, lies and shady truths with a price tag attached, will become harder to conceal behind intentions that purposely delude. As the world gets smaller through the Internet, giants of commerce lose some of their shadowy shelter and their misdeeds are not so easily secreted away. As more corruption is revealed behind the pretense of legitimacy on the wild frontiers of corporate manipulation, the need for oversight becomes more and more apparent. History books are filled with stories about the conqueror and the conquered, about devastating practices that have undermined human values for centuries. Have we learned nothing? Are we destined to ignorantly repeat the oppressive past again and yet again?

The high school I attended in Chicago had a diverse ethnic student body. There were no fights, no competitive comeuppance. We knew we were there to get an education to make our lives meaningful and ourselves able to function in the world outside school doors. It was a great melting pot of humanity, and we cheered the diversity, though that was not a word then in popular use. When we think about the amount of energy expended in abusive competition, with its inhumane efforts to control life for a price, we also see the urgency of giving *people* a new way to survive the future, for we cannot compete in a world where there are no more corners in which to hide. It is cooperate now or perish.

Conflicting beliefs are all that separate the human family. Many people wonder why we can't all get along. There is enough to go around when everyone works together for the good of the whole, for the world is now our neighborhood. Why can't everyone have a place to live and enough food to eat and participate in a world of diverse ideas safely and freely?

The more fear is imposed on Earth's population, the body politic, the more stress and the more sickness we suffer. As we go on, I'll explain why this is so and how physiological responses to emotional disturbances can most often be traced to stress. I'll propose ways to help lower health-care costs and improve the quality of life, because it is time to turn the spigot down on money flowing to a drug industry out of control and to adopt a sustainable approach to healing the world, for the sake of both humanity and the environment. I'll examine in more depth the concept of the corporation as a living person: from it, we can draw strategies and solutions that work with the intelligence of living systems. By linking business to biology, using Mother Nature's own "business model" of cooperative competition and conscious awareness, we can derive a new form of responsible, sustainable leadership.

As quantum physicists assure us, love is the healer, while fear only breeds more fear and its accompanying contempt. To attain a higher level of human achievement, love your neighbors as you love yourself. Respect the differences, for variety is the spice of life. The prospect is good that with an understanding of the biological correlation between the race for money and the physical, emotional and psychological damage that results, we can shift our perception for the good of business, the people of this country and life throughout the world.

CHAPTER TWO

PAY-UPS AND PAYOFFS
Collusion and Collisions

In 2005 Jack Abramoff, an overzealous corporate lobbyist during the George W. Bush administration, was caught with his hand in the cookie jar one too many times. An indulgence may feel good, but done repeatedly, it can shred your world when exposed. While not directly connected to the stock market, trading trips and gifts to influence votes that favor special interests may be even worse. This sneaky behavior affects the whole country, if not the world, as well as individuals' lives, in ways that may not always be obvious. This is a huge problem for big business.

Can companies be ethical, caring and still be successful? You and I know that they can be! But as the disturbing film *The Corporation* shocks viewers with the degree of intentional malfeasance and deception big business is and has been engaged in for profit, albeit legally, it also exposes how some corporations have conspired to beat the system. Since 1886, as we saw in chapter 1, corporations have enjoyed the legal identity of a living "person", a rather silly notion if anybody bothers to ask. This provocative film puts the corporation on the psychiatrist's couch to ask, "What kind of person is this? What drives it?" Many of us might come up with the same answer as does the film: "self-interest", pure and simple self-interest. It is rather like a vulture gorging his stomach on a fresh kill. If you wonder who created this legal entity, and for what reason, recall that the first corporation is traced back to the East India Company and their privatized trade routes. Historians have kept alive for all remembrance the Boston Tea Party, which was all about the corporation and unfair taxes. Now, these "persons" have a stranglehold on our lives as they manipulate our minds to lure us into their lair.

Dirty Work Afoot

Another timely film, the revealing true story *Erin Brockovich*, exposes criminal practices in the Pacific Gas & Electric Company's gas compressor station in Hinkley, California. Brockovich, while working in a law office, discovers medical records in a real estate file where none ought to be found. With her curiosity piqued, she questions the connection between real estate and medical records. Normally, medical records belong in doctors' offices. What are they doing in a real estate file? She asks permission to pursue this anomaly, though not part of her job description, and her boss agrees. Brockovich begins to ask hard questions and learns that people and domestic animals in the high desert community had become sick from drinking local groundwater.

When PG&E's pollution is reported to the government, scared company officials, caught in their deception, begin buying up all affected properties. They then bulldoze 75 percent of the structures, reporting vandalism as the cause. The ensuing scandal reveals that PG&E knowingly endangered the lives of local residents by dumping toxic chromium-6, a known carcinogen, as early as 1965. Not only was the water poisoned, the surrounding land was a toxic dump. The plaintiffs' landmark case was finally settled in 1994 for $333 million: proof that one person can make a difference.

PG&E was circumventing the laws—and causing wholesale chemical poisoning—to cut operating costs to satisfy stockholders and their bottom-line demands. How can you trust companies who cheat on their neighbors and customers?[1]

The Freeport-McMoRan mining company in Papua New Guinea has been breaching environmental laws regarding hazardous waste for well over a decade. The company still lacks a government permit to dispose of the mine's waste. How must shareholders feel about profits earned at the expense of a culture, the environment and our natural resources? I think it would be hard to sleep nights knowing your investment was poisoning what had been one of the world's last remaining untouched landscapes and populations.

Anyone reading about the Freeport situation will find abuses of power and egregious examples of greed. To secure the area, $20 million has been paid to individuals in upper echelons of the military and the police for security, payments interpreted by some as bribes. The politically induced padding of palms for personal gain continues to raise eyebrows. Sticky fingers are in most every available pot, and that is not all that's going on. Increasing tensions between the Indonesian government, the military, the Environmental Ministry and Freeport-McMoRan itself are evident. To operate an American mining company on foreign soil can be testing, especially when proper disposal of toxic waste and tailings related to the project lack oversight.

Unfortunately, there has also been tragic loss of life: 160 were killed between 1975 and 1997. Rioters destroyed Freeport's equipment and ransacked their offices to the tune of $3 million; hence the $20 million in protection bribes. No wonder business on foreign soil is so challenging.

Resource Mining

As a GIA Graduate Gemologist and Master Goldsmith/Silversmith, I can appreciate the wealth and revenues associated with the project, though I doubt customers can appreciate the efforts made by mining companies to extract precious metals and gemstones. In Afghanistan, for instance, gem-hunting in the barren mountains often requires the use of dynamite to extract valuable emeralds, rubies and lapis lazuli, among other stones. Before dynamite, natives used picks and shovels, or an earthquake or landslide could expose previously hidden treasures.

Copper, with its accompanying lead, silver and gold, is a combination of attractive ores formed in veins, unlike alluvial gold and silver found in mountain streams by adventurous miners panning. Hydrothermal fluids generated within the earth are trapped in cracks where silver and other minerals solidify into vein deposits. Silver is a co-product of copper, lead, zinc and, to a lesser extent, gold, though only gold and silver are noble metals used in electronics, on airplane windows, and for making coins and fine jewelry. Copper has a lot of uses. Smelting it with silver and gold strengthens its bond, while leaving it malleable. Some homes have copper water pipes. On extended use, corrosion from salts attack lead-soldered joints and vulnerable hard bends, leaching copper's telltale greenish residue, weakening the bond and causing leaks. Everything has an action and reaction.

Gemstones form in the same general way as metals. Their color results from the environmental influence of neighboring minerals, blending in the fluid state under earth's pressure, precipitating into veins to crystallize where it is mined.

Until recently, our material world has come from natural recyclables. All the metals producing our gadgets, cars and airplanes have come from earth's geologic resources. It is mind-boggling when you really think about it. The trouble is that plastics now replace many of these metals and cannot be recycled. As a result, landfills across the country are running out of space. Of course, these plastic products can be buried, but because they are not natural, they do not deteriorate or biodegrade for at least 1,000 years. With the advent of electronic equipment such as computers and monitors containing toxic metals, it is even worse.

A recyclable product is often better than one that continues to be a problem when worn out or too broken to fix. Atomic energy, with its by-products that we can neither recycle nor destroy, is also a huge problem. Ramifications mount as spent fuel rods sit in the ground waiting to go nowhere. The danger of radiation threatens populations with more downside than up, violating Mother Nature's contract to "do no harm".

The Good, the Bad and the Ugly

Though much is going on in the world of business that is upsetting and disconcerting, there are also worthwhile endeavors. Perhaps one of the most exciting is the remediation of toxic lands by chemical companies and government agencies in a community effort to stimulate tax revenues through urban renewal. Chemicals spilled or left unattended to dissipate in the dirt are finally recognized as persistent dangers. It is as though Mother Nature whispered in the ears of city planners and industry leaders that she could no longer tolerate humans' abuse. She accepts apologies, but money cannot buy her favor. It is action that gets her attention. Earth's membrane, as we will see, is sensitive to changing environmental signals in the field of quantum energy. She knows her inhabitants' thoughts and listens attentively to industry winds of change. It is consciousness that bends her ear with signals of alarm.

Yet toxins persist in some industries affecting workers without adequate protection. We have only to look at the asbestos industry. One of its disastrous byproducts is mesothelioma, a cancerous disease of the lungs that comes from inhaling dust of degrading asbestos particles. At the time asbestos was in wide use, no one gave much thought to the dust-covered clothes of pipe fitters, insulation installers and building tradesmen in factories, shipyards and mines. But the white powder carried home on workers' clothes was the same asbestos packed around heating systems in houses, offices and schools, dust that carried a deadly price, even for the companies producing it. Asbestos is now banned despite much legal battle in the courts.[2]

Industries may not always be aware of the lethal legacy they leave behind; however, awareness is heightening and we see more responsible choices as a result. Companies, like DuPont, accepting the challenge to help in the cleanup are deriving much benefit from their actions. Just as children are taught to clean up after themselves, industry is hearing the clarion call.

The largest settlement for toxic substances used in food preparation was made by DuPont for C8, the chemical combo perfluorooctanoic acid or PFOA, commonly known as Teflon. While Teflon was once thought the answer to every cook's prayer, the fluoride and ethylene nonstick application on cookware turned out to leach into food when heated. Exposure to Teflon has been linked to cancer, though not admitted by DuPont. Even the toxic fumes are sickening.

The class-action suit brought by Ohio and West Virginia residents in 2001 drew a settlement of $107.8 million. But DuPont continues to manufacture the product, denying any wrongdoing—even refusing to admit any wrongdoing when the C8 substance was absorbed by one pregnant worker at the Washington Works plant and transmitted to her fetus through the mother's blood stream by crossing the placental barrier. According to CBS News, "widespread contamination" was found near the plant and never reported to the EPA. Despite the bad press and huge settlement, DuPont continues to sell its product.[3]

As you can see, every action does have a reaction, a result, a consequence, whether in physics, in chemistry or in perceptions of the environment. Biology and business have much in common. Both must be aware to survive. Fortunately, nature is forgiving, adapting to changing environments as a matter of course. Would that business, and humans, behaved more like her.

With living systems responsive to environmental conditions, the intelligence of the natural order will continue. Living systems are orderly: a set of integrated interactions with the ability to regenerate plants on barren land, given the right environment. Mother Nature *knows her business*. She will recover when conditions are right, as did Israel in reclaiming the desert to grow food. Some species continue to propagate in lands with deficient nutrients, deserts with no water or arable land to grow food, as in the Sudan. Business will grow, too, when the right products, the right conditions, the right consciousness and responsive feedback system for self-monitoring are in place.

Often fresh perspectives, especially those focused on a sustainable environment that benefits everyone, are needed to spur growth; the same can be said for personal development. Science is unrelenting in its quest to learn something new about life and its versatile manifestations, about what does or does not work. Discovery is all about making known the unknown.

As seen in the Freeport mining operation, the drive to extract metals from the environment where they form is an expensive operation that shareholders hope to capitalize on when the ores are refined. The downside is that these operations often leave a legacy of destruction in their wake. Without conscious awareness of the responsibilities companies accept on signing contracts, greed, collusion and power can circumvent laws laid down to assure a visible model of civility. The truth is, though, that all of humanity is in the same boat. We will sink or swim according to who is paddling.

Integrated Living Systems

While remote to North America, mining in Papua New Guinea affects the ecosystem by polluting the water that migrates to other lands, poisoning drinking water whose safety is already in question. Stripping the land and dumping wastes affects wildlife by transmitting disease to other species, and because there is no boundary to nature, this action affects everyone. It affects *you*, regardless of who you are and where you live.

In the chapters ahead, we examine fresh perspectives on competitive and cooperative business climates consistent with responsible action, along with the reasons why this is a must to survive the future.

Since the "competitive edge" relates to Darwin's "survival of the fittest", it is clear why beating the competition requires a dog-eat-dog attitude. Darwin also said if his theory did not prove out, that was irrelevant. He must have been hedging his bet, because there has never been a testable case to prove his point. It is possible to be fitter, but not fittest, which implies one species superior to all the rest. And who is to be the judge?

As we examine living systems, it is not surprising to find there is no person, animal or plant that is the "fittest". There is only "survival of the fit". To be fit means you live. To be unfit means you are left behind. In my own family, a brother was born without an anus, to live only a few hours. Once, circus sideshows capitalized on physical oddities that manifested as a result of incorrect genetic coding, thus giving those people a constructive way to earn a living while still being part of the human family.

As we know, not all of us are physically perfect. Most all of us have one quirk or another. Some folks have one leg shorter than the other, one eyebrow elevated higher, or a smile just a bit off-center. I am convinced there is no "perfect" human body. For myself, I recently learned I have a minimal connected palette under my tongue, a condition that leaves some people tongue-tied. Despite the label, I have overcome any limitation it might have posed and I do exceptionally well communicating as a presenter and talk-show host and producer.

Because the body is vulnerable, illness can strike or an accident can happen to reshape life's experience. Stephen Hawking and my good friend Luther Smith, whose diving accident left him a quadriplegic, are good examples. Like many, they have not let their disabilities deter them from living a meaningful life or contributing valued services.

Survival derives from the mind's will and drive to adapt and overcome, to aspire to greatness and to be acknowledged as part of the human family in a meaningful way. Many times, it is the "imperfection" itself that inspires you to go beyond perceived limitations to reach new heights. At least, it may be an instrument of compassion to remind you of your own vulnerability.

The human body is both vulnerable and malleable, and requires a watchful eye on intruders who would have their way with us. Not surprisingly, mankind's experiments with chemical pollutants, prescription drugs and genetic manipulations have fouled the perfected model. Historically, early tribes considered multiple births to be a freak of nature, bad luck. To vanquish the evil spirits, all but one newborn would be smashed against a tree. It was not that long ago in the civilized world that an abnormal baby was allowed to die. Today, they are saved by the miracle of medicine. As a result, a whole new industry of caregivers arose, reducing the able workforce and causing a strain on family resources.

Over the years, there have been multiple transitions in human development, with visions far exceeding perceptions of possibilities. This utility of creative invention is impressive and inspiring. The delivery of goods and services to the world's far shores is a global market today, though begun centuries ago with a carved-out log that allowed travel on water. Christopher Columbus, fueled by the challenge of discovery, capitalized on natural resources to profit Spain and himself. This is something akin to Arthur C. Clarke's vision of the universe and NASA's obsession with Martian terrain as the next planet to exploit when Earth's resources are depleted. From there it will be the Moon.

As long as there are new vistas to discover humankind will continue to make known the unknown. It is the creative juice feeding the intellect and the curious.

CHAPTER THREE

SURVIVAL OF THE FIT
Biology and Business

Botanist and invertebrate zoologist Jean Baptiste LaMarck's position on evolution predates Darwin's theory by 50 years. He said that diverse life forms developed in response to changing environmental conditions, with no grand plan for life's expression such as Darwin's determinism assumed. Behavior is not a legacy through birth, LaMarck said. While genetic tendencies are often touted as reason enough for behavior and disease, there is more to the story.

It is well documented how individual human cells respond to environmental signals. In research laboratories, scientists have learned that cells behave differently in different environments. Simply when the base solution in a petri dish is changed from acid to alkaline, cells in the solution change behavior. This is significant. Consider your physical body as a petri dish. Food can be acid or alkaline. Feelings can be acid or alkaline, loving or fearful. A change in emotion shifts energy. The sensitive body is keen to follow energetic signals, regardless of their quality. Cells always say "yes". The strict model of genetic propensity for disease and behavior is outdated, since it takes a signal from the environment to trigger behavior.

This means human cells are intelligent, *very, very intelligent.* Pharmaceutical companies' advertising would lead you to believe our cells are weak and defenseless, requiring the supervision of a professional. Thus you are encouraged to ask your doctor to write a prescription for the advertised cure-all that you may not even need. But contrary to conditioning by mass-market media, cells in your body are more intelligent than they've been given credit. You are fortunate to have a lot of control over your body, because that makes you boss, and everyone wants to be boss of their life. Just ask them.

I notice that there is no health-care-plan boss governing the birds. They have a lot of freedom, as do the fish and butterflies, and all of Mother Nature's creatures. Clearly, biology is fundamental to life in the same way conscious awareness is to the life of every business. All require awareness of the environment to function and survive. Natural systems are conscious. Cells are smart. They are aware of the environment because innate intelligence is built into the system. Your decisions about life are based upon your perception of incoming signals. This is not necessarily so when it comes to business and government, where so many people are involved in decision-making. But to communicate effectively and take appropriate action in response to environmental conditions, you *must* be aware.

Humans' footprint on Planet Earth has been heavy indeed. At one time, inhabitants cared for the land and nurtured it as it nurtured them, but now, without conscious awareness of their folly, humans act as spoilers. If we pay attention, the efficiency of biological intelligence gives us an alternative: a natural model for sustainability, of which responsible action by business and government is an inextricable part.

Business is like a body. It has its own innate intelligence. It thrives on praise and profits. It is not okay to countermand the system's intelligence for the sake of reporting profits on the balance sheet at the yearly stockholders' meeting. How did we ever sway so far from the path?

Consciousness and energy are twin factors in manifesting reality. How we think directs our response in any given circumstance. As experts conspire to control markets by imposing unrealistic expectations to expand the power of a few, and corporations seek favors as a measure of success, they place profits ahead of social and environmental concerns. But ignoring nature's organizational unity, and the intelligent order of life itself, places humanity in peril. Our irreverent policies and practices are beginning to catch up with us as a lack of awareness of integrated processes poisons our water, air and land.

Evidence of effluents irresponsibly dumped into our waterways is, indeed, disturbing. When oil tankers spill their cargo, irrefutable damage is done to wildlife, as well as Earth's food and water supply. Carbon-dioxide-emitting fuels thwart attempts to reform air-quality control. No corporation wants to admit guilt. Guilt is bad for business. Executive decisions are based on preserving the company's image, not on accepting responsibility for its damaging practices. Meanwhile, the environment and humanity pay the price.

The Body of Business

It is through conscious awareness that nature has survived millennia. In the earliest stages of evolution, when the environment changed, single-cell amoebae spontaneously evolved, banding together to increase awareness as multicellular units of perception. To cover all necessary functions, shared responsibilities were agreed upon by the collective: a good example of cells' innate intelligence. As a result, the human body is composed of trillions of multicellular units of perception. Individual cells contain organelles, small organs replicating the larger organs of the body. They are aware of local needs and respond accordingly to maintain harmony. Thus, conscious awareness is the key to survival.

Working together and sharing responsibilities for the good of the whole is the sound foundation of every business, as it is of every body. Like the body and its cellular collective, business bases its decisions on the input, processing and output of information. In biology, the cellular membrane is the interface between the inside and the outside. In business, the interface can take many forms. Information may be conveyed from outside to inside via hearsay, a phone call, a newspaper item or magazine article, a letter or email. Whatever the source, if it is important to the system it will move through the information pathway to have an effect. You may ask questions like:

- How does this relate to your business and your life?
- What is holding your business or life together?
- What is keeping you in your job?
- What keeps you from doing what you want when you want to do it?

Questions like these evoke a positive or negative response, a yes-or-no signal for the on/off switch to direct your path. Which door to open? You get to choose! Whichever one you do choose will manifest one version of possible outcomes. To put this in perspective, six billion physical bodies on Planet Earth are six billion antennae with collective human cells beyond counting, a body politic.

Generally, suffering is caused by confusion. Which way to go? How to express the pain? Only at death is there separation of mind and body. Until then, the mind and physical body are a collective cellular community of interested parties.

Business and biology share more than B as their first letter. Both are energetic systems grounded in organizational unity. Energetic systems monitor fluid environments to maintain their own efficiency and effectiveness, alert to threats challenging their existence. They rely on cooperation between all interested parties, using efficient feedback loops to report on conditions in the environment, internal and external alike. In this way, energetic systems work for the good of the whole, because they are conscious.

Here's how we can associate the body's organs with different aspects of business:

- Reproductive system (manufacturing)
- Respiratory system (breathing life into the business, enthusiasm, persistence)
- Digestive system (generating income, dealing with daily challenges, assimilating information)
- Excretory system (getting rid of outdated merchandise—what is no longer needed—as in cleaning out the closet or warehouse)
- Regenerative system (customer and employee relations, healing discord, hiring and restocking inventory, as well as developing new products)
- Circulatory system (marketing, sales and distribution, maintaining a continuum)
- Nervous system (maintaining the ebb and flow of harmony, alert to possible danger, sensitive to stress and attentive to trends, and handling bad press and dissent)

The cell's intelligence is at the membrane level—the cell's skin—not in the genes, as some would have us believe. This layer interfaces between the outside and the inside, where signals from the environment are interpreted by antennae called receptors. Like your skin, the membrane is similar to a three-layer sandwich that interacts with the inside environment and the outside environment at once, transmitting signals to organelles (small organs) where information is assessed and acted upon.

This efficient feedback is one of the most significant features of the human body's operating system. Tonsils, for example, function as an important component of the immune system. They take note of every substance crossing its path. If the substance is not known, directions are sent to the DNA to make a new gene. This is equivalent to installing a new program in a computer system. The program must interact with previous versions, assimilating changes to make it unique.

Larger systems, from families to small and large business ventures, share similar concerns and operate in a similar way, though the labels may differ. Large businesses have departments: administration, accounting, public relations, product development, manufacturing, sales and advertising, shipping, security.

There is an orderly sequence of operation in business, as in the body. Everything from automobiles to circuit boards uses the assembly-line process made famous by Henry Ford, which we'll examine in more depth later on. Even in sorting fresh fruits and vegetables, there is a system of conveyor belts in place to label the product, track the quantity for inventory control, and pack it into shipping crates for delivery. In health care, they have even adopted the conveyor-belt principle to manage the supply chain and assign responsibility for patient care.

Machines now do what mankind used to do by hand. Computers collate information once done on bulky labor-intensive data-input systems. This improvement has made it possible to quickly supply the needs of a civilized world, and has allowed the brain to develop beyond survival mode. It is marvelous what the inventive mind has created, all with thought.

Governments work in a similar manner, but are less efficient because of all the bureaucracy. Top-heavy management can also spoil the broth as special interests appease every appetite for profit without considering the flavor and quality of their responsibility to workers or constituency.

Business seeks to attract its customer; not everyone in the world, only those who are self-selected, or through fear or lack are manipulated to believe in a product. For example, insurance companies bet on you not needing their services. Those who buy insurance are hedging their bets by investing in protection. It is a savings plan of sorts. It comes to your rescue when you need it. Except there are limitations. When loss is too high or claims too frequent, the item once covered is cancelled. It becomes the profit/loss item on the financial report, the bottom line of anxiety or prosperity upon which the life of business depends. With hurricanes, tornadoes and tsunamis, fires and the resulting loss of life, limb and property, insurance companies indeed are in a risky business, but that's by choice. The odds are always in the insurance company's favor. That tells us a lot about our belief system.

Natural Intelligence

Living systems have natural intelligence with no needless functions. Organizational unity naturally conserves energy and sustains activity through efficient use of resources. Nature is really in charge. She has no plan to destroy herself any time soon. As the ultimate executive director of life's organic systems, Mother Nature assures us her business affairs are in order, thus insuring longevity at least for herself, unless genetic manipulation of seed supplies alters the trajectory.

Biology and business both require communication pathways to keep the flow of information moving and maintain efficient operations. An effective communication system stays efficient through daily interaction between staff and department heads. The health of your business above the bottom line, in its leadership, integrity, communication skills and progressive thinking, depends upon this energy exchange. The same compatibility standards hold for relationships, healthy bodies and natural environments.

How well you cooperate and adapt to environmental conditions is what makes you a winner, in business and in life. When ideas are implemented with agreement, harmony is preserved. A healthy environment is maintained. Bottom-line profits are assured all around. Everyone benefits.

Business, by nature, is both collaborative and competitive. Darwin's already parsed statement about the "survival of the fittest" has become the driving force behind aggressive top-dog management styles. But if only the "fittest" survived, who would there be to do the work? Rather, as we saw in the last chapter, it is *survival of the fit* in business as it is in life.

To be fit requires cooperating as a living system, efficiently collaborating as a model for community empowerment. As such, living systems are responsive to community needs, drawing on innate intelligence to process incoming and outgoing information. This in/out on/off and all-around sequence is ultimately what sustains life and all its functions. A shift in perceptual reality depends upon how rapidly signals can be transmitted through the brain's neural network to affect the input process and output of the fully functioning cellular community. Living systems cooperate and collaborate just as business and relationships are able to do, given the right environment.

If fear is a constant companion, growth is stunted and harmony is held at a distance. By understanding how consciousness and energy create reality, every individual, business and governmental body can prosper while increasing effectiveness. When there is happiness on the job and in your life, you are likely to enjoy good health, thus reducing dependency on outside forces like the health-care system, doctors and pharmaceutical drugs.

Though billions of research dollars are spent each year attempting to unlock Mother Nature's secrets, nature's inherent intelligence still has scientists baffled. Scientists still haven't learned what turns genes on and off, yet they're playing with them like Tinkertoys, not knowing the outcome. Corporations in genetic research dally with different gene combinations and assume results to be the focus of a new business venture. Investment is high with expectations of even higher returns on implementation—and all that's being done is corruption of the system for profit.

The Corporation Needs Analyzing

How a nation, a business and life itself survives lies in a cooperative alliance. Every form of interaction, whether online inquiries, email, promotions, phone sales, customer and employee relations or other components of business, depends upon communication to be effective.

In the corporate model, suggesting five collaborating parties are a living person is like the dehumanized tin woodsman in *The Wizard of Oz*, who clunks around making a lot of noise. He has no heart and he wants one more than anything. He wants to feel emotion, to be connected with sentient beings. The Corporation has no heart, either. It is only a label given to a piece of paper to protect self-interest while the vacuum of despair sucks believers into its lair. Show me a corporate soul. Taunting magic marketing tricks manipulate the mind, masking meaning with wordy rhetoric. Deluded customers walk right in.

At one time, the Corporation was a good thing. When a city needed a bridge over a river, businessmen would pool their money and know-how to get it built. When the bridge was complete and the debt was paid off, the corporation dissolved. But then, the corporation was not yet a "living person". When it acquired legal status as a living person in 1886, it lost whatever humanity it had had. If the Corporation has the rights of a living person, then it needs to act like one. Right now, the corporate model is eerily close to the cybernetic "Borg" of Gene Roddenberry's imaginative creation *Star Trek*. Half organic (its human creators) and half artificial (its existence on paper), the corporate life form is, like the Borg, a virus, ready to "assimilate" those who can provide it power, money and influence for its own gain. In this scenario, highly favored lobbyists and members of Congress, lured by easy money, bring their political influence to bear.

The money frenzy is evident in sports as well. Has the fever of football completely obliterated common sense, when grown men are willing to run after a ball, be knocked unconscious submitting their bodies to physical injuries that often last a lifetime, just to gain favor with the Money God?

When I went to purchase my first cell phone, a strapping young man in his 20s greeted me from behind the counter. In the course of explaining how the cell phone works and the terms of agreement, I asked what he did before getting this job. He said he had been a professional football player for a team in a nearby state.

I asked, "Did you ever break any bones?"

"Almost every one," he said. Then to prove his point, he raised a pant leg to show me the scars on his leg before pushing up a sleeve where there were more. From head to toe, he listed the concussions and injuries that have left his body with scars and painful memories to haunt him for the rest of his life, all for the money to be made. Sports are big business. From team sponsorships, concession sales of beer, popcorn & candy, sandwiches and more flow revenue into sponsor's coffers. The bet is on for what players will score, which team will win, and by what margins the winning score, and on and on.

As you can see, like attracts like, in corporate life as in daily life. If you are a party person, you will be attracted to other party types. If you are a fisherman, you will easily find others who enjoy the sport. It is quite easy to see in these models that opposites are not attracted to each other. Only when it comes to sexual reproduction or chemical interactions are opposites attracted.

Cooperative Systems

A natural inclination is to live a longer life, and why not? It is a good thing, especially if you have done a good job taking care of your mind and your body. You know from experience not to give your power away.

Once you lose control, it is a whole new playing field. You become the ball fought over by opposing teams of health specialists. The scoreboard registers each test run, with remarks by coaches who hardly know your name, much less know who you are as a person. We sometimes forget our mind is really in charge. What are we thinking?

Every business looks for better ways to serve customers. Each personality has a different management style with unique life experiences. Small business owners generally know their customers' names and needs. They are usually friendly and cooperative and take time to answer all your questions. You feel valued as a customer, no matter the product. It takes everyone doing his or her part to be successful. So, just like the cells in the body cooperate to maintain a healthy body, everyone involved in a company cooperates for the business to be successful.

The terminology for establishing a public corporation was adopted as a business concept with components that similarly worked in concert. Perhaps in the minds of those who drafted this idea there was creative invention at work to birth a lawful entity. Yet there is no life in a piece of paper dead on arrival when the tree went down, nor in a non-living person.

Conscious awareness means paying attention to all signals from the environment. It is a matter of sensitivity to subtle sounds, a musical selection and tiny movement in the trees that could be a bird, squirrel or opossum. It is the subtle breeze brushing your face, uncertain footing on a rocky path leading downhill, blinking eyelids by a fireside marshmallow roast. It is the smell of freshness in the air after a summer shower, or sensing the silence of newly fallen snow. It is recognizing when it is time to move on from a job, a marriage or the place where you live. It is being alive to potential, alive to life.

It is being alive to shenanigans that play out on the theatrical stage of business in collusion with lobbyists and manipulators of futures contracts meted out by Congress. The games continue to play out in high places under rules that say favors can be bought. You see, it is the same game, different house, and taxpayers have to ante up, whether they benefit or not. Teamwork in this case means collusion.

California furniture maker Sam Maloof, by contrast, used teamwork to accomplish a lot of work. Each member of the team knew his job and did it well, which is what cooperation is all about. Maloof credited his success to the three workmen in his shop, who helped speed the furniture-building process because they knew precisely what he wanted them to do. Because of the workers' 40 years of loyalty, Sam arranged to give them the shop when he "went away", having established a foundation to be overseen by those closest to him so his legacy would live on.

The Boeing Company could not possibly get along without teamwork, and so it invites related departments to meet and discuss how best to solve problems. It is teamwork that designs and machines components and pulls them all together in the assembly process. At every step of the process, there is purposeful intention and cooperation. Mother Nature, with the innate intelligence of a living system, demonstrates the ideal of cooperative effort, teamwork at its best. The new biology confirms that her organizing principle is a collaborative process, a model for relationships to be more effective and for systems of all kinds to sustainably function.

CHAPTER FOUR

CREATIVISM
The Art of Conscious Awareness

In the early 1980s I began work on a project in creativity to postulate variations on a theme, only to realize that I first had to answer the critical question: Just what is creativity? The revealing research that followed explored the dynamic connection between awareness and the conscious mind. I named it "creativism". Like activism, creativism is active imagination in practice.

In my study of the human brain and its amazing ability to quickly adapt to changes in the environment, I also learned that it thrives on mentally stimulating activities. As part of the nervous system, axons' synaptic junctions fire excitedly each time new learning takes place, permitting a neuron to pass a chemical signal to another cell. Axons are smart and expand their influence as the brain learns, something it loves to do. It hungers to expand its capacity and presses us to continue to learn all of our life.

Children are like sponges, absorbing every nuance of knowledge to expand their awareness of the environment. Eager to discover how things work, they will spend time watching a caterpillar build its cocoon, only to discover it later transforms into a butterfly. This same kind of transformation is available to everyone, and especially to young minds whose future widens when they lean toward challenging studies. Self-discovery may be the most fascinating of all human experiences, and it continues throughout our lifetime. But despite the "no child left behind" dictum for the U.S. educational system in 2001, the gap between the mind and its potential continues to widen. We must ask, why? More likely than not, it's because education has not kept up with progressive ideas about how children learn, making it more difficult for teachers to do their jobs and for employers to find workers who can think for themselves. We'll explore this more in chapter 13. Textbook learning has limits. Practical applications surge ahead. The way-it-used-to-be complex gets too political for comfort.

India is pointed in the right direction because it approaches education as a lifelong process from birth to death. They educate through innovation, drawing on how children learn at an early age. The Asian News International agency reported in 2006 that at least one school is teaching students to write with both hands at the same time on different subjects simultaneously. The Veena Vadini School at Singrauli in Madhya Pradesh began in 1999, and all 72 pupils, according to principal Virangat Sharma, "can use both their hands to write in two different languages on two different subjects at the same time." One student, Kamla, said: "I know six languages—Hindi, Urdu, English, Roman, Sanskrit and Arabic. I can write in two languages at one time."[1] Beginning this at an early age prepares students for a multifaceted future where language and expression are not limited by stereotyped texts and testing that is meaningless in the long run, except as a standard to measure teachers' ability to effectively teach.

This presents a challenge for the U.S. education system as competition with India sharpens its focus. Jobs are already being farmed out to other countries. When the student dress code was removed some years ago, grades, ambition and self-respect went south, and so did the pants as the waistline dropped to expose more flesh, embarrassingly so. Yet the U.S. is making strides in the right direction, with help from foundations to raise the bar.

Microsoft founder Bill Gates and his wife, Melinda, use their Gates Foundation as a springboard in this regard. What they are working to accomplish with benchmarks and reporting is helping education progress on a steady course. Underprivileged students gain aid and instruction to accelerate learning in a meaningful way. The foundation's stated goal for all students—"regardless of race or family income—is to graduate from high school prepared to succeed in college, career, and life. All students, all schools, everywhere."[2]

Legendary golfer Tiger Woods, using his money and passion to make a positive difference, founded Tiger Woods Learning Center in Anaheim, California, to exemplify the value of hands-on education, coupling workshop team experience with textbook learning.[3] The prospects for goals, career and a rich life now seem more viable. Young minds inspired and young brains stimulated increase neuronal growth, making them smarter and better prepared to meet the demands of the business world.

Here is how it works. During the day, Tiger's "Start Something" character-development and goal-setting program assists students in exploring career fields other than the basics, such as drama, journalism and robotics. After-school programs rotate every two and a half weeks, introducing such subjects as rocket science and flight, audio broadcasting and video production, even tutoring certain school subjects for struggling students. This is a great opportunity for those who might never touch these areas under our present educational system, a chance to inspire them to greatness and their full potential.

However, even a college dorm can birth student ingenuity. Look at Google's Sergey Brin and Larry Page, for instance, as well as Apple's Steve Jobs and Microsoft's Bill Gates. A garage, shed, barn or basement provides a place where thinkers tinker, generally making do with what they have in parts or can obtain cheaply. Innovation does not depend upon having a lot of money, just a curious, eager mind and the will to manifest. Sometimes a school science project is enough to spark the fire and ignite the flame, or an inspirational teacher may meld lessons with practical applications.

It is this curiosity about how the universe works that really spurs growth and invention to create new products for market. Business thrives on product development and the next new idea. Thinking outside the box invites imagination to trigger solutions to problems pestering more than one individual. Creative ideas spin gears into action, and the excitement can last throughout a lifetime. You may be one of those whose vision is already bringing new products to market.

There are lots of areas in which to work, especially in the electronics field. Demand for solutions to planetary pollution and ecological functionality is gaining momentum as awareness of the necessity spreads. Energy is high priority as oil reserves dwindle and we increasingly resent our dependence on a limited commodity. Driving innovation is the public's demand for more fuel-efficient automobiles, pushing industries to develop alternate fuel/energy sources and to keep the price point reasonable. Perhaps for the first time in history, the consumer is pushing the recalcitrant mentality of business to innovate. They expect business to get serious about conserving energy, be more respectful of nature and more responsible stewards of Planet Earth.

This will take a shift in perspective and a unique selling position to satisfy the brain's love for novelty. Clever is sometimes the only route to follow when outlooks are dead-end boring and goals unattainable. Inspired brains think and solve pressing problems. Our understanding of life's complexities tends to increase as we step off the treadmill of conventional thinking into new frontiers that propel us directly to the high-voltage potentials associated with quantum reality.

Creativity invites invention, innovative solutions to pressing problems. More than likely, those involved in the decision-making process are not the ones executing the plan. To resolve difficult situations, to find better ways to do things, requires as much input as possible. Some executives, thankfully not all, assume they have all the answers, but that is changing. It is rather like the human brain making all the decisions without checking to see how the body feels about it. Creativity needs to be a collaborative effort.

Mind and Electromagnetic Fields

The human body is a collective of trillions of cells, a large corporation whose self-interest is a mass of molecules held together by an electromagnetic energy field in the visible light spectrum—an attractive bunch of atoms vibrating energetically, binding together to increase their potency. Even at the atomic level, energy is active. The nervous system depends upon resonating frequencies to interpret environmental signals.

Unique frequency transmissions identify your body with self-markers, just as fingerprints, DNA and retinal imaging exhibit individual characteristics. Global positioning satellites identify you by a similar method. It is as though your body is a radio station broadcasting on an assigned frequency. No matter where you go, you are recognized. There is no place to hide. You are who and what you are, no matter where you are. Corporations are like that, too.

As I explained in an earlier book, *If You Make the Rules, How Come You're Not Boss?*, everyone's thoughts are vibratory signals that boomerang when transmitted to another human target. They bounce back to you, sometimes with a resounding thud, depending on the quality of the signal.

Take two guitars, A and B. When you stroke the E string of guitar A, before long the E string on guitar B will begin to vibrate. Briefly damp guitar

A and the E string on B will re-inspire A to resonate again. The important question is, which guitar started it?

So, who started the argument? Who gave you a dirty look when you made a derogatory remark? If you are not happy in your job, think how it affects others with whom you work. If they avoid you and you have yet to figure out why, look in the mirror and see if you are smiling.

The power of the law of attraction is at work, just as the genie says, "Your wish is my command." When you smile, others instinctually return your smile. Anger inspires others to anger. Happiness begets happiness. Fear pulls fear to you. It is easier to understand now why some people have trouble getting along in this world.

Creativity at Rest

Creative juices continue to percolate even in rest. In fact, there is evidence that eight hours of sleep improves performance threefold over that of the sleep-deprived, according to a German study at the University of Lübeck reported first in the journal *Nature*, then for the general public by the AP journalist William McCall.[4]

Most activity of the day is stored as memories in the brain's hippocampus during the first four hours of sleep, then consolidated in the neocortex (frontal lobe) for easy access. On waking, problems unsolved yesterday often have feasible solutions. A good night's rest is critical to creative problem solving.

If you have trouble thinking straight, you have a good excuse to at least take a nap. Frequent naps during the day are now acceptable. New research on the benefits of two- to three-minute naps may have been inspired by Steve Fossett on his solo record-breaking around-the-world jet flight in 2006, during which he slept only 60 minutes in 67 hours of flight time.

By pacing naps during the day, the body is able to rejuvenate itself, increasing mental acuity and productivity by reducing stress and strains on heart health. Students are advised to take "power naps" to enhance memory and recall and positively affect their test scores. Workers require the same. Multiple researchers agree: power naps are good. This mini-health measure assures that no one can say you are asleep on the job.[5]

We have only to look at the psychic healer Edgar Cayce, who slept on a book to know its contents. We would all learn much faster if we could apply the same principle. Often, when decisions are difficult we avoid commitment until we have a chance to think it over. We hear ourselves say, "Let me sleep on it." In the morning, clarity directs a response.

As William McCall reported for the AP, "70 million Americans are believed to be sleep-deprived, contributing to accidents, health problems and lower test scores."[6] Pierre Maquet and Perrine Ruby at the University of Liège suggest that this study signals a warning to schools, employers and government agencies that sleep is critical to mental performance. Nights are particularly affected when nature's natural sleep cycle is disrupted.

And yet each year the U.S. spends more than $300 billion on stress-linked illness, from heart attacks and stroke to diabetes. Sixty-two percent of American workers report an increase in workload, while more than half feel "overtired and overwhelmed".[7] Included in these numbers are issues such as uncertainty in the workplace and time lost from work. Companies feel it in their bottom lines, both in the U.S. and abroad. England each year loses 13 million workdays as a result of stress-related issues.

Business under Stress

Pressure to improve productivity and profit places workers on notice. Illness is something management can expect if workers have no time to rest and regroup. In Japan, with its high performance ethic, workers' greatest challenge is to avoid dying from overwork. One such death occurred at Toyota Motor Corp., where a worker logged more than 106 hours of overtime in a month. According to government data, "overworking is a serious issue in Japan, where an average worker uses less than 50 percent of paid holidays," report Yoko Kubota and Chang-Ran Kim for Reuters.[8]

Stress runs the treadmill in understaffed offices with increased demands. So, stress can be a killer, especially when workplace trends exacerbate the threat. Swedish researcher Hugo Westerlund with Stockholm's National Institute for Psychological Medicine reports that of 25,000 workers over a five-year period, 7 percent were likely to take sick leave, and another 9 percent would enter hospitals as a result of large-scale business expansion and the instability it engenders. The key stress determinant appears to be workers' degree of control over issues that arise during the period of expansion. More work and fewer people to do the work heighten uncertainty as deadlines loom. These pressures can increase the body's aging process and slow healing.[9]

Low stress, not surprisingly, has the opposite effect. Having a happy marriage with a low conflict ratio may speed healing by 40 percent, according to an Ohio State University study[10] published in December 2005. Couples with a higher level of marital hostility had increased levels of the stress-related cell damage that is linked to heart disease, osteoporosis and arthritis. Another study by U.K. scientists at the University of Birmingham concluded that happily married folks in their golden years fought off the flu bug faster than their lovelorn counterparts,[11] confirming love is the drug that heals the fastest. What an easy way to curb the high cost of health care.

There is a message here: if you hate your job, look for another. Life is too short to spend it being miserable, because your body and its health will suffer. Since cells eavesdrop on all your conversations, spoken aloud or not, it is easy to understand why unhappiness breeds sickness. You are taking care of more than one life within you. Trillions of cells depend upon you, as if they were your children. In a way, they are your children, and as heirs to the title of lineage, they have a vested interest.

If you're concerned about your health, identify your limits. If stress is the biggest block to your success, you may want to find interests with lower demands. Turn your ear to mellow instrumental music that plays well in the background and does not ask for your participation. It helps to reduce your stress in situations that by their very nature tax the system.

Looking at events without emotion is a good way to lower the temperature on seemingly explosive issues. Emotion is a byproduct of perception and therefore personal. So, in a situation where you play a pivotal role, resolve to accept it as it is, and if it needs adjusting, be willing to accept the challenge in good spirits. If something is unsettling, do your part to settle the matter as quickly and harmoniously as possible, as things left undone sometimes affect performance. But leave the issue at the office at the end of the day, unless there's something you can do about it after hours. This is part of the professional style that will help you maintain your cool in the midst of turmoil.

It is common practice among aspiring giants to pay close attention to office politics. When your job is in jeopardy from influences over which you have no control, it's best to be straightforward about your position. Your problem could be an associate who has a differing view of life. Sometimes, it's all about "positioning". Do your best to set achievable standards for your performance and follow through on them. If that doesn't work, you may want to find a position for which you are better suited. The goal here is to be happy doing what you do. Assuredly, if you're not happy, you're more likely to be sick.

Follow Your Heart on Purpose

It's important to follow your heart in all matters. If you're super-sensitive and respond accordingly, your feelings can easily be read as hostile over-reaction. If, on the other hand, you're sensitive to others' emotions, you'll be among the first to recognize an energy shift in their behavior. By being aware that your partner or co-worker is mentally absorbed in an issue that prevents his or her full attention to tasks at hand, you'll be better able to help without getting involved. Perhaps your co-worker needs time off to deal with the situation. Sometimes people are reluctant to disclose highly emotional issues, so exercising compassion is necessary. Everyone has issues, including you. Approaching them with an understanding ear can go a long way toward personalizing a relationship, a point often overlooked in the world of high-rise earnings and breakneck achievement.

If you're focused on achieving a promotion, be consciously alert to signals that will impact your future. If you're determined to make it to the top, be willing to move mountains to make it happen. Generally, such dedication is associated with the will to make a significant difference either in the life of the company, or in the corporate culture of which you are a part. Depending upon your aspirations and temperament, being held accountable for whatever comes your way can be challenging. Yet, the more responsibility you are able to assume, the more responsibility you are given.

Hopefully, you have worthy goals that drive your engine to work each day and build your resistance to office chatter that can turn into gossip with repetition. It saddens me to think that students in school today will enter the workplace poorly equipped in this way because they're deprived of the enriching creative expressions found in the arts. The mental stimulation and sensual pleasure expressed through right-brain synaptic connections is what helps to keep us emotionally sane. The hard factual edge of the left brain must be softened by the right brain's emotional ability to reason and balance. It's the quantum energy of spirit-self balancing your senses, finding expression in the subtle modes of music, drama and graphic arts, as well as three-dimensional art forms like sculpture, jewelry, ceramics and architecture that bring beauty into the workplace, the home and our life. It's the stuff of the Sistine Chapel and artifacts of cultures marking mankind's evolution that fill museum collections throughout the world.

Appreciating mankind's creative efforts and interpretations of life is critical to maintaining psychological balance and connection with spirit. The emotional communication pathways found in the arts bring deep satisfaction as we look to our natural environment for inspiration, aware of the varied expressions Mother Nature conjures to inspire designs in architecture, transportation, home décor—all that we take for granted. Education is shortsighted when it deprives students of access to their creative self, inherent in all human beings regardless of age. That's the stuff of innovative products so valuable to business, for without creative invention, we'd have nothing new on the planet.

Having a hobby adds diversion and satisfaction to one's life, so it is to be encouraged. Building a two-seater airplane can be remarkably satisfying as you pore over the plans and construct the frame. This endeavor entails extraordinary detail and exacting specifications, the same as building a jet plane at Boeing. In work of this kind, as in every expression of imagination, is peacefulness appealing to our "higher" self. Creativity must be encouraged and funded in schools and communities and, if necessary, by business, without attachment to the outcome and not as an advertising opportunity. Nature continues her creative expression in birth and rebirth, the seasons and evolutionary processes. Nature is constantly evolving, and so must we, as humans being human.

Tuning In to Signals from the Environment

As antennae pick up signals from the environment, it is critical to be alert to events that affect endeavors of interest and even life itself. Like human cell membranes, your antennae must be fine-tuned to changes that can affect you and your company's performance and outlook. Whether you panic in response, or carefully consider outcomes and possibilities before blowing anyone's horn, is what makes a responsible pace-setter. Upon the decision you make rests the direction of your actions and of your company, large or small. Is the wind a chilly one, or has the breeze softened? Being sensitive to changing environmental signals can stem the tide of erratic behavior and calm a restless sea. A good night's rest can often solve the problem, as we've noted, and as many a thinker has experienced.

Once you have an idea of how the problem will be handled, you can relax, knowing you've set in motion a series of events to resolve the situation.

Signals will continue coming in from the environment as a feedback loop, like the brain synapses firing, sending information throughout the system. Now, though, something is being done to stem the tide of uncertainty, to yield a possible solution, an expected benefit and who knows what else? Knowing that you have taken steps to resolve a situation that demanded attention is what leadership is all about. It's the same process the human cell goes through, sending information throughout the system of 50 to 70 trillion cells—and you thought some companies had a lot of employees. When the body is in harmony, cells are happy; they don't mutiny unless there is conflict of interests or a virus invades the collective family. In business as in the body, it's your antennae reading the signals traveling through the energy fields: another reason why it's important to stay alert to changes in the environment.

So, how do you really know when you're on the right track? If you don't feel relaxed and happy each day, seek the source of your angst. Whatever the situation, you and your friends as well as your work associates resonate at similar frequencies. In other words, you are known by the company you keep, just by your vibrations.

You are part of the human bar code. Bar codes are frequencies. Each product that's packaged for sale has a bar code recognizable by scanners. Debit and credit cards work the same way. You, too, received a unique bar code at birth. Oh, sure, it could be your birth certificate with your footprint as evidence—but more than that, it is the energetic field surrounding your cellular body, the whole of you, all of the 50 to 70 trillion cells in your body. They are your family. They go with you everywhere. They are aware of your behavior, your bad habits and good traits, and take account of how you sabotage yourself by having one last drink for the road. Nothing goes unnoticed.

The body's five senses signal environmental conditions. The brain is the head of state, the CEO in charge of the body's behavior. To be alert, the brain relies continually on learning new things, new ways to do things, coupling activity with physical exercise and healthy eating. Crossword puzzles, for example, are a great way to mentally stimulate areas of the brain often neglected by routine associative thinking. Excitement usually means you are about to have a new experience or do something you thoroughly enjoy. We'll explore this more in chapter 16.

Inspiring Greatness

I love the artwork of architect Frank Gehry, who plays with shapes and materials to spark creative expression and to make a sculptural statement while still fulfilling function. Gehry's organic architecture is striking in its daring as he manipulates shapes and materials to his will. His thought processes differ dramatically from Louis Sullivan's, whose architectural postulate was "form follows function" and whose penchant was for stacking one floor atop the other to accommodate more business opportunities, which tended to look box-like. Frank Lloyd Wright, on the other hand, designed more dramatic statements, though linear and sometimes awkward constructs, like the caretaker's cottage now serving as Barnsdall Art Center in Hollywood, where I once taught, and the main house next door, called Hollyhock House. While function is a necessary consideration, how that form is expressed is quite another matter.

By all standards legendary woodworker Sam Maloof, whom I mentioned in the previous chapter, exemplifies the creative ideal. Sam and I first met in the 1970s as members of the California Designer-Craftsman's Group, associated with the American Craft Council. We met up again in 2006 at the Bellevue Art Museum in Washington State when he was on tour to promote his collectible furniture art book. Thrilled to see he was still following his heart, I invited him to be a guest on my Progressive Radio Network Internet talk show, *Evolving Ideas©*. Coincidentally, the scheduled date just happened to be the day before his 91st birthday in January 2007. In his sprightly manner, with absolute clarity, Sam said he loved his work so much, "I'd do it even if I didn't get paid."

Sam died in 2009 at the age of 93. For 80 of those 93 years, he designed and handcrafted his now famous furniture. His graceful rocking chairs are especially favorites. Because he was still in love with wood and his craft, with so many happy customers, including former U.S. President Jimmy Carter, he told me in our interview that he had enough work to keep him busy for the next 10 or 15 years. The two-story redwood house that he built so many years ago for himself and his beloved wife, Alfreda, is now listed in the National Register of Historic Places and serves as a museum on his six-acre California property. The Sam and Alfreda Maloof Foundation manages the property to preserve the legacy of a man who followed his heart.

Sam represented the consummate artist, but no matter the field, anyone can have that same passionate connection to their work. I know salesmen who absolutely love sales and could not stop selling if they wanted to. It is in their blood, an integral part of their being. Would that we all could be so dedicated to our work.

Clearly, inventiveness stands out as a significant statement of creative genius. As businesses carve their niche in an industry, each generally has some quality to set it apart from competition. While they cooperate in the marketplace, sometimes providing similar products, some variability is necessary to achieve a unique statement. Companies producing identical products under different brand names capture a larger share of the market, effectively cooperating while competing against themselves for more shelf space and profits. One example is Welch's 100% Grape Juice and the Seneca brand frozen concentrate. Some say one is more nutritious than the other, but when I spoke with a salesman working for the plant, I was told they are exactly the same product produced in the same factory, just two different expressions to compete in two different markets.

Such is retail marketing. Lofty towers everywhere are filled with shrewd business leaders, some with more experience than others, willing to co-operate because they see gain as a net result. So, business is learning that it can no longer compete in a world where there are no corners in which to hide. It is cooperate or perish. That is what Ford Motor Company's Bill Ford is realizing, and so are other companies as they catch the vision of the new economy with heightened awareness.

Meditation Calms and Renews

The latest creative trend for busy executives is taking time to meditate, as Patricia Aburdene reports in *Megatrends 2010*.[12] Stress can cloud clear thinking where balance sheets are affected as much as stakeholder interests. Adapting Eastern disciplines of meditative practice to the busy workaday world can, in a brief time, revive imagination and clarify issues by refreshing the mind.

Sitting comfortably with closed eyes, relax and allow yourself to focus on your breath, conscious of each inhale and exhale. One suggestion by Ayurvedic doctor Virender Sodhi, ND, of Bellevue, Washington, is to slowly inhale for four counts, then hold the breath for four counts before exhaling the same way. This 12-count repetitive practice elevates the oxygen level in the brain and relaxes the body, making it as good as a nap, if not better.

It is obvious that more change is in the air as spirituality enters the business world. Even CEOs are embracing consciousness, finding that it actually improves business relations. They also realize that the dictum Milton Friedman set out in a 1970 article titled "The Social Responsibility of Business Is to Increase Its Profits" is just plain wrong.[13]

"Someday businesses like Whole Foods, which adhere to a stakeholder model of deeper business purpose, will dominate the economic landscape," says Whole Foods' CEO John Mackey.[14] He strongly disagrees that the purpose of business is solely to increase profits for the shareholders. He adheres to the principles of customer service as the priority of business, and cites the difference between that model and the profit-centered business model favoring investors.

Mackey has a six-tier stakeholder list: "customers, team members (employees), investors, vendors, communities, and the environment." His experience has proven that customer happiness must come first, and his team must pursue it with passion and empathy. By doing so, he is convinced his model will far surpass the profit-centered business model. When employees are motivated to provide excellent service, they are also serving the interests of the corporation as a viable member of the community, building good will that brings more business to their stores.

Friedman's profit-maximization model, by contrast, is devoid of emotion or attachment to a community as a team player. It reminds me of the "slam-bam-thank-you-ma'am" philosophy—pure self-interest. Mackey is convinced that Whole Foods' ideas will triumph over time, "not by persuading intellectuals and economists through argument but by winning the competitive test of the marketplace."

Reinventing Business

The shift to conscious awareness of corporate social responsibility is evidenced by a growing number of firms endorsing the ten principles set forth by Ceres, the Coalition for Environmentally Responsible Economies formed in 1989. Ceres's ten principles of accountability are offered as a comprehensive statement of environmental values for business within any industry. They help companies formalize their dedication to environmental awareness and accountability and actively commit to an ongoing process of continuous improvement in environmental performance, dialogue, and comprehensive systematic reporting to protect the biosphere. Their principles address sustainable use of natural resources, disposal of waste, energy conservation, risk reduction, safe products and services, environmental restoration, public information, management commitment and, finally, audits and reporting. By 1993, Sunoco agreed to abide by the principles, the first Fortune 500 Company to do so. Today, Ceres boasts more than 70 companies endorsing the principles, ranging from environmental leaders to Bank of America, Coca-Cola and Nike, even including our own Northwest Timberland Library.[15]

A look at any executive's business calendar reveals challenges and opportunities that demand creative problem solving. These demands trigger brain centers to propel inquiring minds to solve riddles in useful ways. Various scenarios roll around in your head, giving cursory examination to possible outcomes. Our creative juices flow to give ideas form, tangible or not, on every progressive step of mankind's journey to understand the universe and our relationship to it. In every walk of life, in education, the trades and business, creativity gives us options and expands awareness of the possible.

Everyone in business is constantly reinventing his or her self, looking for ways to better serve communities and still maintain the marketplace strength necessary for growth. What markets are yet to be mined? Is your location functioning well? Are there new products coming on board that can expand your presence? Widening the scope of influence is the name of the game. Doing it consciously is an asset when it truly serves the people and the environment in a responsible manner.

If your company is not growing even in a small way, you are on the way to dying. The same is true for the brain's capacity to think and to love. It is designed for growth to keep the synapses firing, just as business grows by taking incremental steps. Growth and satisfaction do not always have to be directly equated with money, though that is often the reward. Many times, satisfaction comes from the kind of growth you are achieving on a personal level. One of the most exciting ways to grow is to expand awareness, to open your mind to new information, to do something you've never done before, to modify an existing product or discover another niche. The best product is one that enhances life, is good for the environment, and is useful or aesthetically pleasing or both.

Creative problem-solving activities actively engage your mind to look for ways to assure a successful outcome through responsible action. A deeper discussion of creative problem-solving techniques with proven tools and methods comes in chapter 17. New ideas are essential to growth. Upstarts jarring the status quo with a vision of new dimensions can be threatening. However, at some point, you have to get off the merry-go-round and stride in a new direction. It's good to remember, as I always say: "Change is inevitable. Growth is optional."

CHAPTER FIVE

PROGRESS ON THE MOVE
An Early Ride on the Road to Change

Any instigator of progress seeks solutions to common problems better than are currently available. As early as 2008, the high cost of gasoline for cars and trucks drove the demand for more energy efficiency. We've been enjoying the comfort of automobiles now for more than 100 years.

According to the French, the first automobile was built in 1884 by Delamare-Deboutteville, while others claim it was built in 1860. "It all depends on your definition of a car," says *Motorera*. Before that, though, came the steam-powered stagecoach, popular in Europe.

Late in the 19th century, along came Henry Ford, a genius and mechanical engineer who later worked for Edison Illuminating Company as chief engineer. He built his first gasoline engine in 1893 and by 1896 completed his first automobile, a crude wooden box with a single seat and steering tiller, with an electric bell sitting on the front of the hood. In 1903, Henry Ford founded the Motor Company. A hundred years later it is still in business reinventing itself.

In the early days, car motors had to be cranked to start, while the squeeze of a rubber bulb sent air to the metal horn. According to historians, Ford's company sold over 15 million Model T cars, inexpensively produced because he believed that "every man, no matter his income, should own a car." Ford was looking out for the customer, a better life for the people, and made a fortune in the doing. That is vision.

To eliminate handwork, stamping machines were built to flawlessly replicate a model. The blacksmith's trade was also incorporated into the mix. Wax or clay models produced molds for casting in iron and other metals, easing production of complicated parts. Each man brought talent to the table as the vision caught fire, making it possible to increase production even more by cutting the time it took to get products to market.

In 1913 Ford was one of the first to apply assembly-line techniques to manufacture his cars, which enormously increased his production ability. Adding standardized interchangeable parts to his product in a sequential manner, usually moved along on a system of chains, with assembly workers standing by in a line at the ready, made it possible for him to mass-produce affordable automobiles. With the advent of his inventive conveyor belt, the speed of production increased exponentially, and Ford was credited with contributing to the creation of a mobile middle class in American society.

Asked about color, Henry Ford said you could have any color you liked as long as it was black. It took 50 years before other colors were introduced. In the meantime, Ford expanded to offer more choice in the Lincoln and Mercury brands. There was also a sidekick, a model named after Henry's brother, Edsel, which had a shorter lifespan.

Soon, other automobile companies sprang up with bigger, roomier insides and varied features. Business grew. Electric starters eliminated hand cranking. Comfort set in and so did resistance to change. While the whole country was mobilized, innovation slackened. Oil companies began driving the U.S. automobile industry, and gasoline prices rose from 12 cents a gallon in the 1930s to more than $4.00 in 2011, sparking protests from consumers.

Mass-produced products like automobiles and bicycles need ancillary systems for distribution, transportation, promotion, marketing, sales, management, and service. Ford could build a lot of cars, but unless he had a way to get them to consumers, he might as well have locked his doors. As news of his affordable fandangle automobile spread across America, demand grew to a crescendo. Investors came out of the woodwork. Dealerships sprang up, especially in towns with high-density populations. Salesmen met the opportunity to make a buck. All could smell the money to be made. Anthills of hungry profit-seekers grew into an orderly mass of associated industries.

Where once the Pony Express sounded the news, paperboys on street corners hollered, "Extra! Extra! Read all about it! Ford's Model T Hits the

Road!" Henry Ford knew it was better to be in the driver's seat than riding on the running board where you had to hang on for dear life.

Comfort was right behind the basics of transportation, and with it came lap blankets, muffs and foot warmers for the women and children, because early cars had no heat. Winters in the North were brutal, especially in snow country. Isinglass windows gave little relief from the frigid wind. Eventually windows of glass rolled up and down to seal interiors off from the harsh elements.

It is interesting to consider how the automobile represents the physical body with energy as the common denominator. Combustion engines need oxygen, fuel to run the system, pipes to carry the fuel to the engine where it propels the vehicle on wheels that turn, and an exhaust that gets rid of the waste byproducts. Again, biology and its cooperative nature provide the model for creative invention. Henry Ford's visionary concept and mechanical ingenuity brought greater mobility to families and individuals all over the country who were once dependent upon slower modes of transportation. In Ford's mind was the beginning, and his dream changed American life, and the world, as a result.

Conversion to Other Industries

Fast-forward to 2011 and everything from sorting apples to manufacturing cars moves by conveyor system. Product tracking codes, which control the flow of inventory for a multitude of products, are widely used by Wal-Mart and big-box stores like Costco and Sam's Club. UPC, uniform pricing code, is still the purview of companies whose mark-ups vary. Companies depending upon efficient delivery of merchandise use trains, trucks and air-service shippers such as United Parcel Service, Airborne Express, Fed Ex and the U.S. Postal Service. Department stores, subway systems and airport terminals employ the same conveyor-belt principles to transport people from one floor to another on escalators, while moving walkways cover longer distances, especially useful for airline passengers with carry-on luggage. The concept spread to other services.

Today, "people moving" is the favored model for processing and treating patients in health care, though the system appears less structured to the uninitiated. Gone are the days of only general practitioners who know about the whole body and see connections that specialists miss. Now, many people feel they are being treated like livestock as they are shuffled from doctor to doctor, lab test to lab test, for diagnostic factoids, whether X-ray, MRI or other authorized sophisticated procedure used to unveil the human body's mysteries. As data accumulates, you soon have a thick file moving down the line inviting more specialists to analyze and prognosticate. Personnel use labels as signposts for further treatment. Every part of your body is broken down into sectors. Forget that the body is a consortium of interested parties with innate intelligence. This process is about analyzing the product in a mechanical way, much like an automobile, though living tissues are more flexible and function 24/7/365 with a lifespan that far exceeds that of any machine. Always, the doctors look for a label, a condition's name that fits the conveyor-belt system of treatment. They follow physician protocols taught at institutions of higher learning as gospel. It all feels like rote programming.

Katherine Baicker, now a professor of health economics at Harvard, reported in the journal *Health Affairs* on the correlation of costs with quality of care, noting that each additional general practitioner per 10,000 people increased a state's quality ranking and lowered spending by $684 per beneficiary. By contrast: "Each additional specialist per 10,000 people lowered a state's ranking and increased spending by $526 per beneficiary."[1]

X-rays, CAT scans and MRIs make the body translucent to doctors, but in many ways, the body remains obscure as an unsolvable mystery. Doctors are taught in medical school to rely on tests, but tests are only as good as the people who read them, and there are plenty of mistakes made. Who would have thought the human body could be so complex that it takes a team of specialists to analyze? And even then, they can still be wrong.

As so many treatments are based on conjecture, a patient's diagnosed disease may be found to have been inaccurate when the body is autopsied at death. *The Physician's Handbook* lists similar symptoms for many types of disease, so diagnosis is sometimes difficult and may look more like guesswork than the truth of what is. It could be this... or it could be that. It is estimated that 2.5 million deaths occur annually in the U.S. due to medical mistakes, according to wrongdiagnosis.com. This is a shocking statistic.

Since 1994, the National Center for Health Statistics has collected no autopsy data. It seems that autopsies expose more than the illness of which the patient died; they may open a can of worms for litigation over malpractice when the treatment is found responsible for the person's death. In 1999, the Institute of Medicine (IOM) reported that up to 98,000 people die from medical errors in hospitals each year, making error the third leading cause of death.[2] Celebrities are not excluded. In 2009, the doctor treating the pop star Michael Jackson was charged with administering a lethal dose of anesthetic and other drugs before he died. The charge was that he "did unlawfully, and without malice, kill Michael Joseph Jackson" by acting "without due caution and circumspection," thus causing his untimely death, reported the Associated Press on February 8, 2010.

Trust is shaken when an estimated 2.4 million improperly filled prescriptions each year[3] are added to errors occurring in physicians' offices, nursing homes and other care facilities. Seventy percent of mishandled surgeries, diagnostic errors, incorrect therapy choices, equipment failure, blood transfusion errors and misinterpretation of medical orders could be prevented.

A 2004 study over a four-and-a-half-month period, which tracked and classified 344 errors in 42 "primary care" clinics (primary care is a fancy name for doctor's offices, as opposed to the ER or hospital), was published in the journal *Quality & Safety in Health Care*. Dr. Jonathan V. Wright of Tahoma Clinic in Washington State is convinced that more occur when there is a large staff. He draws on the assembly-line industrial model for reference to prove when the employee base is doubled there is a four-fold increase in errors—medical mistakes, in this case. Undermining confidence further, 13 percent were due to a doctor's lack of education and/or experience. More importantly, 82 percent were caused by "system malfunctions": office administrative mistakes and/or miscommunications. In one case, a patient died because a message was not relayed.

As Dr. Wright reminds us, this study was but a small sampling of clinics nationwide over four and a half months that either detected or admitted to patient errors. He suspects that many more blunders slip past the watchful eye.[4]

In Minnesota's 2005 hospital report, half of all medical mistakes occurred during surgery, including one death. Of the 106 "adverse health events", up from 99 the previous year, 16 surgeries were performed on the wrong body part, 2 were done on the wrong patient, and 8 patients received the wrong procedure. In 26 instances, foreign objects were left inside the patient.[5] The costs to the U.S. related to medical errors are estimated to reach a burdensome $37.6 billion each year, with $17 billion of those costs associated with preventable errors, according to IOM.[6]

In response to surgical mix-ups in operating rooms reported over the years, Dr. Dennis O'Leary, former head of the Joint Commission on Accreditation of Healthcare Organizations, warns that an M.D. or R.N. after your name does not make you less vulnerable to slipping up. Perhaps the most infamous case was in 1995 when Willie King's orthopedic surgeon amputated the wrong foot. I remember hearing of this and shuddering at the consequences of such an act. How could that happen? Come 2007 in Tanzania and two patients' records were confused. The one due for brain surgery had his knee operated on, while, you guessed it, the man with the knee problem had surgery on his brain.[7]

Trust wavers even more when we learn of instances where the wrong patient receives a heart catheterization or a doctor drills into the wrong side of a patient's skull. Despite regulatory agency warnings to hospitals and surgical centers around the U.S., mix-ups have occurred in at least 275 cases since 1999. Since reporting is voluntary, actual counts may be even higher.

In response to the continuing rise in surgical errors, the Joint Commission announced in 2004 a mandatory checklist to ensure that the correct patient is on the table and the surgical team is aware of the prescribed procedure. The surgeon must initial the incision site while the patient is awake and cooperating. A waterproof marker is used to avoid smudging from fluids and scraping sheets.

Caution is called for as well when X-rays are placed on the light panel to guide the surgeon in the procedure. Should X-rays be reversed, the wrong kidney, for instance, could be removed, as happened in Tom McLaren's experience during his tenure as a surgical services administrator. He has since made a rule not to hand a surgeon the knife until everything is confirmed. One would think precautions like these would be taught in Surgery 101. Yet more than 40 medical organizations are needed to assist the accreditation commission in teaching the new rules.[8]

Even scientists cannot always be trusted: sad commentary on research institutions pressing the "publish or perish" ethic to achieve a competitive edge in institutional funding and credibility. Unethical behavior reported by the watchdog Committee on Publication Ethics indicates that 29 desperate aspirants pushed the envelope for attention in 2003, using varied tactics, from plagiarism to attempted bribery and potential medical malpractice. A few cases raised alarm when found to be conflicts of interest. Though medical journals publish research papers by the tens of thousands, it takes only a few bad eggs to spoil the lot.[9]

In the case of the journal *Nature Neuroscience*, it wasn't publishing research papers getting them into trouble, but a review article that evaluated experimental treatments for depression. In August 2003, *New York Times* reporter Melody Petersen revealed that the favorably written article's lead author had serious financial ties to three therapies. "He held the patent on a lithium patch he described as promising…owned 60,000 shares of stock in a company whose drug he described as effective, was a board member and recipient of stock options and consulting fees from another small company whose product he cited."

Since no one at *Nature Neuroscience* bothered to ask him to disclose any conflicts of interest, he never volunteered the information. As a result, the journal established a new policy to avoid any further conflicts of interest by requiring review article authors to "fess up" to any financial ties to the products they evaluate.[10]

To add to the misery, in 2004 *Newsday* reported that heart-disease experts worked both sides of the fence in urging people to take cholesterol-lowering drugs while they themselves received kickbacks from companies selling those medicines. And they are not the only ones involved in the practice.[11]

Mistaken Identity

The U.S. General Accounting Office spearheaded an investigation into misleading claims in advertisements by Pfizer and other pharmaceutical companies after several FDA letters sent over a four-year period were ignored. But the 8.5 million Americans who each year request and receive prescriptions for specific drugs after seeing or hearing advertisements touting their effectiveness confirm that advertising works. The "ask your doctor if … is right for you" jingle is now adopted by so many advertisers that it is grossly overused and mocked in humor, reducing any serious inquiry.

The white coat and stethoscope symbolize trust and integrity, an iconic image popularized by the 1970s TV medical drama *Marcus Welby, M.D.*, with the neighborhood doctor as good guy. Today's commercials continue to mislead the public into believing drug commercials are actually done by medical doctors, when in truth, they are hired actors.

In fact, the Canadian Broadcasting Company (CBC) online news service says scripts are actually written, not by doctors, but by pharmaceutical company public relations "ghostwriters". The term *ghostwriter* refers to an unnamed someone who likely never sees the evidence, especially not negative findings on the drug in question. It goes so far as to suggest that up to half of any drug's peer-reviewed literature consists of ghostwritten "infomercials". Public disclosure has been notably absent when it comes to conflicts of interest.[12]

Plausible deniability is evidenced in Cell Therapeutics' quarterly report to the Securities and Exchange Commission (SEC) in 2004. In small print the company disclosed their sole marketed drug, Trisenox, and also listed off-label uses lacking FDA approval. A big no-no! While the FDA approved Trisenox as an effective treatment for a rare type of leukemia, it had not approved it for any other uses, including as a treatment for cancer, but the label listed them anyway.

Cell Therapeutics admitted, "Some of our practices intended to make physicians aware of off-label uses of Trisenox, without engaging in off-label promotion, could nevertheless be construed as off-label promotion and it is likely that some instances of off-label promotion occurred in the past." Further, the SEC document submitted by Cell Therapeutics also admitted that "promotion by us of such off-label uses would be unlawful."

The kicker is in what Leah Grant, the company's director of investor relations, said when asked about disclosure. The company received no warnings from the FDA about its promotional practices, nor had representatives been disciplined for inappropriate sales promotion of off-label uses. Which means, if no one complains, they get away with it.

If the government really wanted to resolve the high cost of health care, the FDA would instantly ban all pharmaceutical advertising to the public, which, as you can see, plays a significant part in making people sick. Such a ban would take it away from the frontal lobe of awareness. Sadly, the George W. Bush administration played into the hands of the drug companies by extending the review process, thus undermining enforcement of federal standards by giving the companies more time to market their products unfettered, according to a GAO report. Obviously, no one is watching the hen house!

Trust Defiled

Meanwhile, the medical conveyor belts keep moving. Bills continue to add up beyond just the diagnostic stuff. Kickbacks are inevitable when doctors are taught to prescribe drugs as a payback to the pharmaceutical industry for funding the medical schools and research science labs on university campuses. This allegiance is to be expected, though not abused. With universities functioning more like corporations than like institutions of learning, the interconnectivity plays a significant part in the business of health care.

Since pharmaceutical companies fund medical schools, as I just mentioned, it is quite easy to see why "med" students are taught to prescribe drugs, rather than alternative methods of self-help, although there is an effort now to absorb those into the fold. Medical doctors are not taught to teach people how to care for their bodies naturally, but to put patients on the fast track to the pharmacy for drugs they say will cure you. Truth is, when people use natural remedies the pharmaceutical companies make no money. Today, we see screws tightening on natural products people buy over the counter. Maybe it will take a March for Free Choice to retain control over our bodies and our health rather than play a fixed game of Russian roulette at the drug maker's counter.

The U.S. government estimates that millions of people annually spend more than $27 billion on alternative and complementary medicine. Many people feel betrayed by conventional medicine, disappointed by inadequate care, misdiagnosis, an intolerable drug, failed surgery and lack of careful attention by practitioners. Feeding the discontent are insurance companies' haggles over coverage, conflicting reports from medical studies, deception by drug manufacturers and shocking personal experiences.

In 2004, 48 percent of American adults chose one or more alternative or complementary therapies.[13] More and more people realize that by gifting your power to traditional allopathic health-care practitioners who, in some cases, don't even know your name, you have abdicated responsibility to take control of your own health.

Webster's *Unabridged Twentieth Century Dictionary* defines the term "allopathic" as "...that method of medical practice which seeks to cure disease by the production of a condition of the system either different or opposite to the condition produced by the disease: distinguished from homeopathy."

This realization is enough to convince you to assume more control over your life. It is a helpless feeling to know nobody cares; nobody really cares.

When my father was dying of arteriosclerosis, doctors danced around the test results. I was infuriated by the manner in which they disregarded the integrity of my dad, never addressing the issue head-on. It was a nightmare of impossibility as doctors held out hope to him, while tests and more tests proved inconsequential after the first round. They knew he might as well go home and enjoy the time left.

Watching the craziness in both my mother and my dad's medical care gave me enough insight to realize I would rather take care of myself. At least, if I lack attention, it is my own fault. I saw my mother drugged to the gills after one surgery, her mind warped to another dimension. I saw my dad's frustration when straight answers to his questions were evaded. Who needs that kind of health care?

I thought about the irresponsible surgery I had when the doctor tied off one of the two vagus nerves controlling my body's motor skills, digestion, speaking, and the like; and the lack of information about living with the results of a hysterectomy.

When my husband and I went our separate ways, I no longer had health insurance. The vision challenged me to redirect my life to one of self-care, beginning with a "can do" attitude. I knew if I gave my power away to the medical profession, my life could quite literally end up just like my parents. Amazing what determination can do to power your will.

I learned healing practices and how homeopathic remedies have no side effects, and how, by treating myself as the most important person in my life, I could withstand disease. The power of my thoughts, critical to my state of health, took a few years longer to control. Over time, though, my inner and outer world dramatically changed.

Manmade Solutions to Nature's Problems

Collusion for profit gilds the current health-care model and you wonder who cares about whether you live or die. Feed the machine your money for medical insurance premiums, prescription drugs, steroids, implants, treatments, tests, unnecessary surgeries, and genetic engineering and your life is riding on the conveyor belt. Forget that the human body is a system of interacting organisms operating as a whole.

Our medical care system is still based on Newtonian physics, mechanistic viewpoints shared by science in general. As if by reducing the body to a bunch of parts, like a mechanic analyzing your automobile, science could determine the body's behavior, i.e., performance. With this knowledge, they presume to know how to predict and control Mother Nature. When the machine is broken, all they have to do is replace the parts, or treat the parts as individual components. Forget that these operations are a consortium of interested parties. With the parts bearing no relationship to the whole, our bodies, like our automobiles, are put into the garage for the mechanical fix. In other words, you end up in the hospital with an enormous medical bill that will cost your life or an arm and a leg to pay.

Pharmaceutical drugs are not in the same category as the social drugs law enforcement agencies pursue. Pharmaceutical drugs, in many cases, can twist a mind more easily, and do physical damage by corrupting the body.

In my own case, a number of years ago, in treatment for ulcers, I wobbled down the hall hitting the walls on 75 mg Librium three times a day prescribed by my doctor. My mind was a mess and I had four young children to care for. What must they have thought? I finally flushed the remaining pills down the toilet when I realized life was not worth living if I continued to take them.

Eliot Spitzer, then New York's attorney general, took on GlaxoSmithKline when alerted by a whistle-blower at a medical conference in 1999. For four years, the company had committed fraud by concealing negative results of clinical trials on the antidepressant Paxil. According to a *New York Times* editorial, "Paxil was no more effective than a placebo in treating adolescent depression and might even provoke suicidal thoughts."[14]

Additionally, Dr. Alastair Benbow, a medical director for GlaxoSmithKline, in an effort to address the need for transparency in reporting the results of drug trials, announced that a company website would be established to serve all interested parties: the public, medical professionals and researchers.[15]

To be fair, we honor the sleuthing of pharmaceutical companies who spend billions of dollars on research every year. Very clever advertising by the American Chemistry Council, in an eight-page, four-double-sided-sheet newspaper blast, acknowledged six areas in which chemicals play a significant part in our lives. According to the ad's claims, chemicals are "essential$_2$ ..." living, industry, security, business, discovery and health, representing 80,000 scientists and engineers with an investment of $23 billion in research every year. That ad was not any small change either, and it affirms that business is buzzing in the chemical industry. Certainly, our life is better as a result of chemical combinations of natural elements in proper ratios that produce a bevy of products for home, office and industry. That is the majesty of nature crowning us with her blessings.

But, while pesticides' chemical concoctions have benefited farmers over the years, their effects have been damaging as well, exacting a high toll on the environment and the health of farm workers. Over the last 20 years, Carnegie Mellon University chemist Terry Collins and her colleagues have been developing catalysts that "might safely degrade dangerous stores of pesticides," especially large quantities leaking from storage drums, as well as in tainted wastewater, groundwater and the soil. Precisely because pesticides are so poisonous, it is taking longer than expected to even come close to a solution, which makes you wonder why they are still in use today. Yet success appears on the horizon as catalysts show some common pesticides and other toxic chemicals responding favorably. Only in 2002, by studying the chemical oxidative process, was success reported in *Science*, crediting a green catalyst that nearly completely degrades chlorinated phenols, assisted only by hydrogen peroxide.[16]

The not-yet-on-the-market catalyst fosters other claims as well: cleaning up residues in paper-mill wastewater, removing sulfurous compounds from diesel fuel and, perhaps the most dramatic application, decontaminating troops or gear exposed to anthrax spores, because it is mild enough to leave fabrics and other materials undamaged.

As medical supply and pharmaceutical companies seek to develop a whole battery of engineered treatment and diagnostic equipment, including radiation products, we see a rise in dependency on outside sources for healing. From every possible corridor of maladies, there are new treatments to help take your pain away, some still in trial stage. Most often the cost is prohibitive, with no guarantee they will be effective. With the new science of biology, however, a holistic approach supports a healthy body and lifestyle. Think wellness all the time, and focus on living a long life in good health using a process I call "Youthifying". In my workshops, attendees learn tools to look at life in a different light and walk away with a positive shift in attitude empowered by their experience.

CHAPTER SIX

COLLABORATION
Intimate Love Affairs

With the human brain the powerhouse of thought, imagination and emotional expression, it is a three-pound universe unto itself. As source of consciousness and energy, the brain's control tower is wired for connectivity: connectivity in the neural net with the larger body and its sensory feedback mechanism; connectivity with quantum energy's invisible fields.

Since cell antennae are receptor sites transmitting signals from axons at the synaptic cleft hot-wired for action, they act a bit like telephone relays that allow information to travel to specific destinations. Satellites in the sky bounce signals from one earth center to another, carrying information of import in a matter of seconds. Earth's amazing communication system is similar to the body's ability to transmit information, though human cellular speed is faster.

Your physical body is a vast electrical machine using powerful natural energy voltages in the extended electromagnetic field. According to physicist Thomas E. Bearden, Ph.D., the long-term effects of electromagnetic radiation are more damaging to human cells than heat. One millivolt dropped across a cellular membrane to the next atom is almost equal to a million volts per meter. That is a very strong energy field, unlike heat, which is not very efficient in that regard. This charged electromagnetic field is more efficient at accelerating healing as well, without wasting energy. Focused use of such energies on specific areas of the body, like a laser, is far safer than endangering the whole organism by irradiating the entire body.[1]

The danger lies in the continual bombardment by an electromagnetic hash from atmospheric signals, microwave cell phone towers, step-down canisters on power lines, and the like that are damaging human cells' integrity. These little processes of millivolts and half-millivolts are inflaming tissues in your vulnerable body, penetrating deep into bone marrow to eventually affect the stem cells. A cumulative effect occurs over time. If the population is exposed to continual bombardment of only 10 percent of this kind of electromagnetic hash, you may see 10 percent of an aging populace develop degenerative diseases of which cancer is one. If the jamming gets worse a higher incidence will affect more people, and sooner.

As if that were not enough, commercial industries use neurotoxic chemicals in the manufacturing process of automobile and home interiors, as well as OPs (organic phosphates) and PCP (pentacholorophenol) in household cleaners, gardening pesticides and personal care products that affect your constitution. Not only that, but smoking doesn't help. It is well known that hemoglobin needs 40 to 60 water molecules around it before sufficient oxygen is available through hydrogen bonding. Inhaled tar and nicotine disrupt the hydrogen bonding and inhibit hemoglobin's oxygen supply, causing a serious condition called hypoxia. Alarmed, your body kicks into survival mode. Your metabolism slows down, reducing the need for oxygen. Your body quickly relaxes, misinterpreting this as a good thing, which is reason enough for caution and astute awareness. Bearden himself suffers from this condition, the result of exposure to U.S. military chemical spraying experiments while on duty with his troops in Canada.

Late in 2004, Great Lakes Chemical Corporation began to phase out the potentially harmful flame retardants penta- and octa-BDE, members of a group of chemicals called polybrominated diphenyl ethers (PBDEs), themselves members of a broader class of chemicals known as brominated flame retardants (BFRs). These chemical classes are widely used commercially in TVs, computers and refrigerators, foam mattresses, furniture and automobile interiors; only recently they have been found to exist in fish, house dust, human blood and women's breast milk.

Analytical chemist Dr. Robert Symons of Australia's National Measurement Institute, involved in a study funded by the Australian Department of the Environment and Heritage, confirmed that the top six most egregious flame retardants were present in Australian breast milk, and that Europe and the U.S. had even higher levels. Sweden now has banned these penta and octa chemicals, and for good reason, after the Australian government's National Industrial Chemicals Notification and Assessment Scheme (NICNAS) examined their ability to cause cancer and reproductive problems. The problem appears to be universal in developed countries. These brominated flame retardants behave like persistent organic pollutants in the air we breathe every day and continue to pose health risks. Phasing out these damaging chemicals means new chemical combos; recently, a substitute for penta was found in the flame retardant Firemaster 550, which the EPA concluded is not persistent, bio-accumulative or toxic to aquatic organisms. In 2005, to develop more effective and less damaging fire retardants, as well as specialty chemicals, crop protection, and pool, spa and home care products, Great Lakes Chemical Corporation merged with Crompton Corporation to become Chemtura Corporation.

Many consumer products contain flame retardants, for obvious reasons, but as awareness grows of the inherent dangers of these environmental toxins in consumer goods, it is certain they will leave the market. Keep in mind that living entities must have a balanced environment to survive, and when that environment changes, so do living organisms. It's all evidenced in how cellular organisms respond to the environment.

Every cell in the body is a tiny energy factory. Without oxygen the body dies within five minutes. Since the brain consumes more oxygen than any other organ in the body, it is more susceptible to damage if a continuous supply of oxygen is restricted.[2] As the body grows older, there is even more vulnerability.

The trick is to protect the body as much as possible to prevent further deterioration while enjoying the technology of the 21st century, from which there is no escape; it's pervasive in cell phones, computers, Blackberry devices and electronics of all kinds that pollute the environment. Even the military is involved in hashing the energy field: a joint effort of the U.S. Navy and the U.S. Air Force, called HAARP (High Frequency Active Auroral Research Program) in Gakona, Alaska, bombards our environment with frequencies on a continuous basis. With no end in sight, we may become so wired (pun) that as walking antennae we attract even more charges. Some say the human body is already overcharged.

Energetic Communication

The physical body and the energetic field around it with its intuitive communication capability make up the biological encyclopedia for all we know.

If you think your physical body is not listening in on your conversations, think again.

Notable paranormal research by Cambridge professor Rupert Sheldrake, exploring unexplained powers in animals, proves that thoughts travel through the invisible energy fields to their destination, no matter how twisted the path. Sheldrake's book *Dogs That Know When Their Owners Are Coming Home* probes a connection between people and pets, particularly dogs, that dates back 10,000 years. Cats were favored in ancient Egyptian wall paintings and pottery as early as 4,000 years ago, suggesting more recent domestication. If a paranormal connection exists between pets and their owners, this is likely also true for similar groups in the wild. This paranormal interconnectivity would certainly make sense between species, if for no other reason than as a survival instinct.

We might draw a similar conclusion from the episode in the *Lord of the Rings* trilogy in which the Ents, or tree people, are alerted to danger by the Hobbits (little people). Communicating with nature's subtle forces, the Ents move in force to attack a fortress. It makes a great visual for paranormal phenomena. Not to mention Harry Potter and the owl who comes when beckoned, or the sculpted shrubs in the maze of confusion closing ranks on students in the dark night of their soul, or what seems like magic in the boiling vapors of pretension as they let loose the subtle awareness of an all-knowing intelligence.

We know that whales have a homing instinct, for they return to their pod at mating season and maintain contact with their young. Salmon follow their natural instinct to swim upstream in the same rivers every year to spawn. The turtles of the Galapagos Islands and the small fish called grunion of Southern California beaches also have that migratory instinct. Nomads follow the seasons and depend upon their sense of direction for survival. A collie named Bobby turned up in Oregon a year after his family moved from Indiana, a 2,000-mile journey.

Sheldrake reports there have been numerous attempts to test the hypothesis with homing pigeons. However, "after nearly a century of dedicated but frustrating research, no one knows how pigeons home, and all attempts to explain their navigational ability in terms of known senses and physical forces have so far proved unsuccessful."[3]

Pet projects have, however, collected data on how dogs wait at the front door until the owner comes home, having intuitively received the signal that he or she has left the office. Now, I am certain you will agree there was no phone call between them to alert the animal.[4] Every once in a while, we hear a news story about how a pet alerted parents to their sleeping child's breathing problems or to a fire flaring up in the house, or how a dog dragged a child to safety. It is obvious there is an intelligence that never sleeps, though not so obvious to scientists doing the research, who find living systems more complex than at first imagined and admit there are still lots more things to learn.

Recent research reveals an unusual relationship that a woman and her pet parrot enjoy. The parrot has the ability to read the woman's mind and converse with her in English. This is astonishing to witness on videotape. It means that birds and animals can read our thoughts and communicate in the morphogenetic field. Humans also have the capability to read the field, but we have so many distractions that the clarity of transmission is often blurred.

This sensitivity to energies has relevance to the workforce, be it an office, plant or factory. Energy can be read at home, too, especially when some disturbance alerts your household. You know the minute you walk in the door whether something is awry or not.

Though you may not yet be consciously aware of subtle energy, you are aware that energy is conscious. You feel a sensation when someone is looking at you, even from behind your back, and you turn around to check it out. The physical body's field has comfort-zone distance parameters that can be measured and labeled. Dr. Edward T. Hall, once professor of anthropology at Northwestern University, defined these ranges and coined the term *proxemics* to describe the human territorial space in which we feel comfortable. And the distances vary. We have an "intimate" field, with a "close phase" generally associated with sex and a "far phase" that extends to 18 inches. A "personal" field beyond that extends up to 4 feet, while 12 feet is the limit to our "social" field of physical domination. Anything beyond that is considered "public" space. You may sense someone close to you and someone in the distance staring at you.[5]

We live in cosmic soup. It is proven that clocks in a shop will entrain themselves in a day or two to be in sync with each other, thus creating harmony. When a group of young women are together for any length of time, their menstrual cycles also entrain, creating synchronous rhythms of unity. So something is going on in the energy fields for these things to consistently happen. It is an intelligence that asks us to sit up and take notice.

The Everyday Genie

The greatest computer on earth is your brain, your thinking processor, your inspiration, and the source of mind; a gift of spirit that loves you more than you know. It is not the material world that matters, but what you think about yourself, your life, and those around you that has the greatest effect. The Genie is in fact within you and around you. Indeed, you possess the magic of the Genie to do wondrous things. All you need do is believe it is possible; thinking you can makes it so by entraining energies to your focus. This is the "secret" grabbing everyone's attention.

Your human brain is like a blank slate. Everything you've ever thought is written in your recorded memory. All your emotions and experiences write themselves on your memory disc to play back as a lifelong production in which you star, *This is Your Life*. Training to be human comes early on delivery to free space and continues throughout a lifetime. Each repetition plants the response more securely in your behavior. You tend to fall back on those responses for as long as they work in your best interests.

Given this truism, being receptive to environmental signals is imperative to health, success and life experience. Sensitivity to environmental information can give "heads up" insight into product safety, suggest ways to improve your current status or show you whether to resist products with side effects that could be hazardous.

Key to this scenario is conscious awareness, mindfulness, and awareness of energy, the mind and the quantum field. If Big Pharma's religiosity can convince you of a drug's ability to relieve your symptoms, it will control you and your life. That is what advertising is all about, as we've seen. They profit from your weakness to resist their claims. You have just given your power away, and given your body to the shadows of uncertainty.

We must be carefully taught that an assembly line of medical practitioners awaits us on life's conveyor belt from cradle to grave. At each step there is someone who will take away your pain, your anguish, and your despair with tests and drugs, surgeries, therapeutic aids and the newest product or procedure. The list goes on and on, making a herd of animals happy not to be humans. Unlike Henry Ford, the end result is not the delivery of a new car. Instead, what usually results from the romance with the white coat and stethoscope is something akin to a new home on the conveyor belt.

No one questions the necessity of life-saving surgeries. True, our medical community has come a long way from the battlefields of the Civil War.

However, dependency on someone other than yourself in most cases obfuscates the intelligence of the body to heal itself. Better to cooperate with the body when emergencies are not in order. Even then, there is danger: this requires accepting responsibility for the condition of your body, its nurturing and care, and especially your attitude about life, which allows you to have the human experience.

Human Cells and Their Vulnerability

There is much ado about diseases like cancer, which is an autoimmune disease, a self-inflicted response to an irritating condition haunting a person's life. It can usually be healed if caught in time, by identifying the most aggravating issue in your life that eats away at your tender tissues and dealing with the emotional attachment in a constructive manner. No matter the malady, I have to agree it is not that easy to do. But the body is malleable, yet vulnerable to any invasion, and going to the emotional source *first* works best. Then you are working from the inside out. "The secret of life is to be found in the cells, while the strategy for a successful life is revealed in the dynamics of the cellular community."[6]

This was a very difficult issue for me to accept and deal with when I learned that my son, Terry, had a glioblastoma tumor, the most insidious malignancy of all the cancers that feed off the brain. When the fear of death raised its ugly head, my son chose to have surgery to remove the tumor. Eight months later, he was dead.

So, please know that my comments are quite serious. To avoid maladies in the body, the best and quickest source of healing begins with a review of what bugs you, followed by taking all the time you need to work out your issues at a cellular level. First of all, it is less expensive, it is noninvasive, and it is something you can do on yourself without insurance, without a doctor, but with a powerful belief that you can heal yourself. You must visualize and think every moment that you are well. Find happiness within yourself and share it with everyone around you. See my earlier book, *If You Make the Rules, How Come You're Not Boss?*, for workable self-healing tools.

Dare not let anyone sway you from the mission to heal your body. You are enough! No question about it! *You can do it.* All you need to do is believe in your inner power that has nourished you since birth, always listening to you when you complain, argue, fight, and roll past events over and over on your mind screen, like an old movie that automatically rewinds, never to end. Selective scenes repeat themselves as though they are attached to a repeater button. Over and over repeat the moments when no one listened to you, when so-and-so did not do as you asked, when blame and shame led you to sit on the pity pot to let the steam off. All that energy expended primarily because no one hears your pleas.

No one *really listens*; no one really hears your desperation or the fear associated with survival. No one hears what he or she does not want to hear. Closed minds have no open windows. The Money God always demands more sacrifice for favors, while the most important value of life is to be happy of heart. No matter what! That is the most important value to treasure. The physical body's health depends upon it.

Since the mind reaches everywhere in the electromagnetic energy fields, you are much greater than you have been told. You have a great mind that can do wondrous things. You have just begun. Reach within yourself for answers. Educate yourself, even if the school system was unable to satisfy your curiosity. Take charge of your life. Follow your heart. Do only what makes you happy.

Your three-pound brain thrives on learning. It bores easily and needs constant tending, as does a high-yield garden of flowers. As you express your uniqueness with a happy heart, it fills you with satisfaction. Joe Dispenza, D.C., confirms the power of our thoughts to affect the brain's learning in his seminal book on the subject, *Evolve Your Brain*. Following someone else's lifestyle may be helpful as a guide, but it is really up to you to find your own path, the one with *your* name on it.

As an individual personality living in a multicellular world of life forms as complex as the human body, you can find your path in being and working with others who share a common focus. As a living cell in the body politic responding to the environment, what you think counts. Each individual's life journey is like that of a living cell. Each cell is responsible for its life through awareness of its environment. Collectively, we are all in this together. When seen from this point of view, the obsession with having all the toys leaves something to be desired. None of us takes our toys with us when we leave, but we do take the wisdom of our experiences. I'm beginning to think that's all we take with us and that may be the sole reason for the human life experience.

Your physical body is nothing more than a chemical machine, according to much doctoral thinking, and pharmaceutical companies are all about selling you physical molecules to fix your body when broken. But it is actually in the quantum field of energy where thought creates reality and where the body is transformed. Amit Goswami, Ph.D., writes in *Physics of the Soul*, "Since subtle bodies do not have micro-macro distinctions and their motion is always quantum and never degenerates to classical, even approximately, there is no entropy in the subtle world, and no deterioration."[7]

Your mission as a human is to take charge of your life and follow your heart: to do what makes you happy. This is finally proven scientifically as the quickest way to heal.

Receptors' Abilities to Receive Information

Humans all have antennae to read signals from the environment, such as hair follicles on your head and your body. Other receptors—eyes, nose, ears and tongue—constantly feed you information regarding environmental conditions. You sense the environment through these receptors and respond according to the signal's importance to the system.

As the owner/operator, your brain interprets environmental conditions through signal transmissions coming from your five senses of perceptual reality: taste, touch, sight, smell and hearing. It is the brain's responsibility to interpret this data so that your life can relate and adapt to varied environments. These senses are your connections to the world. Your body is an extension of your brain, your world of worlds within worlds.

Alone, your brain is your body's commander-in-chief; the membrane around each cell, a programmable chip. Without signals from the electromagnetic energy field, there is no life. No matter what advertisers would have you believe, there is only one boss of you: mind acting on the brain's ability to think and respond to interpretations of environmental signals.

The human brain is an intelligent computer, serving a greater mind with unlimited capacity. To assist the body in living outside the womb, the same system of operation is passed to us by our "pair-ents", along with the responsibility of maintaining the system. It is almost as though the sperm and egg rent the womb for nine months and the tenant is forced to vacate when the lease is up. The space was getting a bit cramped anyway when the lady of the house gave us the eviction notice.

With a tunnel to the outside world the only route of natural origin, we intuitively make our way, bringing our baggage with us. We awaken from the comfort of our cozy nest with a smack on our tush and please everyone with our cries. Mother holds us protectively and meets our wide-eyed curiosity with her own. We have safely made the journey from the invisible spectrum to the visible, from the unknown to the known, worlds apart in awareness.

All living beings are entrusted with the ability to know how to get along outside the womb, but only after being programmed. Memories of past events come to our rescue to re-mind us of how we dealt with similar circumstances. Otherwise, we would simply be an analog without a catalog by which to reproduce a known pattern, something akin to the DNA. It is wonderful that Mother Nature includes the patterns to repair and replicate the original model when damage control is needed. This is fortunate for us, indeed.

So there is commonality in the human condition. The assignment for life is to learn as much as we can about this world, investigating every nook and cranny for growth-enhancing experiences before our time capsule collapses, signaling our return to the unknown realm for yet another possible go-around. The temporary temporal body is simply an exploratory vessel especially designed for a Planet Earth experience, and it is not of much use in the otherworld of spirit. This reminds me of Gene Roddenberry's vision of the universe and NASA's obsession with Martian terrain as the next planet to exploit when Earth's resources are exhausted.

To love one another and to work together for the good of the whole is a prerequisite to becoming a wise culture. See for yourself how much happier you are and how much better your endeavors when life works for everyone.

It is the attitude that makes it work. Change your attitude and your whole world changes, and that is the truth. *Your world changes*, for the vista is now quite different. It is as though you just landed on another planet to see the world from a fresh perspective. I find that quite interesting: by simply changing your mind's frequency, your world changes. Very clever of Mother Nature, indeed!

The secret frequency, of course, is love. Everyone wins when you exhibit love and acceptance for your fellow Earth travelers. We are all in this together. Sharing the journey with a happy heart makes this world a better place to live. There is plenty for everyone. Mother Nature makes sure of that. When we work together for the good of the whole, everyone wins. It is called cooperation, and it is the easiest thing to achieve. Mother Nature does it well. If she can do it, so can we. We each are cut from the same fabric of creation.

Tasting the Order of Life

As we've said, your body's antennae read signals from the environment. Is it cold, or hot, or damp or dry? You feel the environment through these receptors—follicles, eyes, ears, nose, tongue—and respond. Food is tasty or dull, hot or cold; the view you see with your eyes is either pleasing or not of much interest. Though you are aware of it all, you give your attention to only those factors important to you. You hear the music of the wind, the roar of crashing waves on the shore, the voice of your beloved and your own when you speak. You smell the sweet aroma of fresh-baked bread and the tantalizing fragrance of pumpkin pie and cinnamon cookies. You taste the full-body flavor of cranberry sauce and the bitter bite of lemon.

But now, it seems that your brain and mine are being hijacked by outsiders, to be managed as though we are incapable of managing ourselves. Mother used to say, "Someone's always telling me what to do." And she did not take to it lightly. It was as though others thought she had no mind of her own making. Usually, she was talking about my dad.

Managing other people's lives became a new category of business sometime in the 1970s to supplant self-management, based on assumptions that people are incompetent and unable to manage themselves. From psychologists to financial planners to the drug companies who know which drug is "right for you", someone is there to tell you what to do. There are tax consultants, health-care providers, insurance advisors, a variety of "specialist" doctors, lawyers, astrologers, nutritionists and psychic readers, oh my!

With no one minding the store, we must all be out to lunch. Which is why there is so much media *programming*, and I am not referring to scheduled broadcasts. They are "helping us out" by telling us what to do, making decisions easier because they fancy themselves mind readers with inside knowledge about our likes and dislikes. It is as if we are not enough, which is silly, since Mother Nature provides all the tools and hardware at birth that we need to survive the earthly experience. When did we become inadequate?

The physical body has rules for survival and for how we adapt to our surrounding environments. There is organization to the body. Each organ system functions efficiently, collaborating with other systems to maintain the physical body's integrity. As discussed earlier, organs like the heart, lungs, liver, stomach, pancreas and gall bladder make up living systems, and organelles, tiny organs inside every cell, replicate the organization of the larger body.

Erwin Schrödinger, Nobel Prize-winning physicist, wrote about his observations of living systems in a 1994 book titled *What Is Life?*

1. When considering the structure of living matter at the molecular level, it is clear that it is more complex than inorganic matter.
2. Living systems tend to preserve their structure over time, meaning that biological systems maintain order.
3. Complexity is somewhat proportional to size, as explained by the randomness at microscopic scales that makes it difficult to develop elaborate mechanisms.
4. Living systems replicate, as in evolution.
5. The hallmark of living systems is that they maintain organization by adapting to the environment.

And Spinoza said, "It is impossible that man should not be a part of nature or that he should not follow her general order."

So when did we become weak and ineffective? Corporations are "Johnny on the spot" with the latest and greatest Product X solutions. You are simply not enough to know which cleanser is "right for you".

The epidemic of "not good enough" is a plague spreading throughout the world. Undeveloped countries and their people yet to be "corporatized" are hotbeds of civil unrest. The clash of cultures is evident. Only the intrepid will forge ahead despite perceived limitations and prove they are enough, no matter what anyone else says. These folks become leaders, founders of companies, inventors, visionaries and pioneers of new directions; they set the pace for the future, undoing the wrongs, and restore the sense of what it takes to live life on this planet in a more meaningful way.

CHAPTER SEVEN

GREEN IS THE NEW FRONTIER
Mechanization, Globalization and the Health-Care Boondoggle

Creative minds and human hands are responsible for a bevy of products and lifestyle enhancements. Yet today, robotic machines in many factories replace humans who previously did the work and contributed to building cities and local businesses. Mechanization, as we've seen, has had dire effects in this economically based new world society. While cost-cutting factors increase profits for investors and inflate already burgeoning executive pay and perks, mechanization has led to increased crime and run-down cities as former employees lack dependable income to feed their families. Everyone in the community is affected. The city and the state are affected, and so are other businesses that supply goods and services no longer needed.

"Build it and they will come" has long been the model for companies siting facilities on lands once vacant. As new communities erupted on barren landscapes, people settled in with their families, drawn by the prospects of a good life. They purchased company products to show good faith. But with the onset of the WTO, World Trade Organization, jobs began disappearing offshore with seemingly little concern for the workforce whose loyalty and labor built the company. Workers now struggle for a living wage, anywhere. Cities like Detroit and Ann Arbor, Michigan, dependent upon a working populace to maintain the economy, also suffer.

As *Seattle Times* syndicated columnist E. J. Dionne wrote in an editorial titled "Paging Walter Reuther", pride often comes before the fall. On a tour of the Ford Motor Company plant in the 1950s, an executive gloating over the fact that the robots paid no union fees received a terse retort from the union boss: "And not one of them buys new Ford cars, either." Business forgets it is a two-way street.[1]

Once there was job security with retirement benefits and health care. Now jobs are outsourced to foreign countries. How will people live now in a monetary-based society that looks elsewhere for hired help? Once we grew our own food, nourished the soil and prayed over our bounty. Now chemical companies goose the soil with pesticides, chemical additives and genetically engineered seeds to reduce cost of production and increase profits, while Big Pharma's busy drugging the population with prescriptions for everything from pimples to senility. And we wonder why health care is a priority. Without a healthy workforce, the country and its people are vulnerable. Where once there was cooperative effort for the good of the whole, now there is divisiveness, confusion and an aging population, many of whom are addicted to prescription drugs as they move toward a horizon of uncertainty.

As if that is not enough, health-care and retirement funds are under fire. To maintain the workforce, companies who once promised health-care and retirement benefits, usually negotiated by unions, have, in part, reneged to cut costs. Trust violated results in hardship.

Health care is Big Business. In the United States, as well as in other countries, affordable health care is a huge issue. According to a study conducted by The Commonwealth Fund titled "Health and Productivity Among U.S. Workers":

> In 2003, an estimated 18 million adults ages 19-64 were not working because of health reasons. Sixty-nine million workers reported missing days due to illness. Fifty-five million workers reported a time when they were unable to concentrate at work because of their own illness or that of a family member. Together, labor time lost due to health reasons represents lost economic output totaling $260 billion per year.

These are staggering statistics. Further, the study claims, "A healthy workforce is one of the most important economic assets as a nation."

In an article by Eduardo Porter in *The New York Times*, August 19, 2004, titled "Rising Cost of Health Benefits Cited as Factor in Slump of Jobs", Sung Won Sohn, then chief economist at Wells Fargo, says, "Health care is a major reason why employment growth has been so sluggish." The article explains that companies are reluctant to hire full-time employees because of the per-worker health insurance sticker price of $3,000 a year. It charges that "health premiums are sapping corporate balance sheets even more than the rising cost of energy."

Nonprofit hospitals admit unfairness exists in overcharging uninsured patients, but abdicate any responsibility for their plight.[2] It is a sad commentary when portions of humanity are sacrificed by a business system that favors the rich with discounts and leaves the poor to fend for themselves.

Canadian health-care services struggle with the same concerns as the U.S., reporting that 15 percent of their population have no family doctor, somewhat better than in the U.S., where estimates run to 20 percent. With a doctor shortage in Canada, local hospital emergency rooms are crowded with the sick waiting in line up to four hours for help or to refill a prescription.[3]

Business suffers when employees are not up to par physically or mentally, which results in production and delivery delays that inconvenience customers. When business suffers for lack of a healthy workforce, a lot of money is spent on temporary hires, which can also reduce efficiency. Then, when rumors fly about internal problems hatching at the source, the cascade of bad press calls management into question. This is not even taking into account other frustrating events that affect workers' health. Wars and the unrelenting fear tactics gripping the U.S. since September 11, 2001, also bear partial responsibility. The more fear imposed, the more sickness there is, which increases bottom-line targets for health care and drug cartels. The more wars between nations, the higher the profits for the military-industrial complex munitions and armaments industries. The more money spent on protection, the less peace there is in the hearts of humankind as every day is lived in a state of uncertainty.

Desperation makes people crazy as they cope with survival. Some seek the feel-good compromise in social entertainment, sex, alcohol and drugs. The more despondent see self-expression in the dead-end highs of methamphetamine. Feeling useless and unappreciated, they hide their fears by losing touch with 3-D reality in another world, out of body. While this escape is meant to be a quiet act, addicts actually advertise their insecurities through irresponsible behavior.

When people are happy, fulfilling their mission to help one another, to make a difference in their community and the world, the automatic response in the body is healthy cells. Most of the time, our physical bodies function on automatic, otherwise we would be spending all our time negotiating outcomes for digestion and heart rhythms and instructing our limbs to move. Surprisingly, the physical body works like a mechanized robot. Some functions are so familiar that we act without thinking. Remember, cells know their job and respond to stimuli at the membrane level, aware of the environment. So, yes, the physical body also behaves like a corporation with its own self-interests, though it can be overwritten through conscious control.

However, we need to distinguish the difference between living systems with awareness and mechanized hardware. To perceive humans as robots with paychecks is unrealistic. The human brain has the capacity to think and problem-solve and take appropriate action.

Falling Short

Admittedly, the world today is not that of our great-great-grandparents, who, not that long ago, chatted over the backyard fence with their neighbors to catch up on the news. Today, with the ease and speed of cell phones, computers and satellite imaging communication systems, we can converse with people on other continents and think not a thing about it.

Ford Motor Company's moving assembly line is now the accepted model for producing almost all products in general use today. With that kind of ingenuity transforming business, you might think other inventive processes would be in the works. But that seems not to be true, at least not in the automotive industry.

With General Motors Corporation (GM) stock listed on the NASDAQ as underperforming, the company is in debt up to its ears. Ford is not far behind. It is because the move that they perceived as fulfilling their "21st-century vision"—acquiring Volvo, Jaguar, Aston Martin and Land Rover—turned out to be a swing away from their branded mass market. Mortgaging virtually all its assets, including the blue oval trademark so familiar to its brand, Ford raised $23 billion in cash. Expecting its legacy to carry it through, the company returned home with its tail between its legs, having suffered defeat at the hands of bloated egos and expectations of high returns on investment.[4] However, in the 2009 economic debacle, Ford was able to weather the financial storm without a handout from the U.S. government, unlike General Motors and Chrysler.

On another issue, skimming profits from the top, paying executives perks and excessive wages beyond their ability to perform leaves workers at the bottom, who actually do the work, out in the cold. How smart is that?

One popular argument is that the United States automobile industry has made little progress in making a more fuel-efficient product, despite the urgent call. Thus, Japanese car production and sales hit an all-time high, while our own legacy automobile industry fell short.

Arguably, tooling is costly. But, as Reuther points out, money is saved because robots on the assembly line require no health insurance.[5] A staggering $9.9-million debt load in 2006 is unconscionable. And the man on the street thinks he has troubles!

The reason the major automobile companies are in trouble is because they have held too tightly to what worked in the past instead of innovating to keep pace with technology. They could have been the first on the track, but they held back, thinking erroneously that the U.S. buying public would continue to purchase the gas-guzzling vehicles, no matter what. The 2005 giveaway year-end sale of SUVs was to get rid of their stock because they had produced more trucks than consumers would buy. Again, prices were reduced, this time down to employee discount rates. What else could they do with yards full of cars, no drivers and even fewer wannabes? By the time the cars, trucks and SUVs were sold, they were old. That could amount to a lot of shipping to foreign markets where there is still demand for U.S. cars, but only if the price is right. Foreign car manufacturers took advantage of the wasteland and beat them at their own game by producing a gas-efficient automobile with style and comfort. They have a built-in market as consumer demand for fuel-efficient vehicles continues to rise.

Honestly, my 1986 Ford Bronco II must have been built on a Wednesday, for it still gives me a comfortable ride with gas mileage as good as the new cars. This means, of course, that specs on mileage have purposely not been changed. Carmakers say it would ruin their business. That could only be the case if they were in collusion with big oil companies. Meanwhile, modular components now replace working parts that home mechanics could repair themselves. When you look under the hood, there is no breathing space. It is as crowded as a subway at rush hour. In this case, technology has not made much improvement, and the cost for this lack of innovation is staggering.

The major automobile manufacturers still have their loyalists, but foreign brands now populate the roads with high frequency. General Motors and Ford Motor Company are making more money as bankers, reported the Bloomberg news service as recently as October 15, 2006. The automakers' financing business yields nearly half its profits, effectively subsidizing the manufacturing sector. GM, however, is divesting itself of investment properties and has finally changed designs, hopeful there is still some loyalty to their brand.

Banks own everything, along with the insurance companies, with pharmaceutical companies not far behind. We look at our measly credit-card debt by comparison and it looks pretty good, except there is a big difference in wages, benefit packages and stock options to collectively tip the books in their favor.

Future Trends

As globalization of jobs continues to drain skilled workers from the U.S. in ascending order, from assembly tasks to manufacturing to computer programmers, it has reached the tipping point with scientists and engineers in research and development laboratories. I cannot help wondering who will be left in the U.S. to do the work when this outsourcing frenzy is over. Will the U.S. become a Third World country unable to take care of itself, vulnerable to cheap shots by anyone's pecking order?

No wonder the U.S. has a shortage in research technicians. Jerry Thursby, a professor at Georgia Tech's College of Management and research associate of the National Bureau of Economic Research, says, "You have to have an environment that fosters the development of a high-quality work force and productive collaboration between corporations and universities if America wants to maintain a competitive advantage in research and development."

Further, Thursby, who has authored a corporate research study financed by the Ewing Marion Kauffman Foundation, suggests that "more and more research work at corporations will be sent to fast-growing economies with strong education systems, like China and India." Their strong educational system stands in contrast to the U.S. educational system that has "dumbed down" curriculums for some years now, teaching to the test instead of focusing on content, critical thinking, rational thought and common sense.

William F. Banholzer, Dow Chemical's chief technology officer, explains the swift economic growth of China and India by saying, in part, "There are so many smart people over there…no monopoly on brains, and none on education either." With American high-school students lacking science and math proficiency, and college graduates reluctant to pursue careers in science and engineering, the needs of business in those sectors slip the U.S. into a lower slot in the economic market.

Yet the University of California–Berkeley sees this situation as an opportunity to become the intellectual hub of the planet by setting up satellite schools with leading technical universities in India and with Tsinghua University in Beijing. Other leading American universities, aware of the profound shift in knowledge workers, are realizing that to stay ahead, or at least stay on par, they must also compete for talent in a global market.[6]

Suffice it to say, keeping up with technological advances while strumming the heart of buyers to orchestrate happy-tune bottom-line profits is the stuff of innovation. It's good to remember that workers are also consumers who act as advertising agents helping to build the business. Therefore, it is in the best interests of business to continue hiring living persons to help keep the supply lines generating profit, and to pay them a living wage.

That will work until a better plan emerges. Futurist Jacque Fresco has such a plan, wildly fresh in its perspective, in which structures for whole communities are built by robots assembling preformed metal units, a process mechanized to eliminate manpower and free people to learn and share the bounty of a living system in practice. His concept will give the people time to work in the garden, to go to school, to experience life and its blessings by participating in the whole of the community. In this community, everything is free, because the system is not based on money.

Fresco's vision of what the future can be for a sustainable New World civilization is based on a straightforward redesign of our culture, one in which human suffering is unacceptable. Neither is there debt, war, poverty or hunger. His perspective is to "declare Earth and all of its resources as the common heritage of all the world's people." Further, Fresco states in *Future by Design*, co-written with Roxanne Meadows, that his vision includes a unilateral

> resource-based economy [that] utilizes existing resources rather than money, and provides an equitable method of distribution in the most humane and efficient manner for all the world's people. It is a system in which all goods and services are available without the use of money, credit, barter or any other form of debt or servitude.

Fresco and his social-change venture, The Venus Project, admit that no government has ever initiated such a plan of action as he proposes. No doubt because it is up to the people to be so disillusioned with their leaders that they will speak up for change and make them seek an alternative social direction. Fresco's organization proposes a feasible plan of action striving toward a condition "where human rights are no longer paper proclamations but a way of life."

This is the first positive change agent that makes sense. Yes, Fresco's a dreamer, but a dreamer with a vision for making this world a better place to live. He says that a different strategy is necessary, one emphasizing scientific method based on biology, not politics, to achieve a dynamic equilibrium between man and nature. No, he is not looking to create a Utopia, as some may suppose, but a viable future based on equanimity and sustainability in place of endless wars for oil and other resources to fuel the money machines.

William Gazecki, Academy Award-nominated filmmaker, calls Fresco a modern-day da Vinci, peer to Einstein and Buckminster Fuller, though Fresco describes himself as a multidisciplinarian or "generalist", interested in how various fields of study interrelate. As a multitalented social engineer and industrial designer, his credentials include broad experience in aerospace, medicine, architecture, automotive design, psychology and even more.

What I love is the way Fresco sees the quality of a total living system in his designs, though the structures themselves are machined and assembled by robots and mechanized for mass production. It is an integrated system, just like the human body. All aspects of it function with a unified goal of a healthy, self-sustaining system.

Fresco's designs also interface with comfort and utility. He bases his concept on the capacity of the human body to be efficient, flexible, strong and enduring, integrally supported by a neatly packaged organized system of blood and extracellular fluids. Each relies on the other, and some cells even multitask when the need is there. Nature must be in harmony to efficiently function, to make the flowers bloom and emit a fragrant perfume. Harmony is our goal in life and in business, just as it is in biology. Achieving this mission means that a lot of problems in business and in the population at large must be resolved. This worthy goal of a cooperative lifestyle invites everyone to compete for knowledge and experience in the fields of endeavor each person finds of interest.

While the success of this model is still years away, it is nevertheless a vision of the possible that will reflect a whole new set of values. Early settlers never dreamed of electric lightbulbs or cities where they could satisfy most all their needs, let alone flying around the world in a jet airplane or into space, yet it is our reality in the 21st century.

Sustainable Concepts

Fresco is not alone as a visionary. Architect William McDonough, collaborating with German chemist Michael Braungart, is calling for a transformation of human industry through ecologically intelligent design.

Leaving a sustainable future for our children and grandchildren is the impetus driving McDonough's designs. He says design must be first; then comes supply-chain integration, energy, and materials assessment based on clean-production qualifications and sustainability. His work uses the pyramid points of Ecology, Equity and Economy to illustrate the considerations that come into play when designing architecture inspired by nature, such as a tall building shaped like a tree. It must consider airflow and breathing capabilities and still be stunningly beautiful. An unorthodox environmentalist, McDonough envisions "factories so safe they need no regulation, and novel, safe materials that can be totally reprocessed into new goods, so there's no reason to scale back consumption or [lose jobs]."

He and Braungart together authored *Cradle to Cradle: Remaking the Way We Make Things* (Northpoint Press, 2002), which is printed on treeless paper "made from plastic resins and inorganic fillers, designed to look and feel like top quality paper while also being waterproof and rugged ... easily recycled in localities with systems to collect polypropylene, like that in yogurt containers." He says this innovation points the way to the day when synthetic goods can be used, upcycled, and used again without losing any material quality—in cradle-to-cradle cycles.

In an interview with McDonough, it is clear that his chemist colleague, Michael Braungart, is an important influence. You can almost see his brain churning out ideas as thoughts pass through the turnstile of his inner vision when he says that at the Rohner textile plant in Switzerland they designed a fabric safe enough to eat.

According to a *Newsweek* interview, "the manufacturing process uses no mutagens, carcinogens, endocrine disrupters, heavy-metal contaminants or chemicals that cause ozone depletion, allergies, skin desensitization or plant and fish toxicity." In the process of testing for 8,000 commonly used chemicals, they ended up with 38. The effluent water is as clean as Swiss drinking water, and the local garden club used the waste trimmings as mulch. Workers no longer have to wear protective clothing, eliminating regulatory paperwork and reducing the cost of production by 20 percent.

Made of worsted wool and the wicking plant fiber ramie, this fabric adapts to the environment to provide warmth when it is cold and coolness when it is hot, so comfort is its star feature. The edible fabric was selected for upholstery on the new Airbus 380.

Adapting architecture to provide a factory full of daylight and fresh air boosted productivity to new heights, and because of the natural light, electrical lighting costs were cut by 50 percent and overall energy by 30 percent. Though the model has been used for some time, China Housing Industry Association is now considering it as a measure of responsibility for building housing for 400 million people over the next 12 years as McDonough Braungart Design Chemistry design seven new cities there. They are looking to building materials of the future, including new polystyrene from BASF, which contains no noxious chemicals but provides strong, lightweight, super-insulated walls. As a result, huge benefits are found in heating and cooling costing next to nothing; and its soundproofing quality means that even a crowd on the floor above will not be heard. Sounds like all apartment dwellings should be using this, if only to provide some sanity in tight-knit community housing.

A bonus to "green roof" planting, in addition to its beauty, is its ability to damp the sounds of jet planes at San Francisco International Airport while absorbing a lot of storm water, a serious issue in the area. Other benefits include oxygen and a natural habitat for fauna. McDonough Braungart Design Chemistry had a great deal of success putting a green roof atop Ford Motor Company's River Rouge plant, saving Ford millions of dollars in storm-water equipment. The ten-and-a-half-acre green roof is the largest McDonough has done, designed and planted to double as a habitat for animals. He also convinced Ford to install "parking lots that absorb water, which then goes into a giant water filter and gets run through constructed wetlands. By the time the water gets to a river three days later, it's pure."[7]

McDonough is a world-renowned architect and winner of three U.S. awards: the Presidential Award for Sustainable Development (1996), the National Design Award (2004), and the EPA Presidential Green Chemistry

Challenge Award (2003). *Time* magazine recognized him as a "Hero for the Planet" in 1999, stating that "his utopianism is grounded in a unified philosophy that—in demonstrable and practical ways—is changing the design of the world."[8]

Green Is the New Black

In 2000, the nonprofit U.S. Green Building Council instituted a green certification program called LEED (Leadership in Energy and Environmental Design). Since its inception, 167 commercial building projects have been certified for this four-tier system, according to the organization's president, Rick Fedrizzi.

On a lesser scale, but equally consistent with the grass-roots movement, Al and Myra Rosen's home in Los Angeles is an example of what homeowners can do to be green. With the purchase of a 4,000-square-foot house in 1997, they began a journey to renovate with eco-conscious awareness, from triple-glazed glass filled with argon gas that lets in sunlight and insulates against heat to windows and skylights that brighten the colorfully enhanced interior.[9]

The move to green chemistry is credited to a change of mind in industry thinking. Instead of continuing to pursue chemical products as they always have, says past president and director-at-large William F. Carroll of the American Chemical Society, their newly stated purpose is to develop better chemical products that use fewer regents and solvents and less energy to achieve the desired end, while generating less waste and increasing profitability.

A Wisconsin-based company, BioIonix, has developed a cylindrical wastewater disinfecting system. Connected to a generator about the size of a microwave oven, it uses the electromagnetic field's electric current to create hydrogen peroxide to disinfect sludge from human feces: industrial waste essentially turns poop into potting soil. Invented by Ken Schlager and Steve Gorski, the system has the capability to kill much of the bacteria and reduce odors. Biosolids are turned into a fertilizer that farmers can apply directly to fields and backyard gardens, another income stream for BioIonix. This young company, started in 2005, holds two patents, with more applications filed, and has generated $1.67 million from 15 investor groups.

Part of the beauty of the BioIonix system is that used hydrogen peroxide breaks back down into water and oxygen, all with electromagnetic fields.

Now we're talking. Here is an example of the power in the electromagnetic field to reconstitute human and industrial waste into fertilizer and clean up after itself. James Tretheway, the company's president, said the system can be used to brighten paper and textiles, as well, virtually "eliminating the expense and hazard of transporting hydrogen peroxide to those plants in concentrated form." As a bonus, it also saves fees for contractors to haul away the sludge to landfills. The environment is the winner in this technology.[10]

Another company, in Oceanside, New York, produces household cleansers so safe that the president, Kevin Schwartz, is not above taking a swig to prove it, and he challenges others to have the same confidence in drinking ordinary cleaning solutions. His vegetable-based Healthy Home Products, free of caustic and toxic ingredients that cause irritation on contact to eyes or to skin, make up a "all-natural" environment-friendly product line safe enough to use around newborns and pets. A bonus: their products have no fumes.

Governor George Pataki signed legislation to go green in New York schools by 2007. Some districts were ahead of the curve, having already experimented with liquid lye bacteria to digest urine salts when cleaning school bathrooms.

The Healthy Home Products use 100 percent recyclable materials, with all ingredients coming from renewable resources. Like BabyGanics, HHP's safe-around-baby products join Seventh Generation, Method, Ecover and Earth Friendly Products. Little by little, the green movement is spreading. As more stores carry "green" products, more environmentally aware buyers will catch the mood to switch, setting the pace for the green revolution to take hold across the board.[11]

In 2009, Ford Motor Company touted Green as the New Black, citing noxious odors from vinyl fabrics used in automobile interiors. Keeping up with the Green movement, interior fabrics will be softer and silkier to the touch as well as sustainable. Other 100-percent post-industrial materials include re-engineered wood, "chrome-free" leather and "renewable soy foam seat bases" and mohair carpet. Their 2008 Ford Escape used 100 percent post-industrial materials, supplied by InterfaceFABRIC, Inc. "conserving an estimated 600,000 gallons of water, an estimated 1.8 million pounds of carbon dioxide equivalents, and the equivalent of more than 7 million kilowatt hours of electricity annually."[12]

Recycling used car tires, glass-bottle bottoms and drink cans from landfills, architect Michael Reynolds of Taos, New Mexico, founder of Earthship Biotecture, has built more than 1,000 sustainable homes. Used tires packed with dirt retain heat and strengthen walls for a sturdy structure, while glass walls allow sunlight for gardens and waterfalls inside the home. Photovoltaic panels, windmills, water collection and onsite sewage treatment make homes sustainable at an affordable price, with a heating bill about $100 a year, since the homes are not on the grid.

When the 2004 earthquake and tsunami hit the Andaman Islands in the Indian Ocean, Reynolds was asked to help rebuild the area. With bottles collected by children, houses were built that could even accommodate food production in the home.[13]

Recycling is not a new concept, but in 2008, converting wood chips, garbage or crop waste into motor fuels became economically and environmentally viable. Even Henry Ford Jr. himself was fascinated with the idea. Corn, algae, plastics, construction debris, forest and lawn trimmings, wood chips, wheat straw, even pine chips and other types of agricultural waste are being considered to produce ethanol. Garbage itself is even under the scope, though conversion problems exist, as DuPont plans to convert nonedible parts of corn and sugarcane. Ideas abound as the human mind churns possible solutions to the excessive waste in landfills propagated by unconscious behavior in a throwaway society. At its new Nevada plant, Fulcrum BioEnergy expects to make 10.5 million gallons of ethanol from 90,000 tons of garbage, while arsenic-laden utility poles are also in line for recycling.

The costly investment in commercializing a process may appear viable at the outset, but time will tell if these initiatives will mature to accommodate a world market. Should electric cars take precedence, and light rail expand as the U.K. and Europe demonstrate and as Warren Buffett's investment projections predict, petroleum products could become a moot point as a major industry and companies could again be in the creative-invention mode.

In 2010, when the BP oil rig exploded in the Gulf of Mexico, it was found that the alarm system had been partly turned off so workers could sleep. It caused an environmental debacle when a pipe five miles deep in the ocean exploded, releasing billions of gallons of oil affecting fish, wildlife, livelihoods and lifestyles. Some workers died as they jumped overboard. Instead of turning the alarm off for a few more winks, the wake-up call for all in this regard means to allow the alarm to sound.

Innovation, then, requires a willingness to experiment and to realize that things do not always work right the first time but future benefits are worth the risk. And take risks we must, for no problem can be solved with the same consciousness that created it, which brings us back to the way we think. Thinking about the future. Dreaming a better life for everyone. That's the stuff of invention.

The Solar Solution

As we seek ways to be more aligned with Mother Nature, drawing on energy from the sun is the new frontier. Solar-energy photovoltaic panels are leading the field, making it both doable and affordable. Joshua Pearce, an engineering professor at Queen's University in Ontario, Canada, conducted two studies to prove the sun's effectiveness as an energy source, showing that it has the same potential to produce power as all the nuclear power reactors in the United States combined. Pearce, a solar voltaic materials specialist, says that in his area of southeastern Ontario alone, 95 gigawatts of potential power are available.

Proving the availability of massive amounts of sun energy to generate power, rooftop photovoltaic panels exposed to sunlight will produce five gigawatts of electricity, enough to power a house and then some. Some communities are banding together, acting as solar-energy suppliers and selling excess to power companies. If anyone wants to get off the grid, this is the answer.

In 2010, I was to speak at the first SICES (Sichuan International Clean Energy Summit) conference in Chengdu, China, where space-based solar power, SBSP, introduced a reliable source of clean energy desperately needed by that country whose energy dependence on coal is everywhere evident. Relatively new buildings were covered with soot. Workers walking or riding bicycles and motorbikes wore masks as a measure of protection from breathing the air polluted by coal dust. The sun never broke through the thick-layered clouds during our three-day visit.

While SBSP is not a new concept, the commercial viability of it is, thanks to technology advancements and current market conditions. The idea is to build large arrays of solar panels in space to capture the sunlight and convert it to electricity 24 hours a day, transmitting the energy back to Earth as radio waves similar to a mobile phone call signal. Solar-power satellites placed in geosynchronous orbit where they are in the sunlight 24 hours a day generate electrical energy with solar cells that are converted to radio frequency energy by transmitters. This energy is then beamed to the receiving "rectenna" (rectifying antenna) on Earth, where the radio frequency energy is converted to DC electricity, then to AC electricity wired into the existing power grid. As you can see, the rectenna is only a receiver of the energy and not a transmitter of any electricity. Captured on Earth by the rectenna, energy is then distributed to power companies who redistribute to customers on their grid.

Indeed, solar technology is the global solution to serve the masses, says Ralph Nansen, author of *Energy Crisis* and *Sun Power*, who led Boeing's team to develop the overall concept of solar-power satellites under the auspices of the Department of Energy and NASA and also participated in the Saturn/Apollo program and the Space Shuttle development. A pioneer in the move to solar, Nansen sees it as "a grand but elegant solution to the problems plaguing our energy-hungry world."

Neville Williams, author of *Chasing the Sun: Solar Adventures Around the World*, is lauded by Sir Arthur C. Clarke, inventor of the communications satellite, as well as Ross Gelbspan and Thom Hartmann, authors who share his vision of delivering solar electricity to 50,000 families in 11 countries and in North America. Williams formed the SELCO (Solar Electric Light Company) group of companies and founded the Solar Electric Light Fund (SELF) in 1990 to transform native communities who had no way to capture nature's energy for their use. This included tribal groups who lived in mountainous regions and suffered from severe weather and inadequate means to heat their villages. With electric lights, they no longer have to retire when the sun goes down, and they can eat foods that need to be cooked—a life-changer for sure.

The twin pillars of sustainability are efficiency and renewable energy. Since Earth is our home, with all the elements we need to survive, thrive and expand awareness through a developing brain, we have a responsibility to be prudent in our decisions in drawing on natural resources to do so. If we consider a subset of such resources, it must be green power produced from solar, wind, geothermal power and heat, biogas, biomass and low-impact small hydroelectric sources. Reducing dependency on fossil fuels enhances world security. Second-generation technologies include solar heating and cooling, wind power, modern forms of bioenergy and solar photovoltaics. Third-generation technologies still in development include advanced biomass gasification, biorefinery technologies, solar thermal power, hot dry rock geothermal energy and ocean energy. In addition, advances in nanotechnology may make it a major player.[14] All of these sources require commitments from related agencies in sustainable energy, as well as public sector involvement. In 2008, a comprehensive cost-benefit analysis review of energy solutions ranked wind power combined with battery electric vehicles (BEV) as the most efficient, followed by concentrated solar power, geothermal power, tidal power, photovoltaic, wave power, coal capture and storage, nuclear energy and finally biofuels.[15]

If BP's Deepwater wells are any indication, we may be in the last throes of fossil fuel supplies, which will bring the developed world to a standstill. When falling supplies of fossil fuels are exhausted, we'd better have an alternative or the world will come to a grinding halt and civilization will return to the Dark Ages. Our dependency on oil must be replaced with reusable/renewable energy sources, alternatives that sustain a viable lifestyle for all peoples on Planet Earth. The siren of alarm is sounding the wakeup call for humanity to count their marbles and be grateful for what they have.

Western societies, accustomed to excess everything, will have to return to simpler ways, beginning by treating Mother Nature with respect, for unless we do, civilization may not make it too much further. The exploitation of nature's freely given resources by profit-oriented corporations who care only about how much money can be made will end then, as they, too, become victims of their own warped self-interest.

CHAPTER EIGHT

THE NATURE OF LEADERSHIP
Knowledge Workers and the Art of Listening

In 2002 the U.S. Bureau of Labor statistics reported that output of goods and services edged up only a modest 0.3 percent at a 1.1 percent decrease in production hours. As the workforce grows smaller, there is bound to be a squeeze. Who will do the work? And who will have a clear enough head to lead if Big Pharma has its way as the biggest drug pusher on the planet?

To model business as cooperative entities, like biology and the human body, workers would be paid a living wage, while the company takes a reasonable profit as its share. This cooperative organic effort would nourish people in constructive ways and show them capable of more than illusory power.

Earth is one body composed of 6.5 billion people, a shortfall from each human body's complex of 50 to 70 or more trillion cells. Each cell has purpose, a job, or it would not exist, for Mother Nature is efficient. She is too smart to waste energy needlessly. The cell's purpose is to provide service, to live in harmony with natural forces, to enjoy the fruits of human existence and to maintain the chemical factory within the nervous system's membrane of perceptive protection.

Without the gifts of Mother Nature, none of what we experience today would be happening. No wars would be fought, no structures would be built, there would be no hunger and no selfish motives on the part of companies thinking they are greater than God. Mankind would have no ability to create, investigate, learn or grow, much less be in business. No money, no economic climate to legalize gambling in casinos or in the stock market. So, with humble appreciation for the gift of life, an intelligent brain and physical prowess, we recognize that no thing or idea lasts forever.

Screwing Mother Nature for profit is not the answer. All living creatures have a symbiotic relationship with all of life and survive by living in harmony. As ecological agencies seek to thwart disease through the use of bio-survival tactics, incited by herbicides and other artificial creations, well-meaning synthetic-pathogen-focused companies are heightening our awareness of the challenge. On the other hand, when you are living a happy and fulfilled life, your health is strong, and your need for health care minimized. When the chips are down, wisdom will carry you a long way. In this context, you are fit to survive.

Business has controls, the government has controls, and there are managers over managers, though they are given sophisticated titles such as President, Vice President, Board of Governors, Chairman, General Manager, Director or Department Head. The titles really mean little, except each has different responsibilities. In the end it is all about oversight, controls that look more like hierarchical parenting. No one person has all the knowledge, for each of us has but a piece of the pie. Depending upon our education and experience, the perspective could be only bite-size.

Now, take the physical body and its nifty organizational system, efficient, easy to manage and functioning well unless we skirt the rules and cheat on ourselves. Cells grow, die and replace themselves in a neat schedule that does not interfere with the system's functioning, all without conscious control. Our brain is the Head of State, sending messages to the body on demand, according to our perceptions. With our five senses, signals alert the body to external conditions, but interpretations are handled in the brain's Cave of Brahman. The input, process and output stations act as a boardroom with members who vote according to how they interpret the signals. The signals are all part of the sympathetic nervous system, keen on staying alert for survival.

Listening to the physical body's nonverbal response to our excesses will in the end express itself either by living a long life in good health or by years of prescription drugs and frequent visits to the doctor. Consider how creativity in business has the same motivating force used to maintain a healthy body, that of intelligent choice. The strong desire to achieve a positive outcome is what drives most leaders. It would be great if products were all beneficial to life and if the consciousness of company executives were always seeking the best for everyone. However, that is not always the case, bombarded as we are with pharmaceutical media advertising, a costume designed to conceal the mental programming shtick to be sick.

For clear thinking, effective communications and high-energy optimism to get the job done, a healthy feel-good attitude is essential. It is body-mind teamwork built on loyalty and a spirit of cooperation, very desirable traits for any serious endeavor.

Consensus works beautifully to achieve results established in the beginning through dynamic group dialogue. When teams feel a part of the process, they are more eager to fully contribute.

Working together for the good of the whole gets jobs done faster. In addition, teamwork builds camaraderie through trust and shared responsibility. Everyone benefits. In this way, teams with a common goal effectively assure success.

Happiness in the body, at work and at home means a balanced life. When companies or organizations demonstrate compassion, setting an example for others to follow in taking care of business on the home front first, they go a long way toward insuring a well-balanced life and continued enthusiasm to participate in the company's success.

Future Thinkers Lay Foundation

Along with Jacque Fresco, visionary architect and founder of Future by Design, Peter Drucker is another legendary forecaster of a knowledge society. Drucker presciently wrote about The Next Society for *The Economist* in November 2001, predicting the new frontier in business to be a knowledge society staffed with knowledge workers. Its three main characteristics are:

1. Borderlessness: because knowledge travels even more effortlessly than money.
2. Upward mobility: available to everyone through easily acquired formal education.
3. The potential for failure as well as success: Anyone can acquire the "means of production", i.e., the knowledge required for the job, but not everyone can win.

The ease and speed of information transference will accelerate in the highly competitive environment via the Internet. Those in the world with access can stay informed, research products and know at what price they may be purchased, all with a click. Knowledge is already available for inquiring minds to accelerate learning, and this will continue to escalate in business schools, universities, hospitals, and increasingly in government agencies.

Prime areas of expansion are knowledge products, health care and education. Manufacturing jobs in America fell from 35 percent of the workforce in 1950 to less than half that in 2008. Outsourcing production to foreign countries attracts workers willing to accept low wages, for they see the jobs as opportunities to move up through education.

Drucker goes on to say that new collaborative frontiers will be built on affiliate alliances, joint ventures, minority stakes, know-how agreements and contracts to create confederations. This is already moving in some corridors, as I myself have experienced.

The effects of this transition will be felt in top management's responsibilities as they balance both short-term and long-term benefits. The same holds true by extension for customers, shareholders, knowledge employees and communities. Empowering people as important brain-thinker resources casts off the old cost-based cog-in-the-wheel percept that demeaned workers as simply an assembly-line necessity.[1]

This organizational thinking model is based on leadership from the inside out, where teams of knowledge workers set rules for engagement. This new frontier in business invites feedback. No longer are orders from the top hailed as Caesar's law. Drucker predicted that knowledge workers would replace the non-skilled. In less formal atmospheres, Action-Learning Teams (ALTs), a concept developed by corporate learning expert Bruce LaRue, would engage creative ideas to problem-solve. This is welcome news for workers who see ways to shortcut processes. In the past, their suggestions would have been met with disdain by supervisors who followed hierarchical orders to the letter. The cooperative feedback implementation system proves its own success. Knowledge workers have more say about how best to do their jobs.

This shift, from the competitive "Don't mess with me, I'm the boss" attitude to working together cooperatively, has spread to the U.S. Army and its combat forces. Major General Robert R. Ivany, presiding over the U.S. Army War College, instituted programs to prepare the next generation of military and civilian leaders to meet cultural and organizational change in a way more in keeping with an expanded worldview. The dramatic transformation in the Army's organizational culture changes the way they conduct business.

Ivany used the Action-Learning Team's art-of-listening model that allows other people's concerns and criticism to be heard and respected in the same way that we all like to be heard. It is a basic human need. It draws on listening without interrupting, which differs from the "Shut up, I know best what you should do" model. When we ignore others' contributions on subjects of common interest in favor of our own, channels are blocked for further discussion.

In the Army's version of the ALT process, called an After Action Review (AAR), facilitators are interested in three main points:

1. What is the unit's mission?
2. What actually happened?
3. What are three capabilities the unit must sustain and three it must improve?

The leaders learn from their subordinates, shifting the culture from a patriarchal model to one of cooperation where shared knowledge is accepted without retribution. Building this culture of cooperative teamwork yields more information, elucidates the talents and skills of the team and allows them to speak up about their superior's shortcomings without retribution.

Huge benefits are derived from this cooperative model. Building trust and honesty is essential to empowering organizations. However, it's cooperation and peaceful negotiation that make this phenomenon possible. Advancements in communications, product development, knowledge and living systems' efficiency make life easier.

From colonels to privates, channels are open to discussion and information-sharing. Everyone learns from each other, rather than having all the commands issued by the lead officer. The generals set the conditions, including assessing anticipated critical moves on the battlefield. This is a far cry from traditional military leadership, where the high command carried all the decision-making responsibility.

This improved knowledge management system expanded throughout the units, inspiring young commanders to set up their own website to network. With their ability to exchange information immediately, discuss operations assessments, exercises, and lessons in real time about operations, the After Action Review encouraged facilitators to cross-pollinate with peers on what did or didn't work.

Certain characteristics are critical to Action-Learning Team leaders. They must be able to:

- Evolve team wisdom and insight
- Model the change they seek
- Secure mutual trust and respect throughout team
- Encourage creative problem solving
- Maintain focus on intention
- Modify leadership style as needed
- Make freedom and accountability high priority

This model provides a clear path for knowledge workers to effectively participate in the success of a venture with leadership establishing the pattern of behavior. Rather than treating knowledge workers as employees, leaders manage them as though they were volunteers. Success results when they are treated with respect, trained to do their job well and allowed to participate fully as part of a cooperative venture.[2]

Leadership

Leadership plays a critical role in demonstrating expected behavior through attitude and performance. To underplay its significance would be detrimental to any aspiring company patterning itself after others' success.

We learn from everyone, regardless of who they are or what they do. In the past, our parents smoked cigarettes and cigars, but forbade offspring to take up the habit. Not to be denied the perceived pleasures of adulthood, stubborn progeny stole away behind the barn and lit up. Many a hind side was bared in reprimand, but that did not stop the mimicking away from home. We mimic teachers in how to read, to write, to speak up or to shut up. We observe and know when words and actions do not match.

In business, no matter the size, from the mom-and-pop store to global corporations, it is no different. Leaders are mentors, like parents. They are more experienced with life, or so we think. Rather than running a family, it is generally the men who run a business or a country, though women are better organizers and multitask more naturally. Their executive abilities are obvious in managing a family, for in some sense a family is a small company enterprise. Decisions influencing the whole are subject to scrutiny, just as risks taken behind boardroom doors, once thought isolated to one corner of the world, take on global proportions. Worldwide communication systems today leave little unknown.

Whether for good or for naught, a company's successful bid to survive in the marketplace will affect the people who run the company, the employees, their livelihoods, the stability of their families' lifestyles as well as the communities where they live and have their business. Often, the effects of such decisions affect the industry, the country and foreign trade. This is much like the U.S. automobile debacle with plant closures and employee debasement.

The Iowa-based company Sky Factory, which creates ceiling and wall art to bring the beauty of nature inside, is a great example of what it means to "build a beautiful company", shunning the hierarchical business model to incorporate everyone with a stake in its future as an owner. Sharing information through open discussions bonds teams to the mission. The vision of its entrepreneurial founder, Bill Witherspoon, a talented painter of landscapes, encompasses five principles: Share information, give everyone equal footing, make decisions as a group, serve each other and share the rewards. With fine art as a model for Sky Factory, it endures as all great art does.[3]

A disaster like Hurricane Katrina, devastating a whole population of coastal residents and thriving businesses, shocked communities into taking another look at their infrastructure, examining weakness and preparedness for disaster. The wake-up call is a stunning blow to our perception of what it means to have a safe harbor. Mother Nature has some level of dependability, if you are watchful and attentive; however, assuming that life is going to continue as it always has is to leave your sails up in a windstorm.

New Orleans, Louisiana, was a test of humanity's compassion. Wal-Mart stepped up to the plate when the U.S. government fell short. They performed admirably in spite of how derisive the attitude toward their stores. Company leadership was awake, aware and ready to lead. They did what our government could not do. FEMA flopped miserably because our government lacked leadership, because no one took charge. There was no plan for emergencies, despite the warning of 9/11. They bungled the situation, as has been proven to be the norm in over-managed operations around the country. Managed, but not led. Everything from food stamps to social services to health care and more are "managed". What does this really mean?

It means people are placed in responsible positions without a clue as to how to lead. They manage to get along and they manage to get by. They perpetuate the managed lifestyles of those they are supposed to lead; manage the department; manage the product, the time clock and the payroll.

That may work until an emergency hits. Then it is soon obvious there is no leadership capable of making appropriate decisions. FEMA's handling of New Orleans is a good example of national incompetence.

Anyone with an idea sounding reasonable will act in the capacity of a leader in a moment of crisis, whether they have ever led before or not. When they act in charge, they rise to the occasion and are ready to make the responsible decisions to save the day. Such examples of leadership occurred at the Twin Towers disaster site, another instance of national incompetence. Natural leaders assume authority and in doing so demonstrate their capability to do the right thing for the right reason. It is leadership of the kind that inspires people to do their best. They think of the safety and security of not only themselves, but of all concerned.

Meeting the Challenge

Dee Ward Hock, founder of VISA, offers a powerful message of change, hope and possibility in his "chaordic" organization model, a blend of chaos and order. Instead of the rigid top-down management style that has been the hallmark of business for more than 400 years, Hock's model for the future of business organizations uses the same cooperative principles of biology discussed throughout this book as the basis for distributed power, diversity and ingenuity.

"We are at that very point in time when a 400-year-old age is dying and another is struggling to be born—a shifting of culture, science, society, and institutions enormously greater than the world has ever experienced. Ahead, the possibility of the regeneration of individuality, liberty, community, and ethics such as the world has never known, and a harmony with nature, with one another, and with the divine intelligence such as the world has never dreamed."[4]

Effective leadership includes self-organizing principles to make the difference in success or failure of an idea, a product or a corporation. Leadership responsive to the environment and to the people makes the world a better place to live, not just to survive to satisfy the bottom line or get a good position in the stock exchange, but to thrive in harmony with Mother Nature.

Part of the problem, as we've seen, is our educational system with its backward "dumb it down" methodology. Reducing instruction to the lowest common denominator leaves little room for the development of mind-stretching enthusiasts. Usually, this is when problems crop up in the classrooms. Challenging students to excel beyond their self-imposed limitations, or those imposed by the system, is what it takes to survive in the jungle of tangled webs confronting education today, and that's why Hock's model of self-organizing principles, ethical and spiritual, could save the day.

This model is an adaptation of nature's innate cooperative-competition structure. Students and administrations cooperate, while students and teachers compete for excellence in education. Families navigate the world best with an open system of discussion and planning. Hock's model of self-governance is perfect for the educational system, where responsibility is shared, viewpoints welcome and collaborative leadership the order of the day.

The key component is cooperation, knowing that each contribution is important to the whole and that leadership emerges from those who understand the principles. Biology proves cooperation works. The whole of nature adapts as needed. As stated in an earlier chapter, the human body's 50 to 70 trillion cells work together for the good of the whole. Leadership is acquired confidence attained by heightened awareness of the environment and correct interpretations of perceptual reality. The good of the whole brings the greatest rewards. At any level, collaborating to seek beneficial solutions is always the best tack.

Lee Iacocca, former CEO of the Chrysler Corporation, takes a hard stand when it comes to leadership. He lambasted politicians, Congress and President Bush in 2007 for their lackadaisical behavior in preserving America. Like so many others aware of the inequities favoring the wealthy with tax cuts, leaving the man on the street to pick up their crumbs, Iacocca wants to know what happened to the backbone to stand up for what is right. When the country is in crisis, Congress takes a holiday. Events continue to plague the country without a pause. To onlookers it is reminiscent of Rome burning while Nero fiddles. In this case, it is Iraq and the Middle East.

"We should be screaming bloody murder," he says. "We've got a gang of clueless bozos steering our ship of state right over a cliff, we've got corporate gangsters stealing us blind, and we can't even clean up after a hurricane, much less build a hybrid car."

Iacocca asks the hard questions: "Where have all the leaders gone?" He restates the pressing question with answers. "Once leaders lifted us up and made us want to do better." And he outlines what he calls the "Nine C's of Leadership". In short form, they are:

CURIOSITY—Listening outside the consensual crowd of head bobbers of the inner circle, being a voracious reader, being aware of the news and of other viewpoints.

CREATIVENESS—Being willing to go out on a limb, try something different, think outside the box. Change is the guaranteed constant, and leadership is all about managing change.

COMMUNICATION—Telling the truth, straight talk about the reality of a situation, even when it hurts to do so.

CHARACTER—Knowing the difference between right and wrong, and "having the guts" to do the right thing.

COURAGE—Without posturing or braggadocio, being willing to take on the hard questions without hiding behind a protective screen. Committing to sit down at the negotiating table and talk.

CONVICTION—The passion to make a difference, to accomplish something worthwhile—what Iacocca calls having "fire in the belly".

CHARISMA—A quality that makes people want to follow you, an ability to inspire because you are trusted.

COMPETENCE—Responsible leadership involves problem solving and doing it well.

COMMON SENSE—Recognize a hole in the wall when you see one. Measure truth against prattle that stirs the pot but doesn't cook the food.

Iacocca says that leaders are made, not born. While theory makes for good conversation, postulates solve nothing. There is nothing you can sink your teeth into.[5]

It is in taking action that you show you have what it takes to lead. To make a positive difference in the world requires taking charge to meet the challenge.

And the World Turns

In 1999, the United States became lopsided, falling into dependency when once our prideful strength of free enterprise had worked for the good of the whole. With the onset of the WTO, the World Trade Organization, the rules changed. No longer was it "keep the workers happy"; now it is about how much more money can be made at the expense of other nations while breaking the backs of workers in service to corporate interests.

This was not taken lightly in Seattle, when an activists' peaceful protest march outside the WTO conference broke out into a riot, provoked by police when they started pushing people around. When bullhorns blared threats to disband or else, it went against the grain as a threat to the right of free speech and the right to assemble. The threatening presence of police dressed in full Star Wars protective gear made it a movie scene with the evil specter and stealth force of Darth Vader. The shocked crowd stood their ground. They had a permit to assemble. Why this? The police increased agitation by poking protestors with their billy clubs. I stood staring at the TV monitor in disbelief.

When the police aggravated the situation by pushing and shoving, the crowd became infuriated. Throwing bottles in defense, they broke windows in nearby businesses, which invited vandalism. From there the scene became a movie script, unimaginable in peaceful Seattle, known for its laissez-faire attitude about life. TV viewers watched this drama play out through rooftop cameras, narrated by newscasters who, themselves, could hardly believe their eyes. As the police became more unruly, it got worse, leading to shameful behavior unbefitting the badge. Seattleites watched in horror as the police beat a protester. Was this really happening in America?

Activists in protest of corporations moving jobs to Third World countries where disadvantaged workers' pay scale is pennies to the dollar also knew that home-front job loss would result as imports of foreign goods flooded the marketplace. Those who could read the writing on the wall saw the portents of evil deeds and unfair practices looming on the horizon, the result of Free Trade, as opposed to Fair Trade, where workers are paid a living wage. It all changed in July 2008 when India and China refused to play the game. In the WTO defeat over the domination of agribusiness and biopiracy, it lost its grip on the control of wheat, as well as other biodiverse crops and traditional knowledge that it hoped to privatize, removing the ability of native people to grow their own food and to feed themselves.

As the independent news service Intellectual Property Watch put it: "Rather than respect the rights of farmers, indigenous peoples and rural communities for whom traditional seeds, native livestock, indigenous knowledge and the local cultures they are intertwined with constitute a collective heritage, it would turn them into corporate property at the highest level yet."

This complex negotiating organization, TRIPS (trade-related aspects of intellectual property rights), is about the recolonization of economically weak countries to profit agribusiness.[6]

With the U.S. losing its manufacturing industry as its economic core, most will agree that corporate greed is responsible. Competitive practices by some multinational corporations devour a market and leech exports produced by Third World countries, repeating the process until, at some point there are no more frontiers to conquer. What will the world of commerce look like when people have all the products they need or will ever want; when the power-starved corporation has gorged itself on its own excesses in a frenzy to increase profit?

As David Korten states in his insightful book about alternatives, *The Great Turning: From Empire to Earth Community*:

> *The difference between human consumption and the regenerative capacity of Earth is made up by depleting the natural capital of the planet—both nonrenewable capital, like minerals and fossil fuels, and renewable capital like forests, fisheries, soil, water, and climatic systems. The consequence is to extract a temporary and unsustainable subsidy from Earth to support current consumption at the expense of our children and their children for generations to come.*[7]

While corporations have expanded their power to megalithic proportions, they see the results of their success as people protest the inequity of a stratified society, where wealth is concentrated at the top. When people run out of money and/or purposely cease purchasing because they are in debt over their ears, will corporations' exploitation end, or will they, like the dinosaurs with their oversized bodies and small heads, be too unwieldy to survive a change in economic climate?

Corporate leaders are smart but easily lured by the money that can be made. The romantic obsession with the corporate bottom line confirms Milton Friedman's dictum that says corporations exist "purely to create profits." Many people see this motive as contrary to how families and communities work, and certainly how biological metabolism and the body as a whole function. The intelligence of the human body would never behave in such a way as to destroy itself on purpose. Had Friedman lived, I like to think he would at some point have seen the folly of his postulate.

CHAPTER NINE

INVENTION AND PERFORMANCE
Spirited Drive for Innovation

Innovative ideas with value, performance and high potential for return on investment can be worthwhile ventures for those willing to take a risk. Such is the case with 3M's Post-it Notes. In 1966 Spencer F. Silver, Ph.D., took a position at 3M's Central Research lab as a Senior Chemist. Two years later, in 1968, he developed a "high-quality but 'low-tack' adhesive, made of tiny, indestructible acrylic spheres." The inventive substance worked well as a temporary attachment, and could easily be pulled from a surface without damage, leaving no trace of its presence. However, its usefulness was initially elusive. Were it not for Silver's colleague Arthur Fry, and his frustration over placeholder bits of paper repeatedly falling out from his hymnal at choir practice, Post-it Notes might never have been born, let alone made it to market in 1980.[1]

Silver and Fry realized that the new adhesive could hold papers together and allow them to be pulled apart again without tearing. Perfect for attaching temporary notes to office documents. They could be used again and again without losing sticking power, so long as dirt did not occlude the adhesive's round pores. Post-it Flags would follow, along with other variations on the theme, as imagination blossomed ideas.

Problem solving is the stuff of innovation and the challenge it invites. Take modes of travel, for instance. Travel in the pioneering horse-and-buggy days meant bumpy rides over rough terrain, but when roads washed out, mud-covered wheels held no traction. How far you could go at any one time was likely determined by the horse's endurance and the traveler's patience. This was not lost on potential businessmen who realized that necessary way stations made perfect locations for inns and stables. Thus, the stagecoach route was born, serving both the travelers' and the horses' need to rest and be fed. As towns sprang up, roads were covered with bricks to avoid the slippery mess of mud-covered wheels. While labor-intensive, handmade bricks smoothed the ride, and many are still in place today, a testament to how well they were made and how well they served their purpose. Boston is a good place to experience the flavor of those earlier times, as bricks can still be found lining areas of the city. Improvements over the years brought cement shoveled in place to harden, later followed by poured concrete and asphalt, still used today to smoothly serve our automobile culture.

Fast-forward to the 20th century and we have gem hunter Gary Bowersox on one of his yearly treks to Afghanistan through meadows up and over rocky climbs into the mountains in search of gemstones. Guides led the way, in part on donkeys, as they climbed narrow paths skirting mountainsides and small villages. Some roads were paved. Once, as they attempted to cross a washed-out road, their Toyota truck got stuck. The Afghan men simply unplugged the distributor wires, picked up the car, carried it to the other side, reconnected the wires, and off they went. It is rather like the gallant gentlemen of more genteel times, carrying a lady across the mud puddle to dry land.

Driving innovation is the creative mind, always primed to problem-solve. Spurred on by imagined success, innovators still take but a single focused step at a time.

Keeping Energy Clean

In August 2006, Bill Ford, Chairman and CEO of the Ford Motor Company, remarked in his *Vision for the Future* report how public awareness of social and environmental issues is gaining public attention:

> We are more convinced than ever that our long-term success depends on how our Company addresses issues such as climate change, energy security, working conditions in our supply chain, safety, congestion, noise and innovative use of renewable resources and materials. Our business connects fundamentally with society and its growing need for sustainable mobility and it is, therefore, in our material interest to anticipate and respond to that need. I refer to this as the sustainability imperative.

He also admits that no single technology can resolve the effects of carbon-dioxide emissions on the atmosphere, suggesting instead a multipronged fuel strategy involving bio-diesel and bio-ethanol in vehicles better known as hybrids.

In 2005, through its National Clean Diesel Campaign and SmartWay financing program, along with the West Coast Collaborative of public- and private-sector groups, EPA awarded more than $2.2 million to West Coast states for diesel emissions reductions. Of this, more than $1.4 million went to projects in Idaho, Oregon and Washington. With projects such as these all over the country, emissions reductions can have a significant effect.

Overconfident, the "Big Three" U.S. automakers, Ford Motor Company, General Motors and DaimlerChrysler, fell behind the curve. In January 2007, Reuters reported that Japan's Toyota Motor Corporation "became one of the Big Three automakers in 2006, using its strong December U.S. sales to oust DaimlerChrysler from the fabled troika."[2]

Responsibility for this shift can be laid on consumer awareness. Fuel-efficient automobiles are more economical to operate and less expensive to buy. No longer can the "Big Three" motor companies ignore the winds of change. Unless they innovate, disenchanted consumers will speak loudly with their wallets by buying hybrid cars.

With pickups and SUVs absorbing 15 percent of the market globally, Ford Motor Company's CEO, Alan R. Mulally, announced in July 2008 that their smaller automobile, Focus, would be their new lead for profits, replacing the Taurus sedan as linchpin. He also created a new mantra to encourage more cohesion among departments: "One Ford, One Team, One Plan, One Goal."[3]

Damaging General Motors's reputation is the fiasco with the innovative electric car. Ten years after the EV1 came on the market in 1996, to be leased but never sold, all but one car had been recalled. GM hauled them to a salvage yard where they were compressed flat as mud pies to destroy the market.

Now why would an automobile company destroy a product that customers loved? Why? That is the question everyone is asking. The film *Who Killed the Electric Car?* exposes the haunting control of products reaching the marketplace and shows what happens when a company steps outside industry comfort zones. Collusion with oil companies corrupted a transition to electric cars, a brave move away from gas-guzzlers. Truth revealed that Chevron Oil bought the battery manufacturer to prevent the EV1 coming to market. We saw the bottom line drop when GM corporate started to act like spoiled brats. After these shenanigans, many people were more determined than ever to buy a hybrid, as we are now experiencing. Now, with the high price of oil and with car buyers moving more toward hybrids, those who killed the electric car are probably wishing they had left well enough alone.

The electric car was among the fastest, most efficient production vehicles ever built. Running on electricity, the electric car, the film tells us, "produced no emissions and catapulted American technology to the forefront of the automotive industry. The lucky few people who drove it never wanted to give it up; so why did General Motors crush its fleet of EV1 electric vehicles in the Arizona desert?" If you asked most people, they would say, "Oil". Too many vested interests have ties to the oil industry. Others would say, "technology stagnation". It is considered to be the biggest blunder in automotive history.

The film proposes that, "oil companies were afraid of losing out on trillions in potential profit from their transportation fuel monopoly over the coming decades."[4]

In 2011, with oil prices skyrocketing, the electric car would certainly win the day for consumers. Not to be discouraged, several industry visionaries have invested in the electric Tesla Roadster by Tesla Motors, co-founded by Martin Eberhard and Elon Musk, the founder of Paypal. Keep an eye on innovations that move us away from gas-guzzling automobiles to more energy-efficient means of transportation. Public demand is the driver on this road to more economical and efficient means of travel. Many companies will look to energy-efficient vehicles for their corporate fleets. AT&T expects to spend roughly $565 million over 10 years to replace or buy 15,000 vehicles, preferring eco-friendly Ford cars and trucks that run on alternative fuels, including natural gas, which in 2011 is plentiful.

And Ford itself plans to introduce five new electric vehicles by 2013, starting with the Transit Connect Electric van already available. Ford is partnering with Microsoft on an application to manage home electricity use while vehicles recharge.[5] With oil depletion on the horizon, especially after the leaky valve on the mile-deep undersea BP pump poured oil into the Gulf of Mexico in 2010, the electric car may yet be a viable solution.

Meanwhile, General Motors was still in the news in June 2010 as it recalled one and a half million cars, including 2006 to 2009 model-year Cadillac and Buick sedans as well as sport utility vehicles, because the company couldn't fix a dangerous systemic malfunction in the windshield's heated cleaning fluid dispenser. GM paid owners $100 compensation each for the inconvenience—worth it to maintain customer goodwill and avoid the image problems Toyota experienced over large recalls and quality issues.[6]

TRIZ—Theory of Inventive Problem Solving

To innovate is crucial for any business or organization. One very useful technique is brainstorming, collective input without reservation. The beauty of this no-holds-barred method is simply to think outside the box. Along the same line comes an inventive process for generating new products. This process, which emerged out of the USSR, is the Theory of Inventive Problem Solving, known as TRIZ, the acronym for its name in Russian; it uses a set of principles to generate new ways to do things that works beautifully for both large and small companies.

Developed in 1946 by Soviet inventor Genrich Altshuller and his colleagues, TRIZ is now used widely throughout the world as a way to brainstorm creative solutions and to forecast technological advances. Over the last 50 years, this process has developed through several stages and been used to examine over 22 million patents for levels of inventiveness and principles of innovation. This research has revealed three key findings:

1. Problems and solutions are repeated across industries and sciences
2. Patterns of technical evolution are repeated across industries and sciences
3. Innovations use scientific effects outside the field where they were developed

When using TRIZ, all three findings are applied to create and improve products, services and systems as well as to solve real, practical everyday problems, including developmental strategies for technology's future. According to the website of the Altshuller Institute for TRIZ studies (www.aitriz.org), hundreds of major companies for more than 50 years have used this process to solve technical problems. Among the companies to use the process in management and service areas during the last 20 years are 3M, Ford, Motorola, Procter & Gamble, Eli Lilly and NASA's Jet Propulsion

Laboratory. An example of its strategic influence can be seen in everyday products like catsup and mustard bottles that have been turned upside down and redesigned as dispensers to be more compatible with gravity—something you and I have naturally been doing for years as a way to use every last bit of a product. Now we see hand lotions, toothpaste and syrups and so much more go with the flow.[7]

Technology and Communication

As technology and the Internet bring us closer together, we search for common ground. Searching for resources is Google's contribution to speeding the process.

Google's youthful co-founders, Sergey Brin and Larry Page, are wise beyond their years. Page is considered to have the brain of a rocket scientist. His inspiration is Nikola Tesla, scientific wonder-boy, whose electrical generating grids spreading light around the world are a model for software information pathways. Certainly, the way Google's search engine functions is proof enough that the concept is valid for other applications as well.

Google's entrepreneurial prowess in creating a unique product is inspiring. Their idea of an Internet search engine allows users to gather information on most any subject imaginable, bringing people and markets together in previously unforeseeable ways. This technology has increased brainpower to change the world of communications. Their Internet search business is also financially remunerative, monetized through Google AdWords and affiliate links.

The Google guys are guided by an admirable informal motto: "Don't be evil" and "Don't be illegal". Though it's not always openly stated, every respectable corporation may also abide by this motto.

Even Google's Mountain View campus is user-friendly. Creating a favorable work environment is another strength. Making it easy for employees to take proper care of their bodies creates a happy workplace environment where respect reigns supreme. As a home away from home, Google offers employees free gourmet meals at several cafés on their campus. There are two swim-in-place pools, massage, hairstylists, on-site computer repair, and playrooms with toys for employees' children. Even dogs are welcome. To speed connecting with others at a distance in their complex, Google provides Segway electric scooters. Their campus even provides pool tables and quirky toys to unwind and relax the mind. This helps to remove stress that could inhibit creative problem-solving activities, the backbone of Google's innovative business.

Clearly, Google's management style is unique among corporations. Since the attitude begins at the top. Google's founders, Larry Page and Sergey Brin, both in their early 30s when they launched the company, along with their adult advisor, Eric Schmidt (CEO from 2001 to 2011), have powered the company's direction and proven the point by example. When top managers, including the CEO, demonstrate their true selves as genuine warm and caring individuals, a healthy environment is created. People want to do their best, because they are part of a firm where employees are valued. They know that their work counts. Feeling appreciated contributes to the overall attitude permeating the firm.

Bottom-line result: production improves, job pride is evident, trust and loyalty become part of the company creed, with layoffs and temporary hiring drastically reduced. Everyone benefits.

Google's formula for success depends on creativity and is a good example of what it takes to build a successful team. To assure innovation, each employee is given a 70-20-10 three-part time-share. 70 percent is devoted to Google's core businesses, search and advertising, 20 percent on related activities and 10 percent on "far-out" ideas.[8]

The speed of information delivery in an easy and seemingly seamless way has transformed societies around the world. To find answers to pressing questions expands awareness through understanding, satisfies curiosity and in the wide scheme of things becomes the stuff of civilization building at a click. To its credit, Google has been judicious in its accuracy of reporting and rapidity of retrieval.

One idea and two people built Google. One idea and two people built Microsoft. One idea and one individual built Ford Motor Company, Wal-Mart, McDonald's and Apple Computer. With Apple's introduction of the iPod and the iPhone, the company is no longer just a "computer" company. It now allows for more innovation and new products, and the new name is simply Apple Inc. Thank goodness Steve Jobs returned to his base. Had he not left the company for a while, everyone in the world today would be using an Apple computer. Steve Jobs continues to innovate and the world awaits further expressions of his inventive mind.

Social Entrepreneurs

Social entrepreneurs are the new breed of innovators: unconventional do-gooders, solution-minded pragmatists educated to think big. And that's just what the world needs right now.

While Oprah Winfrey hasn't won a Nobel Prize, she deserves a great deal of credit for offering a healthy venue in the public arena and championing causes that affect everyone. As a celebrity speaking from experience, Winfrey ensures that others don't have to repeat the pain and humiliation that she did at the hands of a rapist, and she uses her show as a platform for societal change.

When Oprah took on the Texas cattlemen over the mad cow controversy, it nearly brought her to the brink of extinction as she confronted those who would poison us and lie about it. Now, of course, she has been proven right, though she is bound not to speak of it.

Despite that, she continues to champion unpopular causes to demonstrate compassion for humanity, using the Angel Network as a platform for bold endeavors that make a positive difference. She is one to put her money where her mouth is, which is saying a lot about how Harpo Productions, Inc., operates its business. With the end of her television show in 2011, her 25 years of educating, informing and inspiring audiences must be celebrated, for Oprah has made a positive difference in the world.

As government social services implode over bureaucratic incompetence, the need grows for grass-rooters to spring forth with a better understanding of how the right fertilizer grows a healthier culture. While not all are Florence Nightingales or Mother Teresas, change agents are shakers and movers, restless to make a difference. Some graduate from business schools with MBAs, some are teachers with a vision to reach students in urban schools, while some private citizens bank on their experience and wealth to build bridges between low-income earners and a better life. There is enough need to satisfy most social entrepreneurs' vision.

With the collapse of Communism and authoritarian regimes, there is increased incentive for private citizens everywhere to make big social changes. Against this backdrop, social entrepreneurs see that social change is possible with savvy marketing.

J. B. Schramm, founder of College Summit, helps low-income high-school students with B and C averages—college-ready students who are "better than their numbers"—apply to college. Irreversible progress results when the first child in the family goes to college. As earning power increases, he or she essentially puts poverty out of business.[9]

Spearheaded by entrepreneurial zeal, business innovation is the secret to growth. Knowledge increases awareness. Inspiration spurs new ideas. It is the Lewis and Clark expedition mapping territorial paths across a developing nation. It is passing over the Mississippi River to see what is on the other side. It is learning how to adapt the rules of nature in a meaningful way to business and lifestyles across the board.

With the first lunar landing in July 20, 1969, came beautiful photos of Earth seen from space. In the civilized world these photos brought awe and awareness of Earth's special qualities in a cosmos of seemingly lifeless bodies. Though much mystery still exists about how the universe works, despite the proffered views of theorists, astronomers and physicists, humans are better informed, better at understanding and appreciating Earth's natural gifts. Everything needed to live on Earth is provided. All the food, water and tools of creation to survive, obvious and hidden assets, transportation, music, song, even entertainment as we observe the antics of wildlife and the human. Over time, the human brain has expanded. Humans have gotten smarter. They have learned from experience.

Humans, gifted with a thinking brain, now assume they are smarter than Mother Nature. We forget our manners and treat her with disrespect, abusing her gifts and fouling her bed. While her love is beyond measure, she has rules and shies not from having the last word.

Clearly, there is extraordinary magic in organizational unity, as Mother Nature attests. Whether it's rotating planetary bodies producing musical sounds recorded by NASA or a variety of seasonal foods provided for Earth's inhabitants, there is cause for awe and appreciation everywhere. Unless countermanded by human folly, all expressions of nature benefit the whole. Though the mystery of life is still being explored, most agree that a natural intelligence exists.

Organizational unity is key to building a life-giving enterprise. Paying attention to nature and her survival skills is a lesson for everyone. A healthy business survives. A healthy body survives, and a healthy country is one that behaves more like Mother Nature, whose integrity is beyond question.

CHAPTER TEN

THE BUSINESS OF DNA
Risk and Laboratory Folly

At times, life challenges us to step outside our box of perceived limitations and take a risk. Those who dream of climbing mountains end up doing so. Scaling a rock wall takes courage enough just to resist the pull of gravity. Learning to fly an airplane forces us to leave landlubber security and rely on our senses for safety, as I experienced the first time I sat in the cockpit of a single-engine Cessna. The unfamiliar appears scary, but with exposure and practice our comfort zone adjusts. Just think about your first day at school, the first time you sat in the driver's seat of an automobile, your first day on the job. Suddenly, you're in charge of your life in a demonstrable way, and you want to prove to yourself and others that you can survive the challenge and thrive.

Such is the case on a remarkable day in 1954 when Roger Bannister, a young British medical student, becomes the first man ever to run the mile-long track in less than four minutes. At 25 he runs against his old university at the Iffley Road Track in Oxford, England, with a time of 3 minutes and 59.4 seconds. Bannister, who will later become a neurologist and is knighted by the Queen, applies scientific observation and method to his training. Looking at each race as an experiment, he programs his mind to win and trains his body to perform at its peak. By stretching the perceived limitations of physical performance, he proves he can excel by connecting to a higher source through mental suggestion. There, he becomes the energetic "flow", moving with it.[1]

British swimmer Lewis Pugh breaks two world records wearing only

Speedo trunks in the icy salt waters off the Antarctic Peninsula. Despite water temperatures dipping below 32°F, he survives to make the swim without freezing. His first record-breaking swim on December 14, 2005, as the first ever to swim in the most southerly of oceans, keeps him for 18 minutes and 10 seconds in the frigid waters. Two days later, Pugh spends 30 minutes and 30 seconds in water slightly above freezing to achieve the longest-duration polar swim ever completed.[2]

It probably brings chills to your spine just to think about these feats as your fight-or-flight response kicks into gear. In an untrained body, under such conditions, the heart rate skyrockets as gasping breaths ratchet to 60 per minute. All systems are on alert. The shocked body goes into survival mode. Desperate to maintain life and to prevent the paralyzing effects from taking hold, the body's cellular community pulls out all the stops. However, Michael Tipton, exercise physiologist at the University of Portsmouth, U.K., says, "Anybody can develop a habituation to the cold. You can do it with as little as five or six five-minute immersions."

The magic in this process is what sports scientist Tim Noakes, who measured Pugh's body temperature before his swims, calls "anticipatory thermogenesis". The mental imagery prepares the mind in advance so that when the event occurs in real time, the body will withstand the insult. For some, it can be just as frightening to speak before an audience. To avoid the stress of such events, rehearse in your mind the anticipated event. Then the body's stress hormones are not called into play.[3]

Why would anyone want to put themselves into such life-threatening situations? The answer lies in the human need to explore and experience what has not been done before. The thrill of making known the unknown is to overcome perceived limitations, to reach the pinnacle of achievement by breaking a record or making a discovery of some kind. Regardless of circumstance, every success spurs us and others to achieve new heights. We cheer the excitement of the moment, happy for the individual who had the courage to risk, thus exposing our own self-imposed limitations. Consider how crazy people thought the Wright brothers were in building a machine to mimic the birds' ability to fly. Today, we consider flying a necessity when traveling long distances, and we take for granted rocket ships that leave Earth's orbit to go to into space. Every moment a record is shattered, limitations are diminished, perceptions shift and we climb one more rung on the evolutionary ladder.

As a nation, the United States cheers Steve Fossett's flight around the world without refueling in 2006. One year later, at age 23, Jamaican-born Barrington Irving, an aerospace student at Florida Memorial University, breaks three records when he completes a historic solo flight around the world in a single-engine plane he built himself with $300,000 in donated parts. He hopes his achievement is an inspiration to children in poor urban neighborhoods to see that they too can go beyond perceived limitations. Irving says, "I want to show them they can do more with their lives than resort to violence."

Irving's achievement shows what can be done with will and perseverance. His next challenge is learning how to swim.[4]

Clearly, risk-takers' achievements merit acclaim, just as did Henry Ford when he invented the assembly line to accelerate production and speed finished products to market. There are always more mountains to climb, more rugged terrain to conquer, but the greatest achievement of all is in conquering yourself and your perceived limitations.

A Widening Expression of DNA

When you think of DNA, you think of biology and traits you inherit. While your physical makeup is obvious, it is the underlying legacy of hereditary factors that affords variation on the theme. What you do with those traits, the choices you make, are of your own choosing, and they come from your perception of the environment, not from the DNA school supplies with which you're born.

Such is the case when Singapore surprises the world on March 6, 2006, by unveiling plans to construct a helix-shaped bridge connecting to a massive tourist casino complex complete with a giant Ferris wheel. The complex is expected to attract 17 million visitors and S$30 billion in revenue by 2015. Construction costs to build this high-rise DNA look-alike with its three-strand six-lane highway and six-meter pedestrian corridor to reclaimed land are expected to reach S$68 million. This is a stunning example of creative invention, drawing on nature for inspiration.[5]

While Singapore sees potential interweaving strands of the DNA as a bridge design, it is Mother Nature's creativity that really wins the day. She appears to have no limits when it comes to inspiring innovation. She constantly demonstrates her unique capabilities in new species and variations on a theme. Contrasts are everywhere evident, for those who travel the country and the world see terrestrial variations in mountains and valleys, grassland and deserts, lakes and streams, and oceans wide.

However, there is looming danger to Mother Nature's reputation as environmental expert. As Jim Watson said in *Rational Man's World: DNA Modification*: "When you understand something you can begin to control it." Attempting control of Mother Nature is impractical, as she alone holds the ultimate secret of DNA's organizing principles and their unique combining talent. Manipulating genes for profit has long-term consequences with ramifications for both business and living systems, already seen in crop failures and malformed births. Working with Mother Nature, rather than usurping her authority, brings higher yields, more nutritious food, soil conservation and a healthier environment.

Making Mother Nature a partner in your undertakings, rather than the material asset to be manipulated, dissolves attempts to change her character. It makes no sense to change the manager's DNA to improve performance and loyalty. Just as it seems preposterous to even consider such a proposal, it is likewise dangerous to manipulate genes as a solution to man's invasive practices and profligate behavior. Since DNA does not control behavior, time is better spent on product lines consistent with Mother Nature's principles of regeneration, longevity strains, diversity, conservation and wholesome solutions that sustain life.

Four biologists between 1999 and 2001 did experiments involving genetically modified (GM) foods on living systems. In one case, rats fed GM potatoes display tissue and immunological damage. In another, milkweed leaves are dusted with GM corn pollen. When butterfly larvae eat the leaves, large numbers die, whereas in a control group fed non-GM pollen, all survive.

University of California researcher Ignacio Chapela discovers pollen drifting from a field of GM corn planted in Chiapas into Mexico's remote mountains near Oaxaca, to penetrate the DNA of traditional crops and potentially destroy the world's last reserve of biodiverse maize.

In the lab, T. B. Hayes and team expose young frogs to very small doses of the herbicide Atrazine. In one experiment, the frogs' larynxes fail to develop normally. In later tests with the same drug, frogs display serious reproductive problems, including multiple gonads and/or a mixture of ovaries and testes, suggesting that the product might be an endocrine disrupter. Academies and allegedly independent institutions, once prideful

and protective of researchers' scientific freedom, fall away when uncompli-
mentary research threatens bioengineering companies like Monsanto and
Syngenta, who help fund research. Researchers are then abandoned to the
wolves to be discredited.

It's not flawed or imperfect experiments that get these men in trouble,
but results with the potential for damaging economic effects. Without controls, if the communication lines protecting the people are cut, then where
does the public go for truth? As corporations seek to control our minds,
our bodies and our flow of money, each individual must assume responsibility for information gathering and not accept at face value the advertised
product claims.[6]

Determinism and Self-Healing

DNA plays a significant role in shaping nature's expressions by balancing
sexual orientation for propagating species. True enough. DNA is responsible for how you look and how you grow, but not how you live your life.
Darwin's model said that life is a struggle, that we are victims of our hered-
ity and personality is locked in the genes; even life choices are predeter-
mined by the DNA's genetic makeup passed down through generations.[7]

Such determinism, the belief you have no control over your life, is why
the pharmaceutical industries and the medical profession are inclined to
produce physical molecules to fix parts of the body when they go awry.
The "ain't it awful" body has betrayed us. This syndrome is alive and well,
though sick in its premise. The dictum makes us victims with no sense of
responsibility for our behavior, the body's condition or its ability to heal
itself, given the right environment. "Just take these pills and call me in the
morning, or come back again in a week or 30 days, and we'll check your
progress." There is too much reliance on drugs to do the healing. While
they can sometimes help, the greatest healer of all is "self", responding to
a focused mind in action. With the belief that genes control biological expression, our medical community unknowingly ensnares the innocent with
false hope and a belief the medical profession would do us no wrong. Like
lab mice looking through the wire cage at their keepers, we hope they will
be kind to us.

In fact, DNA is a pattern, a model, for reproduction and repair of the
human organism. As first explained to me in 1993 by cell biologist Bruce H.
Lipton, Ph.D., a former Stanford Medical School Senior Research Scholar,

DNA can be likened to a catalog of patterns. For example, you might look in a pattern catalog for a certain style of suit or dress, or an amateur Homebuilt aircraft such as an Ultralight airplane, or a woodworking project to replicate. After choosing the model, you go to the catalog file drawers to fetch the pattern. You have no suit, or dress, or airplane, yet; only the pattern for parts to be assembled.

Modifying the pattern may produce imperfections. In a suit, for instance, one pants leg could be wider and longer than the other, a sleeve tuck could be missing and the coat's body misshapen as one side reveals mis-marked buttonhole positions, making the suit unwearable except by a plaster model made to accommodate. The same is true of purposely altered DNA. Genetically manipulated DNA needs a warning: "GMO Donor not authorized to enter this world."

Commercials entraining viewers to mistrust themselves and perceive every ailment as one of their own, either now or in the future, are a pathetic commentary on corporate ethics. This kind of self-serving behavior is not genetic. No company's DNA is programmed to move counter to the right use of knowledge and human values. That is a choice.

To stop the insanity, all pharmaceutical advertising to the consumer *must be banned.* Direct marketing to the public (something the FCC in the U.S. should never have allowed) is actually creating an increase in health problems. Health insurance is skyrocketing as a result. The FDA is fueling the fire of public trust by playing the fiddle while Rome burns.

When attention is focused on this issue, doctors lie in the crosshairs. They function as intermediaries between drug companies and their patients. They have been trained in medical school to diagnose and prescribe appropriate healing measures; we as consumers have also been trained to seek them out when our bodies are sick. Their advice is often to be "patient", an adjective that became a noun, patience to patients. We depend upon their knowledge and expertise to heal us of our maladies, real or perceived.

Drug companies, once the source of pharmaceuticals sold to compounding pharmacists who combined and dispensed them according to prescription, now play to the urgent cries of patients' fears by capitalizing on standardized formulas, the one-size-fits-all products that line the shelves of drug and health-food stores, as well as some doctor offices. Through advertising to the elderly in *AARP*, *Time* and a bevy of other magazines, as well as billboards, newspapers, television and the Internet, pharmaceutical companies have capitalized grandly on human insecurities. Modern medicine has many magic tricks in its black-bag tool kit of remedies to offer the fastest and most effective treatment possible. Ever since antibiotics came into popular use as a quick fix to shorten healing time, patients have become impatient.

Judged by the high profits accrued by pharmaceutical companies, drug ads are effective. Drug salesmen often leave samples that doctors give to patients. Some doctors do independent research to expand their knowledge base, which is to be expected, especially when increased awareness helps them better perform their services. In emergencies, doctors are a blessing, so thank God we have them. But as with most any profession, doctors practice medicine as they are taught to do in medical schools. Understandably, not all graduate cum laude.

Doctors today also seem confused by the Hippocratic oath of "do no harm", finding it inadequate to deal with the realities of modern medicine. In an age of social change, religious turmoil, scientific discoveries and political and economic instability, when euthanasia is acceptable in some states and not others, when patients' records are demanded by government and health-care organizations how is it possible for a doctor to maintain a patient's privacy? Some are calling the Hippocratic oath the "Hypocritic" oath because the integrity implied in the oath is missing.[8] The "do no harm" dictum could as easily be applied to business in general.

Corporations have themselves been brainwashed. They are experiencing workforce drain as resources and employee absenteeism increase due to illness. Less need for temporary hiring is inevitable when the playing field is level. The health-care insurance issue will largely go away with self-responsibility and awareness of how thoughts create reality.

Being receptive to environmental signals can affect new product development and service. Sensitivity to environmental information (signals) can give heads-up insight into product hazards demanding recall. No company, business or nation can be strong so long as its people are sick and live an uncertain future.

Genetic Manipulation of the Food Supply

Mounting evidence augurs a scary future with genetically modified seeds, says Vandana Shiva, author of *Stolen Harvest: The Hijacking of the Global Food Supply*. In the Philippines, GM sugar imports have destroyed the economy, as has happened with other imported goods in countries whose lifeblood is dependent on export capabilities.[9] Instigated by the World Bank and the International Monetary Fund (IMF), these "structural adjustment packages" of genetically modified seeds are vulnerable to pests and require more pesticides than do native plants.

The USDA and Delta and Pine Land Company entered into a joint agreement to patent a technology called "Control of Plant Gene Expression", designed to license the creation of sterile seeds in all species of plants and seeds by "selectively programming the plant's DNA to kill its own embryos."[10] This essentially forces farmers to buy new seeds every year. Complicity by the USDA is not comforting, for there is a kickback of 5 percent profit from the sales of these seeds to this agency, considered to be the "gene police".[11]

Poor farmers are especially desperate to produce food and money for their families. They buy the GMO seeds on credit, expecting to repay the debt at harvest time. "When the crops failed due to heavy pest incidence or large-scale seed failure," writes Shiva, "many peasants committed suicide by consuming the same pesticides that had gotten them into debt in the first place."[12] In India's Wanagal district, "nearly 400 cotton farmers committed suicide due to crop failure in 1997, and dozens more committed suicide in 1998."[13]

Despite the desperate conditions in Haiti after the 2009 earthquake that devastated the country, peasant farmer Chavannes Jean-Baptiste of the Peasant Movement of Papay (MPP) burned 475 tons (60,000 seed sacks) of Monsanto's Roundup Ready genetically modified seed, preferring to use local seed stocks whose production is dependable. *Truthout* reported in May 2010 that the competitive practice of chemically controlling the food supply is contrary to nature's cooperative interdependence. Continuing down this road will "lead to non-sustainability, violence to animals, and lower productivity when all systems are assessed."[14]

Who knows what else is coming? Could genetically engineering the human race be next? Why bother with sexual reproduction. Why bother to have sex at all? Oh, boy, there goes the fun!

The Council for Responsible Genetics (CRG) came into existence in 1983 to monitor the ethical, social and ecological impacts of genetics biotechnologies and to oppose all forms of patenting life. Their position is that no person, institution or corporation should hold patents for species or varieties of living organisms. Briefly, patents are troubling because they:

- Make important products more expensive and less accessible.
- Promote secrecy and hinder the exchange of information.
- Exploit research funded by taxpayers.
- Promote unsustainable and inequitable agricultural policies.
- Enable First World theft of Third World genetic resources, impoverishing the people.
- View life as a commodity and living beings as "gene machines" to be exploited for profit.

CRG's conclusion is that patents on life forms are ethically and morally unacceptable. See www.actionbioscience.org/genomic/crg.html for CRG's complete position paper.

2004 Nobel Prize-winner Wangari Maathai of Nairobi, Kenya, coordinator of the Green Belt Movement, is the first African woman ever to win this award. In a 1998 essay she condemns genetic engineering and biopiracy by corporate-driven technology on the grounds that the practice is a threat to global food security. Dr. Maathai states: "Under these circumstances, if we thought that slavery and colonialism were gross violations of human rights, we have to wake up to what is awaiting us down the secretive road of biopiracy, patenting of life and genetic engineering. Genocide from hunger, such as we have not yet seen, becomes a haunting possibility."[15]

The lines are drawn and it is time to step up to the plate with a "no thank you" on corporate manipulations of animal and plant life, regardless of the motive implied by the biotechnology industry that GM crops will feed the world. Colin Tudge writes in the *New Statesman* that we can already feed the world, even if the population were to double halfway through the next century. Given the free market, though, things could go downhill in a hurry. He says the claim that GMOs "are needed to feed the world...is nonsense." Current agricultural technology could still easily feed everyone. The problem of starvation is not one of productivity, but rather a lack of infrastructure, poverty and poor distribution. All is done in the interest of corporate profits, hardly a humanitarian effort designed to feed the world.[16]

Feeding the World

Contaminated food sources threaten health safety. Where lies corporate responsibility for feeding the world with good intentions? Where lies corporate consciousness in making mankind dependent on genetically engineered seeds, removing his ability to feed himself? Shame on corporations.

Shame on the patent office for allowing such unethical transgressions. Shame on the courts for their complicity.

The dangers of genes moving to other plants is evidence the biotechnology is out of control. If the corporations want to maintain their hold on the technology, then keep it at home and in a democracy of freedom, and don't allow bureaucratic economics to feed the pockets of special interests. Nature's rules must not be broken to satisfy financial reports.

Feeding the world is not the issue. The issue is favoring the corporatocracy and their need to stay in business. This calls for a closer look at the corruption of nature's gifts for personal and financial gain. We question biotech's chicanery in monkeying around with genes as a cure-all for humanity's future.

The warnings are dire indeed. Dr. P. M. Ghargava, one of the world's top biologists, concluded in January 2010 after researching more than 600 scientific journals that GM foods in the U.S. are largely responsible for the increase in many serious diseases, among them infertility, accelerated aging, dysfunctional insulin injections, changes in major organs and the gastrointestinal system, and immune problems such as asthma, allergies and inflammation. Jeffrey Smith, in *Seeds of Deception*, reports even more problems, including cancer and diseases of the hormonal, immune, nervous and reproductive systems.[17] Smith worked at a GMO detection laboratory, founded the Institute for Responsible Technology, and currently lives in Iowa—surrounded by genetically modified corn and soybeans.

Listen to the people, the plants, the animals and the Earth. Watch the destruction of our biosphere as developers shave the landscape to build yet another subdivision. Watch our planet being starved of a natural food supply. Watch millions of years in Earth's evolutionary journey slip away as native species disappear. Many companies with myopic vision may want to get a better pair of glasses.

CHAPTER ELEVEN

INNOVATION AND INTENTION
How Curiosity, Creativity and Entrepreneurial Zeal Seed the Future

Without inventive minds and nimble fingers to problem-solve the challenges of an evolving world, many of the conveniences we enjoy today would never have happened. Thomas Alva Edison and others before him, like Humphry Davy, Sir Joseph Wilson Swan and Charles Francis Brush, persisted in experimenting with electricity until it was proven that a light bulb could work. The trick was to find the right filament that would burn a long time. Edison finally settled on the carbon filament that would last 1,500 hours. Despite how crazy others thought the idea, these early inventors persisted until they succeeded in changing the world from night to day.

Swedish-born Sven Oldfelt, while working for an engineering company, invented the commercial airplane's vacuum toilet. For him, it was important to design a unit that used little water, for water would add extra weight the plane could ill afford. To get the waste into the tank needed suction of some sort. By creating a vacuum similar to the one you use to clean your home, he came up with a design that worked. Waste is sucked into a central tank at the rear of the plane, where it is stored; the capture tank is easily rolled out and replaced with a new tank at the next scheduled stop. This sounds as if the TRIZ process had an influence, adapting a known use to another product.

Albert Einstein's view of physics, Thomas Edison's light bulb and Nikola

Tesla's alternating current were instrumental in changing our world for the better. Though some taunted them with failure, they never gave up. No matter what others may think, if you have an evolving idea to reshape the way things are done, persist until it works or is proven not to. If you see connections or potential benefits others miss, you have an edge on creativity. In business, that talent makes you valuable. The human brain thinks to problem-solve, which expands awareness as it examines potentials, possibilities in solving the problem. Awareness advances understanding. With understanding comes growth, and that is nonrefundable.

Brave souls take risks to pioneer or modify ideas to create a better life. Revisiting their roots can be a painful reminder of the angst of life without a future.

Such is the story of Starbucks coffeehouse mogul Howard Schultz. His uneducated dad was a World War II veteran who had a blue-collar job as a delivery driver for cloth diapers. He lived with his family in a two-room apartment in federally subsidized housing, loosely called the Project.

One day when Schultz was seven, he came home from school to find his dad sprawled out on the sofa in a full leg cast, the result of an accident on the job. Recovery would be slow. Even worse, companies in the 1960s had no worker's compensation or hospitalization insurance to carry families through this kind of crisis. Aware that his dad bitterly hated his job, he determined to one day own a company in which his dad would be proud to work.

Schultz started out as a salesman selling coffee machines to stores. One of them was Starbucks in Seattle. When the owner announced he was selling the company's three stores, Schultz jumped at the opportunity to buy them. From experience, he knew that the key to expansion lay in branding, and Starbucks already had made a name for itself.

With no capital to advertise, Schultz solved the problem of generating customers by providing equity in the form of stock options to his employees. By partnering in the business, employees had vested interest in its success.[1] Today the company has grown from three stores to 3,500. For seven years, one was in Beijing's Forbidden City adjacent to Tiananmen Square, until a media and public backlash against corporate infiltration into this fabled piece of history forced that Starbucks to close.[2]

Schultz's success provides inspiration to other companies who can learn from his. Rather than treat employees as blue-collar workers with no benefits, Schultz provides worker's compensation, health care and equity, assuring him a place in history as an innovative employer.[3]

But 2008 saw the success of Starbucks's expansion curtailed due to slumping sales, the fall of the dollar, political ramifications of the George W. Bush administration and the forecast of slipping profits, sending stock market values downward and precipitating the firing of many employees. Schultz expanded too quickly and into too many markets, like Starbucks coffee franchises in grocery stores, say the analysts.

Turning Junk Cars into Useful Products

Characteristically, entrepreneurs are risk-takers, inspired by potential returns on investment and the rewards of following their passion to make a difference. You may be one of them.

Former Hofstra University basketball star Brian Appel envisioned a thermal conversion plant to turn turkey slaughterhouse waste into high-quality oil. What could not be converted into fuel oil would become high-grade fertilizer. Despite the naysayers, Appel is now CEO of Changing World Technologies, with a facility perched 100 yards from ConAgra Foods' Butterball plant, where each day 35,000 turkeys are butchered. Pig fat from four other ConAgra slaughterhouses in the Midwest comes through as well. Appel's thermal conversion process can take slaughterhouse waste, municipal sewage, old tires, mixed plastics—virtually all the wretched detritus of modern life—and make high-quality oil. The residual water, to his credit, is clean enough to discharge into a municipal wastewater system.

"To anybody who thinks this can't work on an industrial scale, I say, 'Come here and look,'" Appel says. "This is the first commercial biorefinery in the world that can make oil from a variety of waste streams."[4]

Each year, 15 million junked cars end up at American recyclers with nearly all the metal plucked from them. Of the 4.5 million tons of residual debris, at least 36 kinds of material are plastic, treated fabrics, rubber, and nylon. So promising is the conversion technology that representatives from USCAR, a consortium of motor companies, along with Argonne National Laboratory and the American Plastics Council, arranged a test in which Changing World Technologies ran 3,000 pounds of that residue through their Philadelphia plant.

"The process is brilliant," says Candace Wheeler, a GM research scientist, quoted in *Discover* magazine, April 2006. "There are substances of concern in shredder residue such as PCBs, and traditional incineration of chlorinated plastics can make dioxins." But, she says, the "preliminary test results indicate that the hydrolysis at the heart of the thermal conversion process breaks down the PCBs and converts the chlorine into hydrochloric acid. No PCBs, no dioxins, no emissions," says Wheeler, noting that the principal output of the process is a "light oil" that can be used at an electric power generation plant.

From all standpoints, the process is impressive and the observing groups see its potential. Along with oil, the thermal conversion process can produce a liquid fertilizer that features 9 percent nitrogen, 1 percent phosphorus, 2 percent potash, and 19 amino acids, generally unheard of in organic fertilizers.

At Auburn University in Alabama, Joseph Kloepper, professor of plant pathology, confirmed the fertilizer's potency. Writing in a summary paper after testing the liquid fertilizer, he said: "In my experience, it is rare to find a biological product that demonstrates such a consistent promotion of overall plant growth and root growth on two crops in two different field soils."

Part of the beauty of this high-temperature process is that "there is no coliform bacteria or any other problems often associated with organic fertilizers such as manures," says Raj Mehta, president of Organica Biotech, a manufacturer of nonsynthetic fertilizers and pesticides.

Such science is now being used to extract more oil from existing oil wells, reports *ScienceDaily*. For this to work, it must be economically feasible. Lewis Brown, a Mississippi State microbiologist, in conjunction with the U.S. Department of Energy and a Jackson-based oil company, found that simply injecting plant nutrients into the wells caused microbial growth that forced the once inaccessible oil up to an accessible depth, sweeping it into production from depths of more than 14,000 feet. The microbes, in some cases, will grow at temperatures above 100 degrees Celsius. Brown continues to revive oil fields along with depleted natural gas wells in Wyoming coal beds, using indigenous microflora to produce methane.[5]

But however noble corporations' profit-oriented exploits appear to be, when the BP *Deepwater Horizon* drilling rig burst its cap to release the black gold syrup under the mantle of Earth's rock a mile deep in the Gulf waters off Louisiana, it exposed blatant irresponsibility and incompetence.

Despite efforts to stop the mile-deep well from gushing millions of gallons of oil into the ocean waters, devastating the livelihoods of fishermen who earn their living supplying seafood stores and restaurants, BP engineers had no fail-safe method to cap the well. Unleashed, the well's pressure of 170,000 pounds per square inch was enough to poison all life forms within its path, similar to a volcano spewing its innards.

So unnatural was this disaster that in a *New York Times* op-ed, columnist Bob Herbert sarcastically wrote that the rapacious oil companies' profit-oriented mentality was "choking off the prospects of a viable social and economic future for working people and their families."[6]

Motor fuel from garbage may be an answer, using material like wood chips, garbage or crop waste. To test the waters, so to speak, the U.S. government began offering grants to giant start-up companies as incentives. With a promising outlook of gasoline at $1.01 a gallon, and with the subsidies for corn-based ethanol twice those for conventional fuel, BP, Shell, Honeywell, DuPont and General Motors are among those with a stake in the idea.

The beauty of biofuels is that they don't have to deplete the food supply (corn). Algae, for instance, has been a favorite of the renewable oil and bioproducts company Solazyme since 2003. Any material containing hydrogen, carbon and oxygen, such as wood chips, will work, but so will construction debris, agricultural waste, wheat straw and plastics, as well as forest and lawn trimmings. Of course, there needs to be a balance in cleaning up the forest floor for a fuel source, as the detritus nourishes the land and creatures that depend upon the natural environment for survival.

Seems like there's an abundance of biofuels available from sources that often end up in the city dump. Henry Ford thought it a good idea 100 years ago. Even arsenic-contaminated utility poles in Montreal are a biofuel candidate. The natural energy sources seem endless, so why are we so dependent on oil? Because it takes a while to refine the processes and to assure reliable results before building plants that require significant financial resources.[7]

Design and Architecture

When the documentary series *e² design* was featured on PBS, courtesy of Autodesk and its associates, I saw evidence of creative invention in sustainable architecture happening all over the world, and it excited me. At last, I thought, someone's paying attention to the natural forces of life itself, realizing that to sustain life on this planet with diminishing space for expansion, we need to pay attention.

What a great example of how architecture shapes business with awareness of the new biology. Utilizing recycled building materials in new ways, recombining meaningful artifacts with green design in mind, brings excitement and new opportunities for expression. People behave differently when architecture is aligned with organic forms, the natural rhythmic fields of dance and its fluidity of motion. People feel whole and happy, calm and easy to be with in this comfortable environment. That is why visiting a Japanese garden, with its artistic simplicity of design, offers respite from the world of business commercialism and is a good place to contemplate, to meditate and to restore a sense of calm.

Why is it that most architecture has so many straight lines? It must be because it is easier and less expensive to manufacture, not because it is the best design. Sometimes, I feel like we still live in frontier *Bonanza* land, when the purpose of architecture was simply survival, and have not yet matured into the 21st-century awareness that people buy more when they are in an environment compatible with the natural energies. Employees are happier too, with less reason to complain. Why not build a structure that is both beautiful *and* functional? We talk peace and build structures that lack peaceful elements. Remembering that nature has no straight lines is a good rule to follow; that's why a walk through the forest is restorative. Many executives find respite and relief from the stress of linear thinking, hierarchy and unbending rules when fishing on the lake, away from the office and city life.

When you feel comfortable, there is more calm and peacefulness in your life. Your favorite leather chair that grooves with repeated visits allows you to just sit in a safe place to contemplate. Mellow music soothes the nerves, calms fears and allows your mind to wander in an open, accepting environment where brilliance shines through to solve problems and invent new approaches. It is through your response to environmental signals that the source of creative decision-making promises the planet's future survivability. It is in the natural energy fields that you can think straight. You have been paying attention, haven't you?

Seeing the results of such awareness on a recent visit to my hometown of Chicago made me mighty proud. Mayor Daley's adoption of green architecture as the new model for sustainability reduces mankind's gross footprint by making Chicago's downtown waterfront area one of the most delightful and thrilling statements of progress I have yet to see, from rooftops planted green to Millennium Park's magnificent Pavilion band shell, designed by Frank Gehry. At the innovative Cloud Gate by British artist Anish Kapoor, I stood spellbound by the magnificence of the highly polished form that mimics a bean. Inspired by liquid mercury's organic form, this 110-ton elliptical sculpture, 66 feet long and 33 feet high, looks more like it is actually emulating a cloud than a bean. Its 12-foot-high arch invites visitors to walk beneath it, to touch and to see reflections of themselves on walls of highly polished forged stainless steel, and to experience how peaceful everyone is in its environment.

Listening to the concert beneath the revolutionary outdoor concert venue typical of Gehry-style architecture thrilled my senses. This band-shell of sorts is described on the park's website as "a billowing headdress of brushed stainless steel ribbons that frame the stage opening and connect to an overhead trellis of crisscrossing steel pipes [that] supports the sound system."[8] Eager to experience the music in this marvelous statement of pur-pose, I found my way to one of the 4,000 fixed seats, settled in and closed my eyes. Instantly, I felt my body relax as the resonance of the musical tones harmonized my cells, releasing all the tension of the day. I was in heaven, I thought, as the melodic experience lifted my spirits above the city bustle.

Extending the architectural masterpiece was the Great Lawn, filled with families sitting on lawn chairs and blankets enjoying picnic dinners in the grandest open-air pavilion around, which can accommodate an additional 7,000 people to the seats in the concert pavilion. In my youth, my parents and I used to go to the Grant Park Bandshell at the south end of the park and, like now, sit on the lawn and listen to concerts, but that was a far cry from the elegance of this present structure. It was a most marvelous eve-ning and I was so moved that I couldn't even get out of my seat when the concert ended. I just sat there in my reverie until the hall cleared.

It is this kind of architecture that thrills the senses and replenishes the soul, while reinforcing the marvel of the imaginative human mind. We need more of this kind of flowing architecture that encompasses the spirit of humanity and the energy of the creative mind. I think the absence of this is what disturbs me about the 19th-century-frontier-like architecture seen in many 21st-century shopping centers, almost as if architects have no inventive concepts in their playbook. I look for architecture to reflect new thinking, reflective of progress in building design, and am disappointed in communities whose architecture reflects the linear limitation of unsophisticated minds, whose decisions are based solely on how much money it costs. Only in truly progressive cities, like Seattle, is architecture notable. Looking at Dubai and their fantastic architecture, one has to ask: is there no architect in the West thinking outside the box? Please help us understand why, when China can come up with an innovative structure like the Bird's Nest, home for the 2008 World Olympics, other places continue as before.

Lacking inspiration and pride in innovation just keeps everyone tuned to the way it was 200 years ago. It is definitely not a comfort zone, nor soothing to the senses. Is there no escape? Where is the vision of developing communities? Where is the beautiful architecture? Must it always be in the big cities funded by corporate moguls? You just need architects and city planners with vision to move into the 21st century.

One such visionary is Italian architect Paolo Soleri, Ph.D., born in Turin in 1919, who came to the United States in 1947 to work with Frank Lloyd Wright at Taliesin West in Arizona and at Taliesin East in Wisconsin with a commitment to research and experimentation in urban planning. By 1970, Soleri had drawn over 6,000 people to participate in his concept of arcology (from *architecture* and *ecology*), which proposed communities be contained in large structures with very high population density and very low environmental impact. Construction began on a prototype town for 5,000 people in central Arizona to minimize the use of energy, raw materials and land; yet by 2005 the town was only about 3 percent completed.[9]

Arcologies were used in SimCity 2000, the 1993 version of the city-building simulation game. There were four of them: Plymouth Arco, Forest Arco with a dome park on the top, Draco Arco, which looked like a black dragon, and a fourth, which looked like the Capitol Records Building in Los Angeles. In SimCity 3000 and SimCity 4, arcologies were not included.[10]

Though Soleri's vision didn't make the SimCity cut, at least one architect who moved West to work with him on the arcology project stayed to create his own sustainable-living practice. Rennie Radoccia lives in Clarkdale, Arizona, in an earth berm home. Built as they are, eight feet into the side of a hill, protected from winds, earth berm houses are thermally comfortable regardless of summer's scorching heat—a crisp 105 degrees in June—and winter's snows. But much like a house built on flat land, all the comforts of home are there. Radoccia's private off-the-grid Shangri-la houses his architecture firm's office, his wife's pottery and massage studios, and a organic garden in the front of the house providing much of his family's food.[11]

In a way, cities populating the world are living systems comprised of individual cells, like our bodies, which also respond to the environment. Companies are composed of departments like organs in the body's system while employees are the cells, collectively working together for the good of the whole where all must be in harmony to survive.

With interest in sustainability growing, the human race is sure to survive, unlike the potential downsides of a few years ago that had us wondering. The cooperative dance of camaraderie and respect are met each day in the office, at the grocery store and on the subway. Collectively we're in this together, so take a moment to reflect on whether you and your company or family are honoring nature and her gifts by meeting criteria that assure a continuous healthy lifestyle. Clean air is essential for breathing, for good health and for the spirit of life itself. Without clean air, lungs get congested, inciting sickness. The strength of a company, country or family lies in the health of its constituents. All we need to do is look at the demands for health care and see the effects of our stressful life styles.

Truly, the positive aspect of remediation, whether it's in land, a company's internal operations or the physical body itself, is essential to sustainable living. It is heartening to see the progress from which we can all benefit.

Nanotechnology and New Frontiers

Ideas are like carrots: Go-For's gnawed on for inspiration. Action on an idea tests the hypothesis. Any result is meaningful. If it shows promise, you continue to follow the trail of possibility, for many a success is found just around the corner just when you were about to give up. Such is the case with scientists pursuing Mother Nature's secrets.

As reported in the August 19, 2005, edition of *Science*, as well as *Nature*'s online edition, a promising forecast for business success is seen in the field of nanotechnology.[12] Carbon-60 atoms are used to produce nanotubes, tiny flexible transparent cylinders one-billionth of a meter in diameter, that naturally align themselves in neat rows to form a sheet. Through the law of attraction, an almost magnetic force activates the symbiotic connection. They can also be coaxed to behave as peelable ribbons, enhancing their potential for product development.

Despite this material's delicate appearance, it is 2,000 times thinner than paper and stronger than steel, primarily because of the hexagonal shape of the carbon atoms (named "Buckyballs" after the architect Buckminster Fuller, inventor of the geodesic dome). Because there is no loss of conductivity with rolling the fabric, it is being seriously considered for heated automobile windows and flexible television screens. See how marvelous is the imagination?

For years, electrically conductive nanotubes have been woven into fibers and sheets, but the speed necessary to make them viable for commercial production was lacking. That is, until 2009, when a U.S. team led by Jeremy Levy of the University of Pittsburgh sandwiched two ceramic crystal material insulators (lanthanum aluminate and strontium titanate) and found conductive electricity when a positive charge crossed them to etch a tiny conducting wire which later could be erased; a transistor that acts like an Etch A Sketch drawing tablet.[13]

Meanwhile, another team led by Thomas Russell (University of Massachusetts) solved several problems at once by applying a simple concept using crushed sapphire crystals to align a specific pattern of ridges as a guide for semiconductor film "15 times denser than anything achieved previously." Russell said: "With the densities… you could store 250 DVDs on a surface the size of a quarter."[14]

Nanotechnology may also be able to capitalize on the Casimir Effect, the strange quantum attraction that draws two conducting surfaces together in a vacuum. Nanoparticles have recently been found to *reverse* that attraction, creating forces that are promising for practical applications.

Projected industrial uses for these organic cylinders will grow as they warp the speed to knit even wider fabric, lending itself well to fill an ingenuity gap for creative inventions. This totally new product, biological in nature with innate intelligence, has potential to change our world, as we now know it, to bring us products we have yet to know we even want.

While nanotechnology has promise, there are warnings about health risks, because scientists have no experience with how products made with these nanotubes will affect the health of those using them. In the *Seattle Times* article "Fears grow that tiny particles may pose major health risks", Michelle R. Smith cautions that potential environmental effects of these tiny particles could easily penetrate lungs, brains and other organs, as did asbestos. It is unknown how these organic particles will affect those engaged in the developmental process, manufacturing and usage. To be on the safe side, the National Institute for Occupational Safety and Health is developing guidelines for people working with nanomaterials, but they have no history upon which to base their recommendations. It is generally accepted the mystery will be solved at some point in the near future.

Meanwhile, until more study is done to prove the safety of nanotechnology products such as highly light-absorbent sunscreens, Pat Roy Mooney, executive director of the Ottawa-based nonprofit ETC Group, recommends their removal from store shelves.[15] Not only is nanotechnology on the radar for products to market, research reveals "life-cycle potential environmental impacts may be as much as 100 times greater per unit of weight than those of traditional materials, potentially offsetting some of the environment benefits of the small size of nanomaterials."[16]

Pathologist Agnes Kane at Brown University, with a history researching the damaging effects of asbestos fibers on those exposed in shipyards and the insulation industry, is especially suited for nanoparticles research to see if there is a possible correlation on human and animal cells.

The customary rush to market of untested products to quickly recoup investment is tempered this time, due to the exorbitant sums of money spent by the asbestos industry in liability lawsuits after the fact. While lungs are a priority interest for funding, because they have already been the focus of lawsuits on the asbestos front, there is little focus on the gastrointestinal tract, despite nanoparticle product development for new toothpastes.

The

The structure of nanotubes
membrane. Thin, responsive
by vibrational frequency, the
universe. Nature is revealing
has the potential to benefit m

This is also a good analo
strengthen their bond by sti
we find we are not alone, ar
more come on board. It is t
ness, a flexible bond of inter
poses. Strong teams conduc
make sections work or to cl
it. It is all biology. The nan

are attracted to each other, spreading influence with each individual who learns about it. And, again, much is going on in the quantum field, the invisible world of creation.

Simply the focused belief that this fiber will produce amazing products has the power to make it so. Thomas Edison is a good example of how persistence pays off. He never lost momentum on his belief that an electric light bulb was possible. Most of all, focus shifts the energy to accommodate.

Science journalist Lynne McTaggart, author of *The Field* and *The Intention Experiment,* has set out to prove the power of mind over matter by using an intention experiment that involves a large number of people willing to participate. Volunteer participants focus their intention on achieving a certain end, reinforcing it daily. It is anticipated that the effect will be the desired result. If so, then it is proof of concept. This demonstrates through cooperation that everybody wins in an environment focused on the good of the whole, each taking their share and no more. When the intention is clear, it manifests like magic, as Lynne McTaggart's field studies confirm.[17] Focused intention bears results.

Cleve Backster in the 1970s developed a lie-detector device that could read changes in electromagnetic energy fields and was used in the courts to nab the guilty. One day, Backster was bored after giving a class on the mechanics of the lie detector. For diversion, he decided to hook up the wires of his metering device to the Dracena plant on top of the file cabinet in his office. When he attempted to burn a leaf, the needle moved on his meter. He tried various approaches and found the plant responded each time. Moving outside, he simply *thought* about the harm he might do to the plant, and still the needle responded. He kept distancing himself from the plant by moving up to two miles away and still his thoughts caused a response. With that experiment, he confirmed that thought was alive and able to transmit over very long distances without loss of information.

In these days of rapid communication via the Internet and cell phones, people are better informed, which stretches credulity to its limit. As global awareness expands, cultures will extract wisdom from the chaff and make better decisions for themselves, despite it all. We each are connected as part of the cell body's collective, making decisions based on our perceptions and their importance to the system. It is all energy, and energy is pervasive. We ourselves, our identity, are energy bound by a vibrational frequency.

So, the way you and your associates think has an impact on the whole organization, your family, your politics and approach to business, as well as to the endpoint customer. You will be attracted to people, places and things to help clarify your mission. Information will naturally be drawn to you according to your focus, and you may wonder about the coincidence.

"Why... I just happened to stop by to see Mr. Jones about a new design I have and to get clear on my idea when Dr. Maple popped in. To my surprise, he mentioned the development of his new product, which coincidentally was one I needed to complete my project."

We ask, how did that happen? Is it coincidence? He was there at just the right moment. It must have been serendipity. No, it was meant to happen. You created it that way. You were meant to be there at that precise moment drawn as you were by your desire. That is how it works. Call it coincidence, but your energy and focus brought it to you. It is the Law of Attraction.

Being attracted to situations that invite you to venture into unknown territories, to transcend limitation and to tease growth with gnawing possibilities, is the stuff of the quantum field of physics. It is the unseen energy manifesting itself, and almost everyone has had one or more of these experiences.

You may feel a pull to contact a company about your product, but you do not know exactly why. Call it a hunch, if you like. When you call, the president of the company says they've just decided they need the widget your company offers. And there you are, ready to solve their problem. I think you will agree it feels just like magic. However, it was because you were tuned into the quantum energy field that you felt the urge to make contact.

Hail quantum physics that deals with energy, minutia, uncertainty and probability. It is at the other end of the dimensional scale from Newtonian physics, which works with large-sized numbers and their quantifiable results.

Quantum energy is not like physical matter. Atoms are not tangible like a door you can knock on. Atoms are made of elements with structure invisible to the eye, orderly and holistic, like digital technology. Your wireless cell phone, iPad and Blackberry draw on the quantum energy field to function. It is energy from the vacuum, source of all there is, yet you cannot see, touch or feel it with a palm stroke over a surface. Humans look for similar energies to supplement their own orbiting energy fields. Have you noticed how you migrate to those whose interests you share? The law of attraction is at work again as the symbiotic relationships of thought communicate its presence. You and I know that it is there, causing us to contemplate the nature of matter and how it manifests.

The human mind can come up with even more ideas, with even more potentials. There is no end. This is what growth is all about as we step onto the plank of the unknown to have an experience that could change the direction of our life and that of others, as well. Because of an inspiring idea, someone someplace in the world is risking everything they have to go into business. You may be one of them. If successful, you will reap huge rewards. The more risk involved, the more rewards, even if it is only in experience. It is trusting intuition to lead you on the right path.

Therefore, it is of utmost importance that a company be awake and aware of more than the bottom line as an indicator of progress, buyer trends and satisfaction. With over-inflated stock values, not to mention the strategies of executives wanting more than their share of profits, whoever is minding the store had better look beneath the sheets to make sure there are no dirty tricks being played.

It is sad to witness the recalcitrant behavior of companies whose lack of vision leaves them in the wake of foreign competitors whose outlook is innovative and progressive. The truth continues to be found in this motto: "Change is inevitable, but growth is optional." It all boils down to choice.

CHAPTER TWELVE

SERVING MANKIND'S NEEDS
The Not-So-Sacrosanct Corporation

Service is key to any business. To make customers feel comfortable and workers feel appreciated is the best of both worlds, the proven way to success. Not all businesses succeed, but those that do have an organizational model that works. And, because there is a constant need for workers to do jobs in a variety of fields, people filling those jobs want and need to feel appreciated for their contribution. These workers also need to be paid a living wage from the company's profit. In this way, business owners share their abundance with those who have participated in the business's or organization's success.

Dee Hock, the retired banker turned consultant whom I mentioned in an earlier chapter, brings wisdom and experience to not-for-profit organizations as an individual thinker in organizational design. Hock has coined the word *chaord*, a conjunction of chaos and order, to describe his idea of an organization as building rapport based on harmony and disparate parts coming together for the good of the whole, and expanding programs imbued with these tenets.

As the charismatic founder of the trillion-dollar Visa credit/debit card industry, Dee Hock looked to biology for the answer to collaboration and holistic culture-building: "in harmony with nature, with one another, and with the divine intelligence, such as the world has never dreamed." His vision, shared by many, extends to the regeneration of individuality, liberty, community and ethics. Seeing how far his chaordic principle expanded, in 2007 Hock began working with the Arizona Department of Juvenile Corrections to reform their educational system, a worthy goal given the state of the corporate prison system and the increase in detentions.[1]

Hock was not alone in looking to the prison system as a place to reform people who screw Mother Nature for profit. He found more people incarcerated in the U.S. than in the population of some cities, a dramatic statement that confirms something is drastically wrong with our society. The prison system is like any other corporation looking to increase profits and to expand its successful business model.

However useful, though, punishment without rehabilitation does nothing to change behavior and is therefore *not* a good business model. Reprimanding a child without explaining the benefit in correcting his or her behavior will not reap the reward desired. Hospitalization without medical care does nothing to heal the body. When the values of a society seek to constrain rather than rehabilitate, it is as a cancer sickening the body politic. Not a good business model to emulate.

Ari Cowan, an American social theorist, developed an approach to prevent or dramatically reduce violence in a broad range of settings. This new way of describing and responding to violence is the Violence Integrative Prevention and Restoration (PAR) Model, built on a public-health foundation that treats violence as a disease. The PAR Model has been successfully demonstrated in schools in the United States and communities on the India/Pakistan border. This model has also been applied with success at a Level 5 (maximum security) facility in the United States. During the demonstration, violent incidents were reduced 100 percent, referrals to the Intensive Management Unit ("solitary" or "the hole") were reduced 100 percent, and logged confrontations were reduced 100 percent. In short, the violence stopped.[2]

As a business model, let's take a look at how the rehabilitation process needs improvement. Truth for offenders is, for the most part, like villains living a movie in their head. In a way, Cowan says, they are infected with a malignancy called violence and brutality, which comes from a construct of reality based on depravity. When behavior is disjointed from the individual persona and replaced with a discriminator (another focal point) that offers life-giving choices, this new frame of reference shifts the offender's potential (life choice) to the universal field (unlimited opportunities), which allows reconstruction to begin.

The World Health Organization (WHO) in 2004 stated that the annual estimated costs of reported violent crimes in the United States alone came to a whopping $507 billion. In 2001, the cost to maintain correctional facilities was roughly $38.2 billion, which breaks down to $104 for each resident, according to the U.S. Department of Justice in June 2004. In addition, the estimated cost to society of young people engaging in a life of crime is a staggering $2,600,000 per youth in the United States, according to WHO figures.

The numbers are mind-boggling when you also consider the June 2004 U.S. Department of Justice figures that show 2,121,180 people were in prisons. As if that is not enough to stir contemplation, 1,866,668 children between 2003 and 2005 were abused or neglected, according to figures confirmed by the U.S. Department of Health and Human Services.

Some say the U.S. has taken a wrong turn, citing such reasons as errant laws favoring the rich, an educational system that teaches to the test rather than teaching students to reason and problem-solve through critical thinking, and a disproportion of wealth concentrated in a few. Wait. There is more: conditions of filth, the male/female disparity in hiring and pay, and breeding without a conscience. As men walk away sexually satisfied for the moment, too many women live with the consequences and with children who grow up fatherless. Such inequities undercut progress, even in business.

That these disparities exist in organizational thinking plays a big part in the health and welfare of the body politic. It is well known that a company or organization is only as good as the people who work in it. This is true despite good intentions and how well the plan is designed. To have a healthy business requires the same intelligence as a healthy body, the same respect for humanity as part of the human equation, and since the brain has both left and right hemispheres, it works together like a male/female partnership.

During World War II, men went off to war and women took their jobs, liberating themselves to be part of the global community. Women, who multitask naturally, are more and more treated as equals in a business world predominately run by males. We even see a few women climb the ladder to the executive suite. Women make super executives, organized and efficient. It's also been said that women who have been mothers can do anything. They know how to lead, organize, manage, delegate and discipline, and they are great decision-makers in times of crisis.

That a clear distinction exists between sexes is seen in the development of the brain. Intuition is generally higher for females, whose right brain is more developed than linear-thinking males' left brain that likes doing sequential tasks. A whole brain enjoys the facility of both hemispheres working efficiently, bringing balance to business while seeing relationships missed by others. It is biology communicating through the field of its cellular network in the electromagnetic field.

Performance on Demand

Personnel problems arise in business when executive drivers and competitive managers expect humans to perform as robotic machines that never wear out. This management style leads to workplace abuse. People are pushed around and/or told to meet unrealistic deadlines. Insistence on long hours dulls the intellect. Performance suffers as exhaustion kicks in. Burnout has even taken lives, as reported by *BusinessWeek* in August 2007.[3]

The Paris design complex of the French automaker Renault, for one, experienced a rash of suicides, three engineers in five months. Families reported that the cause lay in unreasonable workloads, high-pressure management tactics based on a results-oriented ethos, exhaustion and humiliating criticism in front of colleagues during performance reviews.

According to a report from Taipei, Taiwan, in 2010, rising public anger over low wages prompted Hon Hai Precision industry to boost salaries by 20 percent after 10 worker suicides called attention to substandard pay at their Foxcorn unit. Entry-level line workers earned a little more than $131.80 (900 yuan) per month before overtime and incentive bonuses, against suicide compensation of 100,000 yuan to victims' families. Corporate operating profitability was still high enough to attract investors, while workers' families struggled to make ends meet.[4]

A survey in 2007 by the staffing service OfficeTeam included interviews with 150 senior executives at the nation's 1,000 largest companies who report that the review process is no longer a once-a-year occasion. Nearly four in ten executives now schedule meetings either twice a year or quarterly, up from 29 percent in 2002.

OfficeTeam has tips for workers to help make the most of the performance reviews:

1. Jog your memory: Make a list of your accomplishments and how your efforts benefited the firm and take them with you to the review.
2. Bring your ideas: Discuss what you hope to achieve over the coming months and whether you need a change in your role. It is suggested that you list necessary support to meet your objectives.
3. Treat the review as a two-way conversation: How you listen and respond to feedback is crucial. Think of the meeting as an opportunity to work with your supervisor to develop a plan to move your career forward.
4. Dish it out—carefully: Use the review to diplomatically provide your manager with feedback. This is your chance to request more guidance or resources.
5. Create an action plan: Always finish the discussion by setting specific goals to work toward. To make the next review more productive, start tracking your achievements and challenges now.[5]

The productivity culture was born here in the U.S. as a means of matching or betting on competition as motivation. It is easy for those throwing out the dictums to compete in a race with time, because they are not the ones doing the work. Often the amount of time allotted to do the work is far less than it takes to accomplish. Meanwhile, executives gloat at the stiff workload as a sign of superior management. It is highly likely that they themselves would collapse under such stress-induced demands. To deal with this factor, companies are adding personalized services so workers can spend more time with their families. Work-life programs are being instituted in many more companies. Google is way ahead of this game, as discussed earlier.

Some companies, like some departments in Microsoft, offer casual hours. The worker sets his or her own schedule with flexibility to choose to work at home or at the office. The responsibility is to get the job done.

Peter Cappelli, who teaches management at The Wharton School, agrees: "Cranking up negative consequences, which seems to be the dominant view of motivation, is not really good for people's mental health."[6] This should not come as a surprise, as any teacher can tell you that praise begets higher performance. If you are already low on the totem pole, what makes anyone think that berating your behavior is going to put you on top? Jack Welch and his "rank-and-yank" policy at General Electric put extreme pressure on workers to meet targets essentially unachievable. When performance reviews are dreaded by all concerned, it makes you wonder if in the long run they are useful. They can end up being an opinion, rather than a record of achievement, like a report card. And under conditions where personalities clash, there could be unexpected fallout with damaging effects.

Other companies, like IBM and Draper Laboratory in Cambridge, Massachusetts, are addressing the stress issue before it becomes psychologically debilitating by giving workers stress tests. Steve Kerr of Goldman Sachs Group Inc. suggests that managers ask subordinates to aim for a target known to be achievable. Unrealistic goals are self-defeating. What seems like common sense is to break up jobs too large and overwhelming when looked at as one goal. No one can do all the required tasks at once. There is a sequence and if not followed it can surely foul the result, first things first.

While it is easy for executives to mete out expectations, it is quite another to execute them in an orderly manner. Henry Ford did not build the Model T in one day, nor did he attack each component at once. Admittedly, competition drives corporate behavior, and money is generally attached as a reward, say, a bonus for the boss who engineers the production train. Even then, workers have to rest or collapse from exhaustion. De-stressing allows time to reflect, to recharge and to appreciate the distance trod, to just kick back and relax after a job is accomplished.

Management consultants Booz Allen Hamilton Inc. came up with another way to address the stress issue: identify life responsibilities and create a work schedule around them. This honors family considerations as a necessity, easing stress on everyone involved. If more staff is needed more hires are made.

More companies have to address this issue, because burnout often causes sickness and the inability to function at peak. In the long run, it is very unhealthy, increasing costs of health care and time off to recuperate. It is a self-defeating policy.

At the Chicago office of Boston Consulting Group, Mark Ostermann had put in 60-plus-hour workweeks for six weeks straight. After this became known to his bosses, they took action to ease the burden. He says, "It's a good check and balance to remind people that it's not all about working the most hours but about delivering to the client."[7]

It should be quite apparent that the role of leader can be challenging.

Some people are placed in management positions when they are ill equipped to manage others; they have enough trouble managing themselves. When promoting employees to management, it is advisable to choose carefully those with potential and to guide them during the transitional period.

Customer Service

While money is bartered for goods as scrip, it is customer referrals upon which business is built. Service and satisfaction go hand in hand.

Long ago, Omar Ruthstrom learned that the greatest advertising medium ever is word of mouth. For more than 40 years, satisfied customers have spread his fame. As a result, his business flourished. Better known as Omar the Tent Man, he operates a tent rental business in Rainier, Washington, 80 miles southeast of Seattle, putting tents up and taking them down for institutions, universities, governments, U.S. presidents, celebrities such as Bill Gates, and private parties of all kinds. He proudly boasts that most mornings, he's up before 5 a.m. and climbs into bed around 10 at night.

What is so extraordinary about Ruthstrom's successful business is that he has never used paid advertising as a way to get customers. He is a complete package with logo hat, jacket and truck signs. He long ago learned that being edgy about life does not suit his style or character. Most often, you will find him with a broad grin making friends of strangers. He takes advantage of every opportunity to spread goodwill. When he hands out his card, he does so with a cheery invitation, "If you ever need a tent, call me." Word-of-mouth advertising is what Omar the Tent Man depends upon, which is why his great reputation spans the U.S. and islands in the Pacific.

But Omar's career did not just happen, or maybe it did. When his grandfather and grandmother and their nine sons emigrated from Sweden to the United States, they left behind land and wealth. After settling in and earning a bit of money, his grandfather purchased a musical instrument for each of the boys as well as for himself, to replace the ones left in Sweden. In the true spirit of self-promotion, they sold themselves to the Barnum and Bailey Circus as the Ruthstrom Family Band, and for many years they traveled with the circus. Omar was named after one of the crew the family particularly liked.

Customer service *is* the name of the game for those with long-range plans. However, not every business handles customer service in the same way. One area of consternation over the years has been the return policy.

Each company sets its own guidelines. Some have strict limitations, while others handle returns without aggravation. Costco has a great reputation for handling customer returns, perhaps because it is a club, but even so there are lessons to be learned from their model.

At one of the major home center stores, a customer bought a pet door to be used in her garage, only to learn when she got home that it did not fit properly. The next morning she went back to the store to return it. This is where it got sticky.

The customer was told she would have to wait 15 days to get a refund because she had paid with a check. She grew more disgruntled by the day, so that when day 15 arrived, her angst was unassailable. Making sure the impact of her unhappiness was not lost, she told the store in no uncertain terms that she would *never* shop there again. She would take her money elsewhere.

You almost cannot blame the company. With bad checks bouncing, it is clear why some stores choose such a policy. Yet it is very poor customer relations for those whose credit is good. The costs involved in losing a customer are enormous. No business can afford that luxury. Bad press travels fast.

One night a family of eight went to the casual Outback restaurant in Kennewick, Washington, for dinner. The first words out of the hostess's mouth were, "There is a 15 percent gratuity to serve your party of eight." Put off by this defining moment, the family vowed next time to go with only four people instead of the party of eight, that is, *if they returned at all.* Lackluster service coupled with a specified gratuity netted the restaurant a loss of four customers.

The tenet of every business is to make customers happy with their purchases and for shopping with you. Putting function ahead of a satisfied customer is not the way to their heart. You yourself would protest if your stomach decided it was not appreciated enough: "No more, I'm not going to perform according to plan. I'm rebelling." Who wins?

Another example is worthy of mention. After attending a late afternoon open-air performance of *The Taming of the Shrew*, two friends, Marilyn and Barbara, and I drive to Snoqualmie Falls in the Cascade Mountains above Seattle to have dinner at the Salish Lodge. After a 45-minute wait, during which we enjoy the beautiful scenery with a walk to the falls, we are seated next to the window with a view, per our request. By now, however, the sun hovers near sunset. Still the beautiful afternoon is a sparkling extravaganza of colorful hues. However, the treasured experience of a table overlooking the falls will soon fall under the shroud of darkness.

Eager to satisfy our hunger, we select light fare and catch up on events in our lives while we wait to be served. And we wait and wait and wait. Finally, two of the three meals arrive, with assurance by our waitress that the other will arrive shortly. Time passes, with Barbara's meal still somewhere in the kitchen, along with the dressing for my salad. We all patiently wait. Sitting on the outside of the table, I seek our waitress, who is everywhere but near us. My request is met with excuses and apologies, which do not salve our angst or satisfy our palettes one tiny bit.

Marilyn and I finish our meals, with Barbara still waiting for her dinner. But now it is pitch-black outside and raining. We have another appointment and have to leave. Again, I am on my feet heading toward the waitress. Obviously, she's forgotten we are even here.

Finally she brings Barbara's dinner with more apologies, saying, "There will be no charge." Yah! I guess not. Barbara is gracious, but the imprint is made. She asks that her food be put in a box to take home. Eating in the car is not an option. Needless to say, we will not go back there again.

When the customer has to find the waitress to get served, it makes you wonder what service is all about. Either this is her first day on the job and she is too flustered to remember her responsibility, or she has far too many tables to handle, or she plainly has no conscious remembrance and lacks the ability to follow the job through to completion. In any of these situations, training is the issue, as well as making sure the applicant is right for the job.

There is a trust factor involved in this story—business serves the public. Having satisfied customers is the goal of every enterprise, regardless of size. It's important to remember that you are also a customer.

New customers rely on a company's reputation. You yourself may have asked for recommendations from those who frequent a business, or one like it, to get a "feel" for satisfaction. Subtleties like tone of voice, actions and facial expressions often count more than do the words, and they too can send a mixed message. Whatever perception, its influence is ubiquitous in the success of every business.

Business owners invest energy, time and money in meeting a need or in bringing a great product to the marketplace. Some products are frivolous, appealing to our playfulness and folly. Some are necessities. Some comply with standards set by government regulatory agencies. Still others apply to our vanity and peace of mind. Whatever it is, the success of the "build it and they will come" philosophy depends on integrity, courteous service and reliability to build confidence and good customer relations.

It is not worth the aggravation and brand slam to produce under-performing products that disappoint end users and give manufacturers black marks on their record. Worse yet is when lax product safety receives bad press and undermines public confidence. Companies cannot afford to produce such products, yet it goes on all the time.

Regardless of which side of the fence companies work, they still gain notoriety, much as aspiring stars do not care what the press says, as long as they spell their names right. "That's show business!"

Dick Spady, however, has the right idea. With five successful Dick's Drive-In restaurants in the Seattle area, his heart is in the right place, evidenced by his company receiving the 2005 Business of the Year award from the Municipal League of King County. His business philosophy encourages young people to do community service four hours a month, for which he pays them their hourly wage. When students work for him for six months, he will even pay their tuition at a community college or an equivalent amount toward a four-year school. How good can it get? He shows what it means to be a good citizen and civilization builder by instilling in these young people the responsibility to get involved in community service and to know what it feels like to find satisfaction in volunteering. He is also serving the children of the community through his active participation and funding of the Seattle Wallingford Boys and Girls Club.

Service and Collective Intelligence

Oprah Winfrey and Harpo Productions Inc. also prove it is possible to impact the world through generosity by enabling social change and supporting positive trends to help the downtrodden overcome limitations. It is a model others emulate. Oprah invites others to give back to the community through her Angel Network and honors folks whose service makes a difference.

The YMCA and YWCA, community-service clubs like the Boys & Girls Club, Kiwanis, Lions, Elks, Zonta International, the Rotary and Shriners Hospital for Children are but a few that also give with a joyful heart to support worthy endeavors. Being a good neighbor is meaningful for communities to prosper.

I am more convinced than ever that we are here to serve, to learn, to expand our minds and to evolve our brains, which is the driving force behind my *Evolving Ideas*© radio and television talk shows, speaking engagements and workshops.

As a natural communicator, getting demerits in deportment in elementary school, the spontaneity of my quizzical mind would remove any complacency I might have had. Teachers recognized this trait and urged me to take classes in drama and public speaking, which I did with great enthusiasm, receiving all A's, leading me many years later to take a TV production class and eventually become producer/host of *Evolving Ideas*©, my own show.

Initially, I approach KCTS, the PBS affiliate in Seattle, and present a program outline to the general manager, expecting to be hired. He is interested and keeps the paperwork and demo tape. This looks promising, but it does not manifest the show. Later, a move to Olympia, Washington, connects me with a local public access station, TCTV, and after a bit of equipment training, I'm on to do 600 television shows with leading-edge thinkers. Dr. Gary Null in New York interviews me several times on East Coast Network radio about my book, *If You Make The Rules, How Come You're Not Boss?*, and later invites me to join his new Progressive Radio Network on the Internet.

Now, many years later, I'm thrilled each week to share with our growing audience interviews with leading-edge thinkers. By expanding your mind, you grow exponentially in knowledge, making you wiser and far more conversant on topics important to the human condition, making your life far more interesting than is possible just listening to the daily news. It certainly works for me and it can work for you. To receive weekly alerts to guests and topics, and to access archives for download, send your email contact information to: radio@evolvingideas.com.

In the same collaborative knowledge-acquiring field, Netflix uses the art of crowdsourcing to overcome corporate constraints borne of hierarchical ladder-climbing to make decisions. The case for collective intelligence has biological roots, different design patterns known as "genes". When applied to the Internet, as in recent examples seen in the paper, "Harnessing Crowds: Mapping the Genome of Collective Intelligence",

Thomas E. Malone, director of the Center for Collective Intelligence at the Massachusetts Institute of Technology says, "It's not magic." Nevertheless, Netflix is an excellent example of crowdsourcing.[8] No matter how clever is your company and your product, marketing relies on a receptive audience willing to embrace innovative ideas and a workable system of delivery.

Beyond Visible Light

Sometimes, I find myself daydreaming through my office window searching for answers to life's mysteries. I attempt to recall conversations with my parents and to dredge up the know-how of my father and my mother. Often, I wish I could ask them questions I did not think to ask when they were living. Most of us take for granted that family will always be there.

I think about Einstein and Buckminster Fuller, great minds that made a difference in the world, and wonder what happened to their acquired knowledge that took them a lifetime to accumulate. Where did it all go when they went away? Yes, I know this is deep thinking, but ask yourself the same question and then apply it to what you know and how much of your knowledge is shared to broaden understanding.

I am curious about children who, at age two, can play a toy piano and make music. And about the young boy who began to write symphonies when he was four, to have them performed on the concert stage shortly after he finished them. I am curious about the blind children whose right brain is so developed they can sit down at the piano and play without ever having had a lesson. How did that happen? How did they know to do that? It is curious, indeed. It is clear that not all learning is done in school, where teachers who are themselves still learning teach you. Much wisdom comes from the human experience, from making mistakes to making corrections, such as the prison system offers. Some comes from experiencing leadership on the job, as VISA creator, or lack of leadership, as we see in the restaurant situation; while more comes from insights gained on the job and in the public arena where the critical-thinking audience speaks up.

It is knowledge and experience that allows you to do jobs other than the ones you initially have been trained to do. If someone were to ask you to write everything down that you know how to do, you would have a very long list. That is, unless you've been hibernating and missed a lot of school, in particular the school of hard knocks where a lot of wisdom is learned. Sometimes I say I've learned things I never knew I ever wanted to learn and done things I never knew I ever wanted to do. You, too, have learned some things you never knew you ever wanted to learn; but in the doing, you gained experience to make you who you are today, and so long as you are living, you will continue to gain knowledge and have experiences. The brain loves to learn and the body loves to experience, and they collaborate for the best effects. This cooperative school is open to every living human being, given attendance on a regular basis.

What is your legacy? You see it is an important question. What if... you came back again to claim the knowledge you acquired this lifetime and just kept going? Would you want to learn as much as you can, to have as many new experiences as possible to add entries into your book of knowledge, and to conquer yourself on the frontiers of discovery, now? Think about what an exciting life awaits the adventurous spirit willing to explore possibilities for personal growth. If you had a choice with no limitations, would you choose to continue what you are doing right now with your life?

More likely than not, unless you awaken to your potential and progress on the road in that direction, the anguishing struggle for self-mastery will continue. Better to bridge the surging currents of torment and indecision, often associated with a sense of oblivion, and move toward yet more challenging experiences to realize all that you are and can be. Dee Hock is a great example of what it means to follow intuition and to make a big difference in the world.

It is not necessarily easy to move through the eye of the needle, nor for the chrysalis to emerge from its cocoon. But the struggle is worth the effort when you are rewarded with the beauty of the butterfly and its freedom to taste the nectar of nature's colorful landscape. An expanded view of the possible sees new horizons to conquer. You are uplifted rather than feeling trapped by recycling ignorance that continues to roll around in your head.

It is the consummate success story. No matter their age, when people pursue their passion, doors open to evolutionary jumps in self-awareness, expression and wisdom. Creativity can enrich the whole of humanity with fresh ways to look at life that are both fun and emotionally rewarding.

Peter Drucker is right. The new frontier is knowledge with integrity, a very necessary coordinate: experience verifies your intention. Life does not give up easily. Neither does the human body. Any ray of light left in life's bulb will brighten with a little encouragement. It is part of the human condition to survive when possible. That is one beautiful thing about life. It wants to express itself, and it will continue to do so until the last ray of light extinguishes. Hope really does spring eternal.

CHAPTER THIRTEEN

GLOBAL AWARENESS
Dynamic Energies for the Future

In the Middle East war for oil looms a failed mission in peacemaking. While oil rights keep the barons' gears lubricated, cries grow louder for renewable energies. To drive innovation is to draw on quantum physics' invisible energetic fields as the most useful and resourceful answers. Yet the severe limitations of traditional electrodynamics restrain progress in developing essential energy needs. T. E. Bearden, Ph.D., says that electrical engineering textbooks continue to reflect the 1800s' obsolete model. Research into energy from the vacuum has been around since the beginning of the 20th century, but as yet, there is not much to show for it. As a result, the U.S. and other developing countries are not advancing technologically, probably because it would leave their current operation in the dust. It's all about control, and profits. Energies pervade every thing, and every nonthing. All electromagnetic fields are energetic force fields with the ability to transcend time and space. Electrical current may follow the line of the wire, but electrons are oriented around the wire to create the field effect.[1]

As Bearden states in his book *Energy from the Vacuum*, we have been using outdated electric energy sources when new technologies will free us from the wires. But then, businesses supporting the model currently in vogue would either convert or go out of business. At this point, the business model breaks down. With oil supplies dwindling, investing in energy available everywhere is the wisest choice.

Perhaps the greatest technological advances in our time are the Internet and the cell phone. However, heavy exposure to electromagnetic energy fields emanating from cell phones to your brain can be dangerous. No longer bound by wires, satellites transmit signals to make instant communication possible. Intuition is even faster.

The Communicating World of Biology

While some may find the marriage of ideologies between biology and business a bit strange, I find them quite compatible. By now, though, you are probably beginning to agree with me there are, indeed, undeniable parallels. To be successful, business of necessity must be resourceful, tuned to marketplace trends and the public's fickle buying habits. Biology is amazingly efficient in this regard. Closely aligned to the speed of Internet conductivity, the membrane is finely tuned to respond to signals from the environment and in a moment effectively translate perceptions into behavior.

No bells ring. Chimes are silent. No verbose language lets us know we have an intimate loving partner within, our own personal bodyguard. Energy fires the living system's communication network. We know it as innate intelligence, a monitoring system that feeds us valuable information about what is going on inside the body, as well as on the outside.

This innate intelligence is very, very smart. Cells constantly talk to one another through a sophisticated input, process and output sequence of commands. Computer chips contain billions of bits of information and travel at high speed to connect people to people, information and products. Through this medium, business is no longer confined to the neighborhood, but is available to global markets around the world.

The Internet cooperates with servers, clients, web users and the marketplace of ideas for mutual benefit. It is the difference between the cell phone that relies on tower and satellite relays and EMF signals and land-line telephone service that relies on wires, predicted to be obsolete by 2016, if progress continues to develop high-efficiency communication systems connecting people to people.

In the human body, the cell's membrane is the interface between the known and unknown, the outside and the inside, and is itself the most efficient of all physical communication systems. The membrane is a liquid crystal semiconductor, the same as is a computer chip, which means that it is programmable. They both share the same characteristics and the same definition, though only the cell membrane is living.

The membrane is the nervous system, the brain of the cell, responsive to signals from the environment, which includes the skin on the outside of our body. The liquid crystal semiconductor membrane is very intelligent, with protein receptors as listening antennae that eavesdrop on our thought processes and self-talk, totally aware of what's going on inside and outside our body. The interaction of communications is what brings to us the reality we call life. Through this vast communication network that processes incoming information, signals travel at the speed of light, 186,000 miles per second, making it extremely fit to run the system. Which means, in biology, that the cellular community responds instantly to stimuli coming from both the outside and within simultaneously. There's no manager or office receptionist to intercept the message and redirect it to some other destination because he or she doesn't understand the transmission.

In 2007, an associate professor at Ohio State University, Dongping Zhong, discovered that water molecules exposed to ultra-fast light pulses link up with proteins and enable them to move and function. Since proteins as complex molecules regulate biochemical reaction and water is their medium of transport, it is imperative for life itself that living organisms drink sufficient water.

This could be significant in treating Alzheimer's, Parkinson's, cataracts, cystic fibrosis and diabetes. Drinking water assists clear thinking and better protein digestion, as well as cell membrane signal transmission, and also alleviates physical stress.[2]

The human body is efficient and knows the path of least resistance to accomplish the task at hand. Even as I write this page, the brain takes the thought that has carefully been formulated in the vast network of neuronal connections and aligns with muscles that move my fingers over the computer keyboard, making sense out of my mental construct. It is like magic, don't you agree?

Whether you write by hand or use the computer, the human brain is the organ with the know-how to accomplish the intended result. It is a marvel of organizational unity, and so little gratitude is expressed for its efficiency. If business wants to improve its operations, it should pay more attention to the membrane of communication awareness and apply this model of integrated processes.

As the physical body's trillions of cells adapt to environmental conditions, so must those corporations with satellite offices and a global presence. As economic climates shift from hot to cold, depending upon political agendas not always in the best interests of humanity or effective and efficient commerce, the confusion and uncertainty factors make it difficult to know where to place your cards. If mankind struggles for identity, so do entrepreneurs and executives of big corporations. They hold fast to safety nets made of bottom-line numbers that connect the moves on the chessboard with merchandise sales and Internet commerce, all once held tightly as pride of ownership. Volatile markets in resources kick security into competitors' lanes to score striking advantages that unseat confidence in future wins.

Of course, you're going to have those that cause problems. Look at all the stuff you have on your plate. Even the physical body depends upon parasites for proper digestion. Our bowels are active participants in processing foods. We depend upon bacteria that feed on our waste to break down the nutrients for proper absorption. Creatures of the night in small places devour leftovers and turn them into a profit. Unusable portions are eliminated to make way for more on the way. It goes down the tube, so to speak, to be pushed out for another round of services. Foods have been transformed, masticated, digested, absorbed, and the dregs discarded as unusable by the body. It is the waste of living creatures. What goes in has to come out. It's the input, process and output of creation. An idea that comes to you is developed, and the results speak for themselves.

Cooperative Spirit in Business

Biology is very efficient, using no more energy than is necessary. In an emergency, some cells will differentiate, meaning they shape-shift to briefly assume tasks other than their regular assigned responsibilities. In business, we might call these "floaters", or "temps", or "jacks of all trades", as they move with ease from one job to another.

The biology of business is comparable to the biology of living organisms. To function efficiently, the whole system must cooperate. Living organisms are efficient, malleable and honest in all their dealings, and they can be relied upon to always fulfill their mission, given the opportunity. Living systems demand no time off for good behavior, nor holidays and weekends to rest up for the next round, though a bit of rest is helpful. That's what winter and nightfall are all about. They are nature's rest periods, to cool off from the day's hot sun, and to sleep in winter until spring awakens the seeds and soil again. Though the seasons change, nature adapts and keeps growing. It keeps creating and duplicating itself by hiding its secrets in the seeds that spring forth in the next season's renewal without reminder. Winter provides cover to germinate seeds. Snowfall and rain supply water for sustainability. Every season provides a necessary component to balance the ecosystem.

While the body is busy taking care of its business, interpreting environmental signals in the communication relay system important to the care and nurturing of the organism, it is also carrying on activities of interest to the property owner. Running a business requires the same attention. Business itself is an environment, and minding your body's business is even more critical.

The human brain is capable of discerning incoming and outgoing data streams according to their importance to the system. The power of the mind can decide whether a food is good for you or not, based upon previous experience. When you make a decision about what you want to eat, the body will signal yea or nay. In other words, the body will be sure to let you know how it feels. You can override the body's innate intelligence by choosing foods emotionally and eat something that makes you sick.

With an insatiable appetite to make things work, the body's survival is also the cell's. There is definitely a symbiotic relationship at play here, just as in an office environment where cooperation is critical for a positive outcome. A business, like a body, will sound the alarm when there are too many fires to put out, ignited by a series of events not always in a company's best interests. For example, an order requiring special attention is ignored, the parts' delivery date is delayed, internal production slows to exacerbate the problem. Worse, the impatient customer needs the unit to complete their own production quota. Your reputation is on the line. Future sales are at stake. Your budget is dependent upon being paid for the completed order, and now payroll is at risk. By all accounts it is a bad hair day. But when it is assured that all departments are cooperating and functioning at peak performance, the company as a fully functioning system can carry on its business in a reliable fashion. Thus, cooperative competition wins again.

How Wireless Power Could Work
Fuel for cars, lighting, home heating and cooking is a fertile field for innovation, as is electronic gadgetry. Business accepts this technology so long as it is market-profitable. Turn to "free energy" and they tenaciously hold on

to current energy streams, regardless of efficiency. Suppliers of electricity, for example, want to maintain control of their market, and any new power source that is not under their grasp threatens their survival. Unfortunately, it is this kind of protective thinking that retards innovation. Novelty threatens the status quo. Of course, wireless energy is not necessarily monetarily "free", but it does remove tangibility as a necessity to function. Costs of operation are negligible compared to wired technologies. As we learn more about the quantum energy field, the more we want a way to control it for profit. However, when money is no longer the determinant of wealth, but innovation is, you'll see dynamic inventions materialize that will propel us into the space age and beyond. Cooperative competition will make it so.

In November 2006, Jonathan Fildes, science and technology reporter for BBC News, titled an article "Physics promises wireless power", positing that "the tangle of cables and plugs needed to recharge today's electronic gadgets could soon be a thing of the past." He reported that a team of researchers at MIT experimenting with the acoustic vibrations familiar to musicians as "resonance" could have hit upon a possible way for wireless energy to work. Some may remember the opera singer shattering a glass goblet when she sang a note that matched the resonant frequency of the glass. In the MIT study, "instead of using acoustic vibrations, the team's system exploits the resonance of 'electromagnetic waves'. Electromagnetic radiation includes radio waves, infrared and X-rays."[3] Marin Soljacic, an assistant professor of physics at MIT, suspects this effect could be adapted to work in a factory.

Professor Soljacic presented the MIT work, done in collaboration with his colleagues Aristeidis Karalis and John Joannopoulos, at the American Institute of Physics Industrial Physics Forum in San Francisco in November 2006. Applications of wireless energy transfer have been proposed in other quarters, too, including a "SplashPower" pad made by a U.K. company to recharge wireless gadgets such as phones and MP3 players, which uses electromagnetic induction, the same process used to charge electric toothbrushes. Ceiling hubs in each room are envisioned to serve as phone and laptop chargers constantly in operation.

Perfecting Practices in Biology and Business
To feed the urban multitudes without individual family farms, which were once the norm, collective farming communities now depend upon

distribution channels to buy and sell what they produce. To give such products as ready-to-eat sliced meat and fish, fruit and other edibles a longer shelf life, the Sweden-based company Avure, a subsidiary of Flow International, developed an improved version of the high-pressure processing system introduced a hundred years ago that effectively destroys most major food-borne pathogens. By dunking prewrapped foods into tanks of pressurized water "four to seven thousand times higher than normal atmospheric levels" for less than 10 minutes, the new process kills salmonella, *E. coli* and listeria without heat treatment or chemical additives, effectively lowering the amount of added preservatives the foods need.[4] Companies whose labels are familiar household names, like Hormel Foods Corporation and Perdue Farms, are using this process, maintaining food's nutritional quality without sacrificing product flavor or integrity—a big advantage for the high-pressure process.[5]

The business community can learn a lot from biology, especially when applied to better business practices. When the human body says one thing and the mind says another, it is a signal that the body politic is stressed, out of ease with itself, and needs time to rebalance. The human body certainly could not have survived this long if it functioned indiscriminately, for it is the ultimate expression in efficiency. Opportunities are everywhere. Mother Nature is the greatest inspiration. The variety of nature's expressions is truly awesome, and it seems inappropriate and unwise to fool around with her creations. Therein lies the problem with genetic engineering. The consequence of purposely manipulating her creations for profit is that she will bite back, sooner or later. "You can't fool Mother Nature," proclaimed an ad in the 1980s comparing butter to margarine. She will have her way, regardless.

Look at what happened when someone made the decision to reroute the Mississippi River. Look at the devastation when Hurricane Katrina hit shore. Why do some think that Mother Nature needs to be improved upon? Rather, working *with* Mother Nature is the better course of action. She has done a good job over the millennia. Genetic engineering is already corrupting the purity of the process. The truth of GMO will be a horror film that no one will want to watch.

Look what some drugs have done to babies, causing all manner of deformities. Oh yes, there will be natural genetic defects, errant programming at conception, but to deliberately manipulate the perfected human organism is folly. What scientist wants to play God, and for what reasons? We should have learned something from the atomic bomb.

The grand scope of the human body to perform multiple functions simultaneously is a demonstration of a perfected model. The business of the body is carried out with patience and persistence. It does not do stupid things, but immediately reports an error message when things go awry. The more genetic manipulations, the more we can expect weird results. Money made with these mental constructs endangers the human race and makes more people dependent. There is something wrong with the system when whole new sectors open up focused on increased drug dependency.

It is good to remember that creative producers are what make the market work. Why do we have to go to countries abroad for minds that can think? What have we done here through our mechanized educational system that fetters progress without reason? Leaders must set an example of how to create a better, healthier world where everyone benefits. When students see a world that does not work led by elected officials who cannot lead, or do not lead with the good of all concerned in mind, they lose confidence. Learning must be fun and meaningful. Rote learning is not the answer. Memorizing facts without comprehension can be useful for the spelling bee and game show, but may not be useful in life.

Rather than rote learning to meet prescribed tests, teach students to develop their minds. Emphasize critical thinking with interpretations from differing perspectives, weighing facts for analysis. Teaching reading without understanding leaves students ill prepared for life, work and community service. Critical thinking and logic are necessary components for effective decision-making. Weighing options and considering outcomes with consequences is essential for stable lifestyles, communities, families and businesses to stay on track.

There is cause for concern when students spend more time watching television and text-messaging friends than they do in personal interaction, missing opportunities to develop relationships face to face, where emotions are experienced that round out developing minds.

Demands on student performance slip through the cracks without accountability, with habits of study a bit too casual for the intense workaday world of business for which they are being prepared. Employers still look for educated minds willing to work to move ahead. One of my television guests met the challenge when she founded the Read Right program, which teaches people of all ages to read in a comprehensive manner. Dee Tadlock, Ph.D., a reading specialist, redirected her focus when she learned her own son could not read, having been taught in the traditional manner. Biologically, her son was capable. There was nothing wrong with his brain. It was just the way his brain took in information. Strongly motivated to help her son, she developed a program for training students to read with comprehension. It was not long before her son and many others like him could read and excel in their studies.

I was heartened in our TV interview when Tadlock brought in a reading specialist from the South Puget Sound area, along with a Texas high-school principal whose student body went from the lowest-performing in the state to excellent in four years, as proof that her method works. She explained how young students' brains are malleable and how, with appropriate guidance, even students from low-income-earner families can excel.[6] Tadlock says: "If you can talk, you can learn to read." If one can do it, others can too.

Herein lies an opportunity for business to participate. By creating a fund for financially strapped school districts to help pay teachers to train young minds to read using Tadlock's successful method, business can go a long way toward accelerating learning. This is constructive to society, to student achievement and to the whole of business in the long run.

Principles of Business Have Primitive Origins

In September of 1977, as I mentioned at the start of the book, I traveled to Papua New Guinea on my quest to experience as many existing primitive and underdeveloped societies as I could in order to better understand humanity's evolutionary journey. This Neolithic culture, 10,000 to 30,000 years old, was one of the most fascinating of my world travels. These people are naturally intuitive and use their innate antennae as a resolution pathway to problem-solve in the wild.

When we visited the Highlands Asaro tribe, they told us the legend of the origin of the Mudmen, the mud-masked figures who have become iconic images of Papua New Guinea. While there are many versions of the story, most agree on a few key elements, similar to this rendering found in the German travel series DuMont Kultur-Reiseführer:

> *During one of the many tribal fights, the inhabitants of Asaro came off worst. The survivors saved themselves on the muddy banks of the river,*

where they hid until nightfall. When they, completely covered with light mud, tried to sneak away quietly, the enemy, who thought they were the avenging ghosts of the killed, observed them. The enemy panicked and fled. The Asaro, surprised by the effect of their unintentional make-up, developed it as a war strategy, a kind of psychological warfare, and created mudmasks.[7]

It was a business decision, of course. Even in the bush there are problems, just like business today. What do you do when your life and all that you have is threatened, and there is no place to go? Use your imagination. Think creatively.

Though this quick thinking was an innovative solution to a pressing problem, it was not preplanned strategic behavior, as might be the case in a company. Despite that, the age-old wisdom that actions speak louder than words again won the day. What saved the Asaro was the enemy's perception, a belief that these mud-covered forms were actually angry gods.

The key is to understand that problems can only be solved when the creative process is central. Like the Asaro tribe in Papua New Guinea, every business today is challenged by how to survive in a hostile environment when threatened by the unseen, or by unknown forces. The tried and true may not always work or be suitable in each situation. While this is true whenever we are pressed for answers, the solution is simple: relax and in the quiet of your inner knowingness allow your subconscious mind to bring you the answer.

In the Asaro tribe, the legend and the popularity of the mud-masked natives made them the symbol of Papua New Guinea as a travel destination, and they appeared in tour books and posters throughout Australia and other parts of the world. During the 1970s, the demand for Mudmen performances was so high that another tribe was asked to participate also.

It was precisely the year of my visit to PNG that representative Mudmen were sent to New York as a promotional stunt to advertise travel to their primitive world, reflected in the historiology of the mud-masked natives of the Kominive village. It must have been a huge shock to the senses when the natives saw the contrasts in lifestyle.

With their identity established and advertised by tour companies, the Asaro head man, Ruipo Okoroho, began to extract a fee from tourist agencies who wanted to sell their "product", which allowed the agencies to arrange village visits where the Mudmen would dance and wave leaves to chase bad spirits away. Additionally, they would demonstrate traditional fire-starting with sticks and dry grass to show how easily it can be done. Each Mudman who participates in the performance receives a certain payment in kina, so the Kominive villagers function as an emblem of unanimity and a much-valued source of additional income. While the Mudmen have a group identity, each dancer is encouraged to express his handicraft personality in the making of his mud mask.

The business organization entails "intellectual property" to describe the ownership of immaterial things such as stories and rituals. Specific groups or individuals may own the exclusive rights to recite, perform or organize them.[8] In the case of the Mudmen, a performance may not be staged without permission of the big man, Ruipo, who also earned money for licensing and as late as 1993 still retained his chairmanship.

Thus, even in the wild, business deals center on proprietary rights, tradition and a wise elder who looks out for the "company" and takes high compensation for his negotiating skills. The perception that Mudmen have value is a simple belief that makes it so.

CHAPTER FOURTEEN

BOTTOM-LINE TRENDS
Fueling the Money Flow

Every endeavor draws on the history of events to reshape the way things are to be done in the future. Companies that have been around for a while know to be patient, for trends shift like ocean currents to mark periodic change. In today's world, there is a lot of stress as big companies get even bigger. They compete in the market by cutting prices to increase the money flow. Though bottom-line profits may suffer, at least merchandise is moving, which makes it look good for investors. It had better best last year's record sales, else how do they justify their projections?

How long can that go on without cycling to the other end of the ledger? The fire may get bigger and hotter, but there is always a cool-down. It is cyclic, as we have seen over the years. Everyone in business adjusts, and if they don't, they soon go broke.

Having survived for millennia, nature makes an excellent model for business to emulate. One of its traits is that it doesn't cheat on itself. To manipulate the books is to cause irreparable harm to your company, yourself, your family and associates, the business you own and those for whom you work. With integrity lacking, intense competition sometimes means cheating is acceptable to stay in the game. Those involved play as though they will never get caught. If money is the god of business, then "In God We Trust" has problems. While it may seem to be worth the high stakes at the time, cheating does not go over well in business or in nature, as the downsides can be lethal in either case.

Since perceptions are a personal reality, each person has them. Each corporation, each company acting as an individual cell in the business body, as in the physical body, has a perception about what good their product brings to a customer's life. Reputations are damaged when companies seek to undermine those they serve with products that endanger life, and that includes companies producing harmful drugs. A lack of integrity is a sickness that eats away at more than the bottom line, to the detriment of companies, and of governments as well.

When too much money is siphoned off by improper accounting or subversive activities that manipulate numbers for self-aggrandizement, the whole of the company suffers, as does the human body when the behavior of one organ compromises the whole. The Enron case illustrated this well when it was exposed that their downfall came because executives manipulated financial prerogatives, misappropriating insured funds, bad loans and conflicts of interest, bringing scandal to JPMorgan Chase & Co. and to a whole lot of investors and corporations.[1] In 2010, Bernie Madoff, in a financial "who done it", admits in court his deliberate Ponzi-scheme business, explaining just how he did it.

Deceptive practices and underhanded ploys by politicians, lobbyists and corporate power brokers still run rampant because they are emboldened by their titled positions, brazen and without shame. When the violated trust is exposed, the jig is up, and officials with friends in high places are tapped as scoundrels, subsequently scandalizing the institutions once thought impenetrable. The trillion-cell body suffers as well, sometimes a painful death, as promises are broken. Whom can you trust to walk the line without selling out for a chariot ride? Caretakers of industry and government play a dangerous game, doing things the human body and Mother Nature and its intelligent systems would never do because they are contrary to its innate wisdom.

When private interests take precedence over responsible action, it is embarrassing to business. It indicates the seed of a bigger problem with the money machine, the ego, desperation to sustain status through symbolic corporate success, to spend beyond means—including the U.S. government, which is not exempt either. If the human body spent its energy the way some corporations spend money, it would be dead before nightfall and would certainly not reproduce itself as a model endeavor.

Living systems do not cheat on themselves. Like the human body, living systems are built on integrity fully integrated with a common interest.

When cells mutiny, they overtake the body and endanger survivability. The result is dis-ease.

Outsourcing and New Trends

Outsourcing to developing countries is the latest trend in lowering costs to boost the bottom line. Resisting the temptation, Network Solutions, a web hosting company and domain holder, continues to maintain its employee base in the U.S. The field will level at some point, if companies can survive the challenge.

Wal-Mart, seeking an economic advantage, is on the move to provide banking services on their premises, ostensibly to handle credit-card transactions. According to *Time* magazine, April 24, 2006, community bankers are worried. Dan Coup, president and CEO of the First National Bank of Hope, Kansas, said their small-town bank might not survive Wal-Mart's competition any more than the local grocer whose store is for sale. Community and small-town banks depend on high fees and interest to make loans to small businesses, and the threat may change the way banking is done.[2]

In addition to the large centers with more variety, Wal-Mart is going small with community stores spreading like a virus across the nation. The nation is afflicted with consumption. When Mom and Pop cannot support themselves with their small business, then who will buy Wal-Mart's wares, or the wares of anyone else, for that matter? If the trend continues, the forecast is sobering.

The rush to own all the money, controlling lives and livelihoods, can change the face of business in ways many are not expecting. When the banks hold all the money, poverty ensues. When the customer base is enslaved, who or what will save us from ourselves and from the greed that lines the corporate pockets of Scrooge? The default in low-prime home loans that began in 2007 demonstrates the vulnerability of doing business by fiat. Loaning money on a signature without viable resources to back it is fraud. Because the U.S. put money in the banks, instead of in the hands of the citizens, after the credit default debacle, the country's recovery may be slowed for years to come. Had they given the money to the people, the U.S. would be on solid ground today with debts paid off and money to spare. The banks, mortgage companies and credit-card companies would all be solvent. The people would be happy and commerce would again be flourishing.

Consumerism is a dangerous disease attacking the body politic, an unsettling surge by companies playing to the ego. To have all the goodies advertisers say we need to feel good about ourselves and to be part of the in-crowd—that is the carrot taunting us with promises they cannot fulfill. Even when the economy is in shambles, the pursuit of the status ladder calls like the siren.

Wealth, placed in the hands of a few, distorts the picture. As seen in Africa and South America, it makes for a gross imbalance of power. The great divide between the rich and the poor is widening as the middle class is squeezed from both directions. The multinational corporation in its present construct may finally be seen as the worst business idea ever created for the whole of mankind.

Not only is business out of balance, the world is out of balance, as reflected in the health and well-being of its people. It is a symbiotic relationship. Employees are happy when the boss is, and the boss is happy when employees meet the deadline and do a great job. When everyone is happy, things flow naturally in harmony, as does the river when unobstructed.

Today's World Is a Sick World

Planet Earth is home to six billion people; six billion thinking brains, each with a position about the state of affairs in their neighborhood and the world. Today, we do not have to go far to hear someone say that our world is sick.

We poison our planet's water supply by inappropriately treating it as the toilet of creation. Hospitals and manufacturing processors, for example, flush contaminants into the rivers and streams, including needles and chemical waste. Chemists combine elements on the periodic chart and produce all manner of useful products for society and the military war machine; many of their byproducts end up in sewers that feed into our oceans, one water supply for the planet. Danger also lies in toxic chemical combinations that in breathing make you sick.

A *New York Times* editorial on February 25, 2007, titled "The Truth about Coal", noted that new construction of coal-fired power plants is brewing unrest, though the Dallas-based utility TXU (the focus of the editorial) is using the latest technology to emit fewer pollutants. Still, the company persists in "burning coal, with no ability to capture and dispose of immense amounts of carbon dioxide" when "costlier...technologies are available that could capture greenhouse gases before they enter the atmosphere."[3] Besides, it is a dangerous industry, as mines collapse to trap workers. The rescue of workers in Chile is an exception to the rule.

One damning insight in the *Times* editorial is that "everyone is using the atmosphere like a municipal dump, depositing carbon dioxide free." A carbon tax is one suggested solution. Companies with a conscience want to do what's right for the environment and take care of our air quality responsibly. After all, they breathe the same air. To preserve the atmosphere with nearly 150 coal-fired plants still on the drawing board nationwide in the U.S. at the time of writing, the editorial strongly suggested that a law to restrict carbon emissions be enacted globally. Countries like China have the same problems. Laws and taxes seem to be the preferred way to enforce standards for doing what seems like common sense.

Other magic combinations have new products' potential written all over them, along with their accompanying hazards. Take plastic, for example. It does not biodegrade. (Oh, maybe in a thousand years or so, but who knows that for sure?) Uh-oh! Too late! Huge amounts of energy are expended in plastic water bottle disposal at transfer stations and landfills across the U.S. Mother Earth is being poisoned so some among us can make money at her expense. Unable to use normal methods of degeneration, she is confused and does not know what to do with this artificial "stuff".

In Britain, it is estimated that 10 billion plastic carrier bags are used each year, and that is considered conservative, says Dr. Richard Swannell of WRAP (Waste & Resources Action Programme), a not-for-profit company. In 2005, the company initiated a pilot educational program in Bristol and Edinburgh to encourage plastic-bag reuse as a matter of course. Other countries, like Australia, reduced their use to 25 percent, while Bangladesh, Taiwan and South Africa, along with some states in India, have banned the manufacture and use of plastic bags outright. Ireland charges 15 cents (10p) per bag, while Germany has taken a softer approach: customers can choose between buying a sturdy reusable bag or one of the lovely linen bags.[4]

In January 2009, shoppers in Seattle, Washington, were to begin paying 20 cents per paper or plastic bag they used in grocery, drug and convenience stores, with the Seattle City Council also set to ban polystyrene, or Styrofoam, food containers, like the clamshell variety used by takeout restaurants, along with plastic utensils used by food-service businesses. However, the ban was defeated through big-money efforts from Progressive

Bag Affiliates, an arm of the Virginia-based American Chemistry Council.[5]

It's easy to see how the business membrane's perception of the environment protects businesses from losing their advantage, even when their own lives and those of their families and friends are affected. Stores did have to shift to biodegradable or recyclable all the way in 2010, when Styrofoam food trays used for raw meat and seafood in grocery stores joined the ranks of the bygone era. With awareness, fewer plastic bags used would mean the landscape is no longer coated with polythene. This is a good thing, because plastic bags are a huge litter problem, responsible for the deaths of 100,000 marine mammals and a million birds each year.[6]

To the rescue comes a Canada-Wide Science Fair in Ottawa awarding top prize to Daniel Burd, 16, a student at Waterloo Collegiate Institute, for isolating microbes that "lunch on plastic bags." Having to deal with plastic bags falling out of a closet when he was doing chores gave him the idea for his project. He already knew that eventually they would biodegrade, and that microorganisms must be behind it.

Grinding the plastic bags into powder and mixing it with ordinary household chemicals, yeast and water to encourage microbes to grow, plus a bit of sodium acetate as a ready source of carbon, Burd found that at 37 degrees centigrade, 43 percent degradation occurred over six weeks. By comparison, under normal circumstances, some bags might take as long as 1,000 years to degrade. Burd claims that industrial use should be easy: "All you need is a fermenter … your growth medium, your microbes and your plastic bags." Using nature to solve a manmade problem is a huge leap in restoring the planet to greater sustainability.[7]

Unfortunately, humans have also created chemical bonds that do not recycle, meaning they cannot be used again as a prime resource. Oh, we can change the end use, like using plastic bottles to make clothing. That may be good. But will changing products' end use change the way the material is processed by Mother Nature? What about the unconscionable behavior of chemical dumping that poisons the water and contaminates the land, making it unfit for growing food? What about putting an aluminum byproduct, fluoride, into our drinking water under the guise that it is healthy, when it is really toxic to the body? How conscionable is that? Who thought that one up, and why? Is it possible that the aluminum business is selling the waste to cities as a way to dispose of their toxic mix? Seems a bit strange, which brings us to yet another aberration.

Abid Aslam of *OneWorld* reported on February 5, 2006, that $100 billion is spent every year on bottled water, labeling it "Nectar of the Frauds?" Erroneously, the public has been programmed to think that bottled water is safer than what comes out of the tap. At $10 per gallon, the cost of bottled water is more than the cost of gasoline in the United States.[8]

In 2004, 41 billion gallons of bottled water, costing up to 10,000 times more than tap water, were consumed around the world, representing a lot of money that could have been better spent improving native water supplies and sanitation, which plays a large part in curbing disease.

On a trip to Mexico a number of years ago, informed of the unsanitary conditions existing in remote villages, we were encouraged to drink only bottled water when we stopped at roadside cafés. Dutiful to our instructions, we insisted on buying bottled water. Upon taking our order, one of the men left the small building. Upon his return, he plunked down the bottled water. I thought it strange that he did not pull one from their refrigerated showcase next to where we sat.

What really happened was that he filled an empty plastic bottle with tap water from a faucet outside, recapped it, and came back into the café to charge us for bottled water. Now we know that bottled water is not anything other than tap water. In fact, it was brought out on a weekly radio newscast on March 24, 2006, that the brand name Evian in reverse spells *naïve*. And that suits us real well. This is boldly creative and simply addresses the myth that water flowing from the faucet is unsafe. Wisely consider that if your neighbors are not sick, then it is likely the tap water in your area is safe to drink. The opposite is also true.

You can always have your water tested by your county water department and receive a printout of the analysis. Common sense tells us to use our "noggin", a favorite term of my dad's that meant to use your brain to think things through rather than acting out of ignorance.

The corporate appetite to privatize groundwater to generate profit is another controlling mechanism. The body consists of 90 percent water and is dependent upon this natural resource. This will, of course, be a boondoggle for the poor people of the world who stand the most to suffer the most.

Vandana Shiva writes in her book *Water Wars: Privatization, Pollution and Profit*, "In less than a decade, sugarcane fields converted groundwater into a commodity and left people and staple food crops thirsty for water."[9] In India, the move from tube wells to electric pumps that feed from tube wells brought water to irrigate the fields planted with sugarcane. Shiva, reporting on sugarcane water consumption in the province of Maharashtra, cites a report of the Poona, India, Groundwater Surveys and Development Agency from 1984: "sugarcane ... consumes 80 percent of all irrigation water and eight times more water than other irrigated crops."

Mark Tonkin of Design Technology & Irrigation, based in Brighton, UK, developed an efficient system that waters just the roots. He says that once the pipes have been laid, the system will require little maintenance and therefore no significant costs. This is partly because it's fed by gravity from an elevated supply tank, and partly because water diffuses through the porous pipe walls, so there are no holes to get blocked up. Ingenious ideas have been exploited before, with sprinklers and plastic perforated pipe strips laid adjacent to the plant's base, where the excess is reabsorbed into the atmosphere. Now, large-crop farming operations can conserve water by reaching the roots where the water is needed. The benefit of the network of plastic sub-surface pipes is their ability to retain virtually all contaminants, allowing almost any quality of water, whether pure, brackish, salted or polluted to reach the plants' roots, even watering crops with salt water, previously thought impossible. Regardless of water quality, Tonkin's dRHS irrigation system can take most industrial wastewater and use it without the need for a purification process.[10]

Resources for Sale

Encumbered by debt to the World Bank, countries are selling their natural resources to corporations for privatization while Monsanto's Terminator seeds, which do not reproduce themselves each season, are maniacal products of a "Frankensteinian" mind, dead-set on profiting from the destruction of earth's biosphere. The end result could be their demise, victims of their own creative horror story.

Just look at how much money and how many resources will be available to peoples of the world when there are no more wars. Unfortunately, that may be a dream unfulfilled, as war in itself is very big business. We understand the motivation; wars are about territorial rights, resources, water rights, oil, gas and coal reserves and so much more. Concern for the common good must become the prime motivator. What is at stake is the commonality of human needs. With cooperation, everyone can benefit.

It is heartening to learn of the backlash from communities in Maine when Nestlé, multinational corporate owner of the Poland Spring label, and Nestlé Waters NA (a subsidiary of Nestlé S.A., the world's largest food and beverage company) were denied their request to privatize groundwater resources and well drilling in the state. They already pump millions of gallons of spring water from aquifers each day to bottle for public consumption. In June 2009, activists successfully put a halt to a proposed 50-year contract between Nestlé and the Kennebunk, Kennebunkport and Wells (KKW) Water District.

Essentially, the new law strips corporations of their status of "personhood" obtained in 1886 courtesy of a judge's ruling without debate, a strategy long used by corporations as a ruse to block pro-environment and pro-worker measures; a measure giving them dominance over the supply of water for the commons, for one.

Masquerading as a "good neighbor", the company's tactics were directed purely to delude the public as to the extent of their intentions. This included the company's natural resource manager, Mark Dubois, threatening (on video) "to show their hand" when the community passed a 180-day moratorium prohibiting Nestlé from testing wells and preventing the signing of a proposed contract between Nestlé and the town's selectmen.

Like Erin Brockovich, the whistleblower on PG&E's leaking chromium-6 into the waterways in Hinkley, California, it was a resident of Shapleigh, Maine—Ann Wentworth—who became aware when hiking in the Vernon Walker Wildlife Preserve that Nestlé had illegally drilled "test wells" without notifying the townspeople.

This is a global issue as multinational corporations seek to own all the water in the world for financial gain. As if we don't already have enough plastic bottles floating in the waterways, Nestlé wants to make Mother Nature the repository of their material corporate legacy. It's not enough that Nestlé has drilled test wells on the sly. There is complicity here as well when the selectmen agree behind closed doors to sell resources to profit the corporation.

Attorney Thomas Linzey of the Community Environmental Legal Defense Fund, who helped write Ecuador's new constitution, pioneered the concept of the rights-based ordinance giving entity rights to ecosystems. Ecuador is a model for the rest of the world as the first country in the world to protect its natural resources from corporate exploitation in this way. When citizens of the world encounter similar invasive practices by corporations seeking to exploit their natural resources, it is critical that they craft rights-based ordinances to ensure that decisions made by citizens for their communities will not be overruled by the legal clout of corporations like Nestlé.[11]

Human-to-Human Concerns

Clearly, despite our savvy progress in robotic technology, our understanding of human-to-human concerns is still in its infancy because our awareness is not yet heightened. Perhaps religion has blinded our vision of the possible, keeping us focused on unworthiness and the condition of "not good enough".

Primitive cultures still hold secrets to the other worlds of "mind" and its knowledge of herbs and potions that have kept them alive for millennia. Now, province-seeking corporations with profit-hungry Goliath appetites seek to destroy not only these cultures but also the natural sources of life-giving remedies.

It all boils down to attitude and how we view the world. Take artists, for instance. Artists respond to different drummers, whose lure is the gift of spirit, the vision of possibility. From a creative mind with imagination, perspectives and desires pour forth in tangible and intangible forms to express insights that guide their artistry. Artists inspire us to see the world through a different lens and from different perspectives to understand viewpoints other than the conventional. Creativity expresses itself energetically, and we often feel emotion as a result. It touches our soul, and we benefit from the experience: right brain–left brain communication in mathematics, music, drama, two- and three-dimensional art, the written word, literature, the Internet and so many other ways.

Without imagination, nothing comes into existence: no art, no inventions, innovations, products or business. Together, humans and business depend upon the input, process and output sequence of energy in the quantum, just like living cells in biology.

Beliefs are products of our mind's perceptual reality, driving our lifestyles, relationships, business and body as unseen energies of thought. In the mind is the beginning. Whatever we do affects the quantum field, for we shape it moment by moment with our attitudes and desires.

Biology is intelligent. When the amoeba became aware that the environment was changing, it awoke to possibility. Driven by innate intelligence to survive whatever was to come, the amoeba joined with other amoebae in community. As weather changed, so did the food supply that had been stabilized for a very long time, arousing the desire to pay attention to potentials. Cells banded together, dividing responsibilities so that they could all survive the changing environment.

There is plenty of evidence to prove that there is a reaction to every action, even if subtle. Thought acts upon itself as vibrational frequency. Consciousness and energy do create reality. Clearly, the stock market operates in the input, process and output mode as it measures business from an investment point of view. Buying and selling commodities, gambling on futures and "puts", are largely based on the perception of the environment.

The Corporation, with no affinity for human life, exists as an idea, which makes it just as vulnerable. Designed to protect assets from government infringement—well, there's an idea worth examining—it feeds itself upon the less structured, garnering property for its own aggrandizement by whatever means it takes, legal or otherwise. Governments produce nothing. They consume resources from constituents, producers, creators and the inventive mind, for without a constant funneling of money, the government would go bankrupt. When the U.S. looks at the national debt, people shudder at irresponsible spending habits. The U.S. Congress sets a terrible example of fiscal responsibility. Talk about accountability!

When talents and resources are drained, the business of governance, the running of business, and all those playing some part in the process become vulnerable, threatened with annihilation unless something is done about it.

The same goes for the human body. If we abuse our bodies, then the total of what we think we are suffers. Corporations can be destroyed in a moment by abuse of power. The same also holds true for governments, such as we've seen in Zimbabwe.

With just distribution, everyone wins. As speaker Les Brown says, "It's not over until you win." Winning is what life is all about. Winning at life means to take responsibility for who and what you are. When only one person wins, however, everybody loses. Everyone needs to win.

Cloning Business Models

Obsessed with the bottom line and spreading the corporate gospel of more and bigger everything, business cloning has taken on megalithic proportions. Wal-Mart has grown exponentially compared to other big-box stores and has set the pace for rapid expansion of a global consumer base. Outlying areas where no right-minded business head would even venture now seem viable. On one of my cross-country trips, I noticed a Wal-Mart situated out in the country, miles from town. Again, no right-minded businessperson would have looked twice at this location. Even if it were a handshake community, a business in the boonies would not have a chance of getting a tip of the hat or a nod. Who would have thought people would be willing to drive miles out of town to shop, when their own communities pretty much met their needs, except for major purchases?

But Wal-Mart proved that given enough publicity they could actually expand communities. In a way, the stores have brought people together who never would have met, or ventured too far from the homegrown turf where they lived. However, neighboring towns with their small cafés and Mom-and-Pop stores often dry up, resulting in dilapidated buildings and deteriorated lifestyles, when corporate entities invade the community. The death of a town is depressing to see. All over America are ghost towns, remnants of better days, sitting lonely as cast-off outskirts of remembrance. The body of business in this case is broken, and so is the spirit that kept these towns alive for so many years. Breaking the spirit is not a good thing to do, and you see the sadness in the body's stance as dejected residents lazily scuff their shoes to the nearest pub. The only lively chat in some small towns is when locals commiserate over the fallen advantage of big business.

The spread of Wal-Mart is equal to the casino craze. Both feature great rewards: just give me your money and you will see how great you feel. You might win back some of your investment, but it is merely a redistribution of profits. True, business is about serving the people with products and services that communities desire. Debt is harbored as a way of life. No one really owns anything. It is all on loan from the big bank in the sky that grows taller with each interest hike. Where will it end and when?

Most people can see how dysfunctional is the U.S. government, a corporate entity holed up in Washington, DC, inside a protective boundary within the living body of the populace. It is a small organ within the larger body of the country that depends upon the rest of the body politic to feed and keep it alive. In a way, some think it is the brain; however, it depends upon the intelligence of the body, or states' representatives, to manage affairs. We wonder about our lawmakers, who create rules and regulations for those of us living outside its membrane boundary to which they are not bound when in D.C. Unable to provide for itself as a living entity unto itself, government depends on the producers of the U.S. to fill its coffers so it can continue as it always has. We put up with the rules, expecting our representatives to look out for us, as would good parents. But unfortunately, parasitic behavior feeds off the weak and defenseless until it is, itself, consumed. The compromised cell body that had so much promise for a healthy life now suffers from its own gluttony. Again, Enron and the Abramoff scandal come to mind, as well as Bernie Madoff and his Ponzi scheme. But this model is much the same in other countries as well.

As business and special interests grease the palms of legislators, the populace suffers from invasive laws that remove the hard-won freedoms that let them live in peace and harmony. Airport security is becoming increasingly invasive, photographing bodies and patting them down, sometimes requiring private searches as they move through the conveyor belt of checking luggage. Who's to say the workers hired are honest?

The more restrictive and repressive the laws, the more corruption; the more pain inflicted, the more citizens become prisoners of these devices. Real or perceived, the more crime there is, the more rebellion is evidenced and the more behaviors are questioned and restricted. Restricted freedom brings its own problems, and soon you have a prison planet under a dictatorship. Surely, Ari Cowan and others like him are on to something BIG. Treat the crimes as a disease and rehabilitate those involved by instilling another vision, one that is wholesome and equitable for everyone. All agree, the prison system is broken, and the way it is being run is an embarrassment. Prisoners are better off, in some regards, than they were outside the prison walls. They have a clean bed to sleep in, three meals a day, and an opportunity to get an education at taxpayers' expense. The staggering size of the parasitic prison population continues to grow as a big business.

Manipulating the mind is the job of advertisers who constantly create new ways to convince us we need their products. Companies stay in business by generating sales. The never-ending climb to the top of the S&P 500 is the driving force behind corporate business. To live peaceably and have enough money to do what you want to do when you want to do it is the goal of most people, especially small business owners. For a Scrooge, · whose eyes never leave the counting table, there is only emptiness inside.

Humpty Dumpty is vulnerable to being toppled from its high-rise glass wall when a misplaced potshot cracks the egg of illusion. Happily, some corporations realize that their role in society is to help others help themselves, to uplift people to a height where everyone wins. Thank goodness for that. However, attention is too often focused on multinational corporations, when many small companies/corporations behave as good citizens. Only a few bad seeds spoil the harvest. Again, it is the structural qualities of the corporate model, bred to benefit investors at others' expense and to avert taxes being paid to a government that serves the whole, or is supposed to serve the whole. When the big multinational businesses and big-time executives pay their real share of taxes, the burden on those who actually do the work will be lessened.

When misguided efforts are reconsidered, the irresponsible behavior that's destroying the environment for the money that can be made will be redirected toward sustainability with the conscious intention to do what is best and right for everyone, regardless of who they are.

CHAPTER FIFTEEN

QUANTUM MIND AND BUSINESS
The New Frontier

In the quantum energy field lies probability. Beyond space-time is perception. Perception is how we view our world and our place in it. Thus, some see Earth as a place to exploit, to ravage for personal gain. Others see Earth as a living organism, a Garden of Eden with everything provided to sustain life. Still others see Earth as a space ship traveling amongst the stars.

Gene Roddenberry's space travel for the common good played out against a backdrop of human travails in the long-running television series *Star Trek*. We marveled at characters' ability to teleport, to disappear and reappear in a totally different place at the "Beam me up, Scotty" command. Science fiction is unlimited by protocols that say it is impossible. Now, however, teleporting is in the works for real.

In October 2006, according to Reuters, physicists at Denmark's Niels Bohr Institute at the University of Copenhagen succeeded in teleporting information over a short distance, from light to matter in a split second. This brings quantum communications and computer science much closer together. It also confirms that thought as energy has the power to communicate, transferring information by light as a secure transmission without the weakness of eavesdropping.[1]

Now the brain can control electronic devices without lifting a finger: devices such as a train. In Hitachi's Advanced Research Laboratory in Hatoyama, Japan, scientists apply electroencephalographic principles with a twist.[2] Similar to an EEG with probes attached to the scalp to read and graph electrical signals, optical fibers connected to a cap can map changes in subjects' frontal-lobe blood flow. The "brain-machine interface" device (BCI) then links these electric signals to move a toy train via the control computer and motor.

The mere act of *thinking about problem solving* is enough to stimulate energy signals in the frontal cortex to move the train. Even doing simple calculations or singing a song demonstrates effectiveness.

Underlying Hitachi's brain-machine interface (BCI) is optical topography. Sending small amounts of infrared light through the skull to the brain's surface is enough to visually map shifts in blood flow.

While medical uses are high priority, Hitachi and Honda Motor Company are collaborating, envisioning potential use in intelligent cars. The technology could replace remote controls and keyboards to operate electric wheelchairs, beds or artificial limbs for the disabled; it is already useful in monitoring paralyzed patients' brain activity, allowing them to answer questions with a "yes" or "no" simply by thinking.

Earlier signal technology developed by other companies required implanting chips in patients' skulls to gain such information, while Hitachi's BCI technology is not invasive. Another application on this kind of brain machine is under consideration that will link patients and allow them to "speak" to each other.

To give the disabled an increased sense of independence, a wireless device called a Tongue Drive was devised at the Georgia Institute of Technology to operate a computer or steer a powered wheelchair around a room. With the tongue directly connected to the brain by a cranial nerve and the magnet about the size of a grain of rice, the team was able to move a cursor on the computer screen. Because the "tongue movements are fast and do not require much thinking, concentration or effort," the Tongue Drive offers a sense of "rich, active independent and productive lives."[3]

Smart homes of the future have been developed using virtual reality to interface with the brain-computer to remote-control light switches and TVs. The technology can also be utilized to replace house keys, granting increased autonomy to people with physical disabilities, or even to TV couch potatoes, who can channel-surf just by thinking about it. This, according to Christoph Guger, CEO of g.tec, the Austrian medical engineering company developing the technology's EEG equipment, could help patients learn how to use prosthetic limbs and allow people in wheelchairs to experience walking in virtual reality using their thoughts.[4]

What else is possible? It took only a few years to become accustomed to working with computers. Today, most everyone has one. Youngsters as young as five are joining the ranks in record numbers as they learn to hunt and peck the keyboard, once the province of secretaries. Today, we move a mouse across a virtual desktop, point to a folder where the file is stored, click and, without having to sort through file cabinets stuffed with documents, retrieve exactly the one we want in a moment. Yet there is nothing tangible to confirm our efforts, like a typewriter with character keys stamping inked tape marks onto a sheet of paper. To have a wired telephone in your home once was a luxury. Today, wireless cell and computer telephones make it possible to call anyone anyplace on the planet, via satellites. As Marshall McLuhan famously said, "The medium is the message."

Each day, you and I are confronted with opportunities to traverse dimensions in parallel universes, as explained so well by scientists in the blockbuster movie *What the Bleep Do We Know?!* A beam of light is both a particle *and* a wave, explained Fred Alan Wolf, Ph.D., theoretical physicist. Both are valid, just two different perspectives depending upon your focus.

When Mother first told me that my bedroom dresser was not solid, but composed of molecules held together by frequency, this made no sense to me at all. I could touch the dresser, run my hands over its polished surface, hear sound when I knocked on it, move it around the room and put things inside the drawers without protest. As I matured, this conundrum made more sense. Nothing is solid. Yet, for some, it is still a challenge to wrap your brain around the concept. It seems so contrary to what we see and feel.

Is what holds molecules together, then, a thought-form with a similar frequency? Is it truly real or a fabric of our imagination? Or is it, as David Peat suggests in his Introduction to *Superstrings and the Search for the Theory of Everything*, "a free-flowing play of the mind...like patterns in a kaleidoscope moving and transforming until some new pattern swings into perception"?[5] Molecules attract each other in the same way as a focused mind manifests reality.

One exercise has convinced me of the mind's ability to read energy. Try it yourself and see if it works for you too. When you're looking for something eluding your eye, pause and say aloud: "Reveal to me the location of...the red pen," for example. Then wait for an energy pull to draw you to it. You may walk into a room, pick up something innocuous and spy the object nearby or a few feet away. Or you may pick up an item and see the object in question underneath. It could be right under your nose and you fail to see it.

A flash of memory may reveal that the item was left at the office, in your car or even in another room in your house. This has happened so many times for me that I now depend upon it as a sure thing. If, then, whatever you want does not appear, you may get a nudge triggering your recollection of having given the item away or loaned it to a friend. With a little practice, this amazing interconnectivity with universal energies will soon make a believer out of you. The secret is to let go and let the energy direct you, allowing space for the universe to manifest. Try it. If you doubt its effectiveness and get impatient or frustrated, it only stands to foul the transmission. Focus on what you want and it shall be given to you. What you see in your mind's eye is truly what you get as a manifestation of the power of attraction. Be careful what you wish for.

Gut feelings are those innate sensations that nudge you with knowledge you might otherwise miss. These sensations inform us through our inner knowing whether there is truth, danger or caution to be observed. With practice you grow into a heightened awareness called "knowingness". No more guessing, no more playing dumb. You just know, though you may not know how you know.

You may think of someone and then receive an email, a phone call, or a postal card or letter. They may even show up unannounced at your front door to seal the premonition. In the quantum world of mind/matter connections, the energetic pull is strong enough to get your attention. Attitudes of co-workers, as well as clients or customers, are felt as strongly as if spoken aloud in words. Adding a voice as another dimension confirms your intuitive sense. Being attuned to energetic forces aids effectiveness and goes a long way toward keeping you apprised of environmental conditions. I now respect this "feeling" as a trusted ally.

As David Hawkins, M.D., Ph.D., so eloquently explains in *Power vs. Force: The Hidden Determinants of Human Behavior*, kinesiology draws on a weak and strong muscle response as direct communication to unrevealed sources over which we have no control. While force is evident in war, power is far stronger in negotiation. Power is in choosing a higher road of conscious awareness that benefits all concerned. Weakness is experienced in the lower realms of perversion, like cheating and lying. Ignoring obvious insights of subjective awareness is not the choice of those who exercise power. Moving from fear to joy is a leap, but Hawkins says: "Once this realization occurs, life becomes effortless and the sources of suffering dissolve; suffering is only the price we pay for our attachments."[6] Such intuitive abilities are available to everyone, though not everyone develops them.

Interconnectivity

In his book *The Web of Life: A New Scientific Understanding of Living Systems*, Fritjof Capra caused us to rethink our world and all of life as interconnecting systems. He reminds us of the stunning mathematical example of life's repetitive patterning made visual in the Mandelbrot set, inspired by Gaston Julia in the early 1900s. Through high-speed sophisticated computers, the beauty of one mathematical formula is brought to life with colorful forms expanding without end to repeat again and again the same pattern, as in a coastline, for example. It reminds me a bit of the kaleidoscope, when with a simple turn of the revolving tube, colorful shapes reposition themselves into beautiful patterns. However, the Mandelbrot set is a sophisticated mathematical expression of variations on a theme that repeat themselves ad infinitum: life without end.

We see the same repetitive pattern in the human cell and even in our lives as we move from one location to live in another. We tend to repeat ourselves in so many ways. Behavior is repetitive, though expressions may vary, which allows us to identify personalities and their patterns.

The human thinking brain tends to massage ideas in the natural process of resolving a problem or meeting a challenge. While every cell lives in symbiotic relationship with the whole, not a single cell can make it alone. It is in collaboration through heightened awareness of the environment that cells survive the shifts in perceptual reality. All work together for the good of the whole. Cell communication is as effective as a network broadcast system in meeting everyday needs, though the speed of transmission for human cells is faster.

The physical body has differentiating cells to do necessary repairs and functions when cells are damaged or put out of commission. Robert O. Becker, M.D., writes about his discoveries in *The Body Electric* that patients who have lost bodily limbs can still experience sensations of feeling in the space where the limb is missing, as if it were still there. Sensations in the phantom limb's electromagnetic field prove that quantum energy does indeed exist.[7]

In this world of "seeing is believing", doubters shun such evidence, but that is shunning the existence of energy fields confirmed by physics to surround every cell, organ and body in the invisible world of quantum reality. Rather than dismiss the spiritual aspect of the body that makes us more than we think we are, embrace it as a truth of what is. By doing so, you expand your awareness of how thought communicates to experience the marvels of the unseen world in everyday life and in business interactions.

Pure energy is electromagnetic radiation traveling at a constant speed of roughly 670,000,000 miles per hour. Materiality, however, is in the visible light spectrum's energy field, the narrowest of the seven acknowledged levels. It would be a mistake to ignore the other levels as unreadable by the body, since the body is vulnerable to those fields, 24/7. No one argues the reality of X-ray images unseen until photographed or radio waves appreciated for the communication highways that keep us connected. Satellites transmit cell phone communications. Gamma rays with the shortest wavelengths are the fastest. Generated as they are by radioactive atoms, they have the ability, when focused, to kill living cells. Cosmic rays are highly charged particles that interact with Earth's atmosphere to affect weather and provide information about energy in the cosmos.

So what's the big deal, then, that the body is matter suspended in a field? The big deal is that now we can understand how thought travels so fast, and how each cell in our body is held together by synergistic energy in the seven levels of the electromagnetic spectrum. Understanding that no thing is solid captures the imagination of how the self-aware universe works. It is all energy, held together by frequency vibrations.

Since everything has this energy bonding, all things work in harmony. The tie that binds us is our affinity for completion, for inclusion, for connection. Thus, like-minded people are naturally attracted to each other. Again, the law of attraction is in play. Clubs, organizations and companies have a bond of sorts. Unions collectively act for the benefit of their members. Even the term *membership* signifies selectivity, requiring specific qualifications to become part of the group that shares common interests, like cells, or like people living in community within the larger body of a town or city. There is no difference, only the expression.

It bears repeating how knowledge of the new biology can revolutionize your life and that of business by drawing on the quantum field of energies. This gives you power. Thoughts, transmitting as bits of information, travel through the ethers to antennae on cellular membrane receptor sites. Each cell has millions of receivers, like hairs on your head, fine-tuned to receive signals from the environment. Each human is an antenna on Earth's crusty surface, along with each flower and tree. We feel the wind and see the trees wave to and fro responding to the unseen forces, bending to their wishes, as in a hurricane. Spiraling winds of a tornado rearrange everything in its path, scattering buildings across neatly organized landscapes into piles of debris, disordered and dismembered from an organized state. Mother Nature does not ask permission to reorder the universe.

Everywhere we see the effects of unseen forces, yet deny that the physical body can have phantom limbs, or that thoughts can be manipulated through frequency. Mind control drives this home for deeper reflection.

Yes, you are more than your body. You are spirit energy, and Spirit is not the province of religion. Spirit was here in the beginning, long before factions formed to promote belief in an outside entity.

Belief is at the core of limitation: "family values", legislation by lawmakers "for our own good", whatever that means. Who can claim the truth for another when each of us has the same power of knowing? We give it away to others, our power to control ourselves. Listen to your own thoughts and accept responsibility for your choices. We are persuaded to do things we would not do on our own. We are manipulated by clever advertising to buy products we do not really need, to go to parties we do not want to attend or to embark on business ventures we feel are unwise. We shop at stores we think have the best quality merchandise, with pricing carefully selected for their target markets, or have the best policies of operation. You see we are at choice.

Collectively, the human corporate body is vulnerable to frequencies of all types, including cell phones, cell phone towers and transformers on telephone poles emitting low frequency signals to which cases of cancer are attributed. There are also smart meters, smart cards, barcodes, retinal imaging, fingerprinting, DNA identities and more that impact life and its charges.

Even our name has vibrations that identify who we are. The U.S. government is involved with implanting RFID (radio frequency identification) chips to track humans, the same technology currently used to track lost shopping carts up to a mile away from a store, as well as pets and Alzheimer's patients who become disoriented and wander off.[8]

Vulnerable to Change—Does Mind Really Matter?

Clever advertisers study human behavior and purposely choose words and images appealing to the psyche to gain entry into your mind for their benefit. Companies employ clever artists and marketing professionals to coin slogans and copy, convincing dialogue and images, to persuade you to dig deep in your pockets for money to give them. Advertising is designed to bend your mind to their will. Companies know very well that the mind is adaptable and can be manipulated for profit, so vulnerable is it to suggestion.

It is these very traits upon which some advertisers base their operation. They appeal to the human mind's vulnerability to acquire and to experience the pleasurable sensations derived from purchasing products and services. Manipulating photographs to include suggestive sexual images appeals to our base desires, as has been explored in depth by Wilson Bryan Key in his two books, *Subliminal Seduction* and *Media Sexploitation*. For instance, embedded sexual organs positioned in one Seagram's ad in ice cubes and even clothing are reinforced with the word SEX repeated multiple times in various disguises, a common practice. Even the mirror on a motor home ad is not exempt. Sex drives the world of advertising and the creation of some products. It's the feel-good essence of pleasure seekers.

Rapid flashing of digital images on television screens entrains your brain below the conscious level. Aimed at the subconscious mind, they appeal to emotions that betray your vulnerability. It is all cleverly planned to induce product acquisition by eager participants in a purchasing frenzy. And it works!

You will never have enough. You will always want more, better and bigger items than the last. You will always want to look better, feel better, wear the latest style suit, drive the newest car and use the latest in shampoos when soap does the same thing and is cheaper. Even toothpaste is enamoring. But let us be clear. It is not about simplifying your life; it is about being the first on your block to have the latest and greatest: the ego's desire for one-upmanship. The mind games are carefully planned with convincing storyboards targeting the brand and market to sell to you in the most convincing way.

There is a lesson here about mind control and the ability to manipulate thinking. It goes on all the time with TV and radio advertising about how vulnerable the human being is to disease, which is not true at all.

Perceptions can be manipulated by expectations. In other words, if we expect something to happen, it usually does, no matter the subject.[9]

Tricks of the Mind

Altering consciousness with mood-enhancers is the stuff of snake charmers and magicians, so some think. However, we have only to look at the work of Dr. Franz Mesmer, a German physician, who in the 1700s used ethereal music played on a glass harmonica in a dimly lit room as a way to cure people suffering from unexplained medical conditions. His technique became known as "mesmerizing".

Hypnosis was used as an anesthetic for surgical procedures long before ether was discovered. According to a March 19, 2006, article in *Time* magazine,[10] India used hypnosis in 1845 and abandoned it for ether the following year. During the Civil War, amputations were the territory of butchers who knew the anatomy but whose tools were crude. Even barbers were recruited for help. On the battlefield, it is uncertain any means of anesthetic was available. Soldiers had to use their minds to dull the pain, or they would simply pass out. The power of suggestion is truly amazing, and it is unwise to take it lightly.

I myself use self-hypnosis for dental work and preparation for crowns. The anesthetic makes me sick, and it is less stressful for me to just close my eyes and use my mental forces to quiet sensations. No aftereffects—I am good to go when I get up from the chair. It is only the fear of pain making one a victim of sedation. Use your imagination to change the picture in your head. Go for a visit to your childhood playground and romp on the ground doing somersaults, see how high you can swing and how many times you can go around the merry-go-round, or swing on the overhead bars, or walk their length with your hands. I guarantee you will not even be aware of the drill or of any pain unless the dentist hits a nerve. In truth, you are saved from root canals should a nerve be hit, because you will instantly respond. I find that dentists must exercise their best skill when you hypnotize yourself. They must be more careful, which is very good for you.

Hypnosis can be used for surgical procedures of all kinds, as well, with fewer side effects, allowing the body to recover more quickly. According to the *Time* article, "pain travels from the brain stem through the midbrain and into the cortex, where conscious feelings of pain arise." When you block the sensory cortex with mind or thought energy of intent, there are no sensations of feeling. *Time* reports that Shelley Thomas used hypnosis before receiving a pelvic operation. When she was thoroughly relaxed, she was rolled into the surgical theater for a 30-minute procedure without anesthetic or pain. Dr. David Hawkins, too, has had two major surgeries without anesthetic, using his mind to maintain calm.

Realizing the benefit of having patients awake and alert during some complicated surgeries, medicine has begun to use energy to advantage in cutting-edge alternative techniques. In 2001, Cheryl Hogarth entered surgery for an inoperable tumor in the brain nearly the size of a ping-pong ball. Instead of the knife commonly used by surgeons, she received hundreds of high-intensity beams of gamma radiation from a bloodless device called the X-Knife, designed to shrink the tumor cells and deter their growth. In a single session of radiosurgery, without anesthesia, without a scar between her ears as in a traditional craniotomy, she went home that evening. The downside is that this Sacramento mother of two was advised to also have chemotherapy, "just to be sure."[11]

The key to this procedure is the blast of radiation, spread into 201 fine beams targeting the affected site, with fallout in surrounding tissues minimal and immediate. This blast of radiation attacks the DNA and cuts off the blood supply to essentially starve the tumor. Of 150,000 patients with metastatic cancer, only 10 percent receiving this radiosurgical procedure delay death two years. While this technique is not foolproof, it is an alternative worth exploring. In the future with more acceptance of radiosurgery it could become standard practice.

It may also come as a surprise to learn that an actual gland in the brain's frontal lobe, the pineal gland, sometimes called the "third eye", is associated with psychic knowledge. Opening the "third eye" brings heightened awareness. The pineal gland is a small organ I always thought of as my directional guide. If I became directionally disoriented, not knowing whether I was heading east, west, north or south, it would detect the energies and direct me to move in the right direction in order to reach my destination.

The pineal gland is the only gland in the human body containing quartz crystals, *real* quartz crystals. They act as antennae, so to speak, to open doors to other dimensions. The early quartz radio receivers brought signals in from the outside for the first time in the early 1900s. History books show pictures of families gathered around early radios to hear voices coming out of a box through speakers—now but a memory against the backdrop of personal radio receivers worn on the ear.[12]

The journal *Nature Biotechnology* recently released findings verifying that quartz crystals can "hear" viruses. Researchers learned that quartz crystals vibrate when exposed to an electric field and as the field strengthens vibrations increase. They suspect that physicians in the future will use quartz crystals to listen to ailments in the body, rather than using the current mode of listening to heartbeats through the stethoscope with which we are so familiar.[13]

Perhaps intuition is connected to the frontal lobe's quartz crystals by resonating frequency vibrations transmitted through the electromagnetic energy fields. After all, the human body lives in the invisible soup of electromagnetic energies, the same systems responsible for powering the universe. With the visible light spectrum the narrowest of all in the collective range of energetic electromagnet fields, our physical body is a manifestation of sound and light, which is why we can see and why we can hear and why we can feel. It is fascinating to realize that only in the physical realm of creative invention can we generate and recognize possibilities yet unborn.

Intuition and Decision

As a part of nature, we are so much more than we have been taught. We are frequency generators, drawing on universal energies to make tangible the imaginings of our mind. We are no small accomplishment, and yet we tend to think we are insignificant.

In a *Wall Street Journal* article, "Follow Your Intuition: The Unconscious 'You' May Be the Wiser Half", Sharon Begley reports on research by Timothy D. Wilson, professor of psychology at the University of Virginia, Charlottesville. While not the first to probe the power of intuition—such luminaries as Jose Delgado and Russian Madame Blavatsky dot the landscape with well-documented research—Wilson sheds new light with his work.

Wilson and neurologist Antonio Damasio of the University of Iowa, Iowa City, conducted experiments focused on "gut feelings" and skin response. Wilson's research involved a moving "X" in a quadrant field. When volunteers figured out the hidden rules intuitively, their ability to discern the next place the "X" would show up sped their efficiency.

Damasio's study involved subjects drawing from four decks of cards marked with an amount "won" or "lost". Two decks reflected big wins and losses, but, when played consistently, yielded a net loss. The other two decks with smaller wins and losses over time rewarded players with a net gain.[14]

Volunteers relied on their intuitive feelings to avoid the losing decks, though they could not articulate how they "knew". On the other hand, their bodies sweat when choosing the losing deck as a response to environmental stress. Intuitively, participants "knew" but did not know why they knew which deck's cards would yield them a net loss. Volunteers with brain damage to the ventromedial region of their prefrontal lobe could not process the environmental cue of body response and never learned to avoid the bad decks.[15] Obviously, this has ramifications for gamblers who will probably have more luck paying attention to their "gut feelings" than letting their conscious minds lead them astray. Conscious decisions are not as dependable as going with your intuition.

A study at the University of Amsterdam, The Netherlands, supports this position. Ap Dijksterhuis and his colleagues did a study of IKEA customers and found that the simpler decisions about housewares or generic clothing can be made in advance of purchase, while a furniture decision requiring a more complex thought process is best made on the spur of the moment.[16] In other words, the best way to make a decision is to go with your gut feeling after resisting temptations to jump into the net. Put your feet up and think about something else to free the mind to connect the data points for coherence. It is rather like pushing yourself up the hill when there is no steam in the engine. Idle a while, take a walk, and the task will appear less daunting. Take the easy path to enlightened decision-making without costing yourself a gazillion in consulting fees.

Of course, emotional decision-making is not always the right path. Intuition can be hijacked by other forces at work, like hormones. Too many people rush into marriage, only to awaken to the realization that they have not really thought it through enough as to the real-life consequence of the ins and outs of an intimate relationship. Spurred by the molecules of emotion in the sexual centers of attraction, wildly racing to reach the climax of awareness and satisfaction, the ego abruptly deflates when reality sets in and the dishes need to be washed. Is that all there is? It is the age-old instrument of reward and punishment; the same motivation used by scientists to nudge results from experiments. What does this mean?

This kind of research provides verification of the accuracy of Sanskrit literature. Consciousness-research pioneer Christopher Hills identifies the brain cavity through which electromagnetic signals travel for interpretation as the "Cave of Brahman" where ancient sages located the focus of consciousness; it denotes the input, process and output of the pineal, thalamus and hypothalamus, and pituitary glands in the third ventricle of the brain.

How this works is similar to your telephone, as I explained in *If You Make The Rules, How Come You're Not Boss?* The phone rings, you answer, you hear information and you determine whether it has importance for you. If it does, you take action. The comparable decision-making taking place deep in the brain confirms that mental processes inaccessible to consciousness do influence judgments, feelings and behavior.

Our ability to empathize with the pain of others, especially when it involves our loved ones, is because the mind/body connection is hardwired. Feelings associated with pain in the body and the body's remembrance of experienced injury correlate into a sympathetic response like wincing. One study using functional magnetic resonance imaging (fMRI) to study brain activity of volunteers responding to a painful shock administered either to them or to their partners showed that the same areas of the brain important for pain perception had increased activity.

Another related study, also using fMRI, confirmed expectations that treatment with a placebo reduces the experience of pain as well as activity in pain-responsive areas of the brain. This means that perceived pain without actually experiencing pain is not differentiated by the brain. The pain-related brain centers confirmed the same neural correlates.[17]

Additionally, the *New England Journal of Medicine* released a report in March 2003 about hormone replacement therapy that had no significant effect on postmenopausal women, which is understandable, since the therapy tested was not a bio-identical product. The reason is that Wyeth, the manufacturer, combined estrogen with the artificial steroid progestin made from horse urine, in place of bio-identical progesterone. What is so interesting about this research is that when the results were compared against the placebo group, the women on the Wyeth product had no better clarity of mind, sexual pleasure or memory retention. The human body is really smart—it knows the difference between animals four-legged and two-. Research supports the idea that most women are estrogen-dominant, so it is understandable why the women taking the pills with more estrogen, received no benefit.

As a result, in 2002, federal health officials halted a large study of hormone replacement therapy of estrogen and progestin because the pills caused more women harm than good. Women were jeopardizing their lives with "greater risk of breast cancer, heart attacks, strokes and blood clots than other women, and the damage was not offset by a small beneficial effect in reducing the risk of colon cancer and hip fractures."[18]

All this evidence of how smart the human body is, with its ability to read signals from the environment through the sophisticated process of the input, process and output intelligence, should be enough to convince anyone that there's more to being "alive" than once thought. With all these signals traversing the energetic field, it is no wonder that impulses striking our frontal lobe are read and often acted upon without consideration of their source. Vulnerable as life forms are to these signals, we need to be more aware of what goes on in our thinking brain and how our thoughts manifest reality. Look at the results and see the direction, as one would follow a map to a given destination. Hindsight is always 20/20. As you can discern, a shift in perception becomes a shift in reality.

CHAPTER SIXTEEN

BRAIN POWER AND CONNECTIONS
Birthing Change

As the executive branch of the physical body, our brain is a three-pound universe, which is responsible for coordinating and simultaneously operating multiple systems seamlessly without too much awareness on our part.

It has been presumed that brain circuitry is hardwired by adolescence and is inflexible in adulthood, but this is limited thinking. Since life has an in-built processing plant, dependent upon growth and heightened awareness to accommodate changing environments, it is exciting to consider potential adaptations that we may yet see. Trainable, subject to new ideas, the brain loves novelty, and anything exciting the imagination is game for exploration. This makes mental stimulation the challenging key to unlocking the brain's potential. Growing minds eagerly seek ever more knowledge.

Unfortunately, television sitcoms keep rolling the same old dice on neighborly satires and leave nothing new to stimulate the brain. Bored, the brain's neurons contract, synapses fire slowly and intellect is dulled with a big ho-hum yawn.

Which is why I was so fascinated with the July 1994 *Life* magazine cover story about the Sisters of Mankato brain research study. It pointed out how brain cells increase with meaningful activity, how longevity is assured when brain cells are kept busy learning new things, and how the nuns refused to sit still to let their brains drain.

A professor of preventive medicine at the University of Kentucky, David Snowdon, conducted the study over several years in the 1990s for the university's Sanders-Brown Center on Aging. Working with the 700 nuns of the School Sisters of Notre Dame in Mankato, Minnesota, he learned that those with advanced degrees and teaching experience, and those who continued to actively challenge their minds, lived longer and in better health than nuns less educated who worked in the kitchen and cleaned rooms.

The Mankato nuns maintained their youthfulness and agility into their 100s, tapping feet, clapping sticks to music and learning to play musical instruments. They also knew that crossword puzzles develop cognitive qualities, while jigsaw puzzles are great for expanding spatial relationship abilities.

The Sisters of Mankato made a conscious decision to donate their brains to research when they die and are the largest group of donors in the world. Longevity is evidenced in the more than 90-year life spans by avoiding common problems generally found in the population.

They are an example of what a purposeful, intellectually stimulating life can do to expand the brain, causing brain cells and neurons to branch wildly and spawn millions of new synaptic connections. All of which means more intelligence. You can do more things more quickly. The beauty and bonus of living an active life is that age-related signs of debilitating brain disease are less apparent. The incidence of dementia, Alzheimer's and other such diseases among the Mankato nuns is very low.[1]

Activity and Rest

Dr. Antonio Convit of the New York University School of Medicine admits that the accepted notion of brain degeneration as we age is no longer valid. Now known is the brain's ability to regenerate itself, just like the rest of the body, given stimulus to do so. One of the factors is fitness. For instance, cardiovascular exercise over time tends to maintain the strength of tissues, instead of reducing the amount. Even a 30-minute walk a few times a week may be enough to tilt the scales in its favor.

Square dancing, ballet or tap is preferred for brain calisthenics, as changing moves and quick thinking are necessary to keep the mind actively involved and interested. Harvard brain researcher Marilyn Albert says, "We suspect that moderately strenuous exercise leads to the development of small blood vessels. Blood carries oxygen, and oxygen nourishes the brain."

Stan Colcombe of the University of Illinois at Urbana-Champaign discovered dramatic differences in his research sampling of physically fit people 55 and over when their MRI scans revealed that their brains' gray matter was in better shape than presumed.[2]

The most pleasant way to increase dendrites, Albert suggests, is to meet and interact with provocative, intelligent and interesting people. I know for myself mentally stimulating conversations with knowledgeable people excite my brain. Energy generated by such encounters lifts my spirit, too. I walk taller, imbued with greater understanding as well. This is what I do to grow new dendrites in my brain. Which is why, in 1992, I created a mind-expanding television show, *Evolving Ideas*© (www.elainesmitha.com/archives), and why I continue the show on Internet radio (www.progressive-radionetwork.com/elaine-smitha), speak professionally, consult and coach as ways to help others increase their own awareness. It truly is education beyond the classroom, but without having to take any tests for academic grades. Communications is in my blood, and the circulation keeps me alive and well.

Added to mental exercises to maintain brain function is the pause that refreshes, which the brain needs to assimilate experiences into its data bank. A study found that in such a pause, rats' brains replayed their experiences in reverse order, presumably to reinforce cell memory. Inserting a "pincushion of fine wires" into the rats' skulls allowed researchers to monitor specific brain cells in the hippocampus, an area of the brain involved in learning and memory.

As the scurrying activity paused for the rats to eat, groom and wipe their whiskers, brain-cell activity increased as reverse-order repetitive replays cemented the experience. This groundbreaking discovery is revolutionary, for it offers insight into why "coffee breaks" and rest stops are essential. The brain needs to rerun the just-made movie to ensure that all the essentials are correct. It is the retraced sequence of how we got to here from there, rather like reviewing the path we took in the forest that will take us back to the start.

David Foster and his colleague, Matthew Wilson, scientists at MIT, who conducted this study, propose that workers must take periodic rests to be effective. Without them, efficiency is lost. Companies insisting on long hours without breaks are working counterproductively. Instead of getting more work done they actually exhaust their employees to the point where they are numb-skulled. They cannot remember what they have done or in what sequence. Exhausted, they will often lay their heads down on the most convenient surface and take a snooze. The body and mind have spoken!

This is exactly what my eldest son would do as a child. One day I heard a knock on the door from a passerby who had stopped to tell me that my son was lying in the driveway next to the street. When I went to check on him, he stirred from his sleep. I picked him up and brought him inside. Later, when he was in his teens, concerned about the lateness of the hour, I phoned his friend's house to check when he was coming home, only to learn he got tired working on his buddy's car and fell asleep in the back seat, too weary to drive home.

Wilson and his colleagues discovered that in sleep, the brain replays the internal movie, this time in forward motion rather than reverse, presumably to edit the electrical firing sequence for computer errors.

This exciting discovery has unveiled hitherto unknown secrets of how the brain learns, supplying new knowledge that may unravel answers to why hyperactive children often have learning difficulties. It suggests that idle time is beneficial as gazing out the window refreshes thought and staring into space shifts brain waves from active beta to calming alpha. The brain's subconscious mind has its own viewpoint.

Edvard Moser at the Norwegian University of Science and Technology in Trondheim, whose specialty is the study of memory, excitedly declares, "It's absolutely original; no one has ever seen this before at all."

The Foster/Wilson study points out the importance of food in the rats' mental replay from reverse to start, noting that the first brain cells to fire were the ones closest to the food. Perhaps this has significance in terms of why we look to food as a reward for our efforts, and why punishment is in its being denied.[3]

There is something else to be said for chats by the water cooler, where breaks are the pause that refreshes. Drinking water does more than quench your thirst. The brain depends upon water to carry electrical signals through the cerebral fluid to axons whose dendrites fire the synapses. Without water, there can be no communication in the physical body. That is why dehydration is looked upon so critically. The body dies without water. Every body requires 8 to 10 glasses of water a day for life to sustain itself. Without it, knowledge cannot get through the system. Organs cannot do their job transporting nourishment and eliminating wastes. A plugged system cannot survive.

Feeding the Mind

As I've noted, students who spend more time watching television and text-messaging friends than in personal interaction miss opportunities to develop interpersonal relationships face to face, learn to interpret subtle body language, round out their minds and make crucial human connections. A cell phone offers no comfort when you need a friend at your side to give you solace. Is there a danger these students will become isolationists and anti-social? Perhaps not with all the Internet social networks—yet unless there is personal interaction face to face, human connectivity may suffer.

Students are poorly prepared for the world in more quantifiable ways, too, as school performance slips and habits of study become too casual. Combined classes where language is a barrier can thwart student progress as well. Employers look for educated minds, willing and able to work. Will they be able to find them in our current model?

As we've discussed, part of the problem is our lowest-common-denominator educational system with its emphasis on teaching to the test. John Taylor Gatto resigned after 26 years of award-winning teaching in New York's Manhattan public schools. Since then, he has traveled around the country promoting a radical transformation of state schooling, because he says the cookie-cutter teaching style imposed on teachers and students alike, stamps out self-knowledge, curiosity, concentration and solitude so essential to learning.[4]

Schools' regimented rules for behavior, curriculum and performance, Gatto says, have damaged the independent thinking so necessary to well-balanced human beings and effective community leadership. He argues that school policing, surveillance and numbering students for tracking allow little time for students to contemplate, make independent discoveries and play with classmates to learn essential tools of creativity and self-discovery that benefit the family, the community and the country. Children need to play, to sit under a tree and think, to discover by inquiry the little things in life.

Growing the brain is exciting when the stimulus is there. Expanding awareness with knowledge is key to a healthy brain. To avoid Alzheimer's or dementia in later years, it is imperative that minds continue to be challenged. While silly sitcoms are entertaining, they do not challenge the intellect.

The brain forms new neuronal pathways when it is expanding

consciousness. It would be terribly dull to be caught in the revolving door watching boring life movies over and over, yet again.

Craving opportunities to learn leads us down exciting corridors where we meet new people, make new friends, learn new things, solve problems, conquer ignorance and excel through expanded awareness. No matter your age, this is true. No matter where you are right now, this is true. When your mind is not excited to learn from those whose areas of expertise differ from your own, then turn at the next opportunity in the direction of self-reflection. If it were me I would soon learn I was going the wrong way on a very busy street.

When you consider how you know things, without ever having been trained by another human being who had to learn from another human being, and so on into infinitum, where did that knowledge come from? How did you acquire the bedrock of information that you utilize on a daily basis?

It took a transmitted picture of Earth from the Moon to change the way we think of our planet and of ourselves. Our beautiful planet provides the right atmosphere to support an infrastructure compatible for life forms of infinite variety: safe, nutritious food to eat, animals to provide skins for warmth, birds to sing their lovely melodies and waters to refresh our water-based bodies.

Everything composing the human body is earthly interacting on levels unseen in colorful bodies of different hues. What limits our understanding is our connection, or lack thereof, to other energy fields in the electromagnetic spectrum in order to know things we never knew before. Quieting the mind from the hustle and bustle of daily life and business are precious silent moments valued by the wise as a way to rejuvenate the body and outlook on life. By taking time for yourself, you open your mind to knowing on the grand scale of design; there is order to chaos.

CHAPTER SEVENTEEN

SOCRATIC METHOD
Good Business Practice
Hears Everyone's Voice

Many years ago, I took a class in Listening at Orange Coast College in Costa Mesa, California, and found it quite useful. How well we listen to others without allowing our inner thoughts to block transmissions is something to think about. The art of listening allows concerns and criticisms to be aired, which expands our awareness of viewpoints we might not otherwise have considered. To be heard, to express opinions and to share experiences and outcomes is the basis of the art of dialogue.

Effective problem solving is critical to business and relationships of all kinds, and to understanding how to make the next step better. The time-honored Socratic method is a respectful and effective way to self-examine ideas and emotions regarding issues at hand by reaching into the recesses of participants' minds for insights. Showing mutual respect for the ideas presented is critical. Everyone benefits when all interested parties are reasonably drawn out concerning ideas and potentials. The art of inquiry is an exploratory tool to examine how others feel about the problem at hand and to find ways to resolve or improve upon the situation. When we are not learning, we are not growing. This makes growth the essence of life itself and of business, if it is to be viable.

A good example of the success of respectful inquiry is seen in the Higher Horizons 100 experiment in Hartford, Connecticut, where IQs increased 20 points when teachers actually listened to their students and valued what they had to say. Another university experiment in 2002 found that IQs dropped in just a few short weeks when students felt rejected and unaccepted.[1]

Group dynamics can be observed and evaluated in a session where each takes a turn listening intently to what others have to say, which means to listen without allowing the prattle of contrariness to foul the transmission. The test is to experience someone respecting your point of view as a person of value, though he or she may not fully agree with your position. I can tell you from experience that it feels mighty good. A lot of discord can be averted using this technique. We all want to feel we are making a contribution and are respected. When positions are held tightly as the only way to go, it is difficult to come to agreement. I found myself in such an environment when a participant stalked out of the room, slamming the door behind him. This, of course, resolved nothing, only demonstrated how quickly a conversation can suffer and decay.

With small or large groups, this dynamic format to purposefully draw out thoughts calls for two flip charts, one for progressive ideas and the other for objections. In this way, everyone has his or her comment heard and noted. Tackle the biggest challenge first by immediately going to the formal problem-solving activity.

A successful working model for this activity comes from Alex Osborn and Sidney Parnes, who established a system of protocols as the architecture for creative problem solving (CPS) taught through the Creative Problem Solving Institute, an arm of the Creative Education Foundation.

CPS at a glance refines the brainstorming process on two fronts: *Divergent* implies differing or dissimilar ideas, while *Convergent* implies accepted views and common practice. Divergent or differing points of view often delay agreement until resolved. Convergent ideas are focused clearly in agreement. In the CPS brainstorming process, both have a role: divergent thinking is geared to generating options and convergent thinking entails deciding among them. Each mode has its own "rules":

Divergent Rules	Convergent Rules
Defer Judgment	Be Affirmative
Strive for Quantity	Be Deliberate
Seek Wild Ideas	Check Your Objective
Combine & Build on Ideas	Improve Your Ideas
	Consider Novelty

After establishing these ground rules, the CPS process moves on to problem solving in three stages.

Stage I—Explore the Challenge
  Objective Finding
  Fact Finding
  Problem Finding
Stage II—Generate Ideas
  Idea Finding
Stage III—Prepare for Action
  Solution Finding
  Acceptance Finding

In practice, the plan works as follows. Stage I starts with a mess: you identify a situation that presents a challenge; identify all known facts related to the situation; seek out all the information essential to the situation, and identify the underlying problem. In Stage II, you identify as many solutions to the problem as possible. In Stage III, you choose the best solution(s) for action from this list; gain acceptance for the solution by working out a plan of action, including lists of resources needed and steps to be taken; and then implement it.

Problem solving draws on participants' abilities, experience, intelligence and critical thinking, tools of everyday living. For instance, how can we solve the problem of using all of a product at the bottom of the container? For examples, refer to the discussion of the TRIZ process earlier in this book.

Problems are often most effectively solved in a team where brainstorming allows for more ideas to be generated. Thinking of many ideas is critical to effective problem solving using the Osborn-Parnes model. CPS is flexible, and its use depends on the situation. The steps can be (and often are) used in a linear fashion, from start to finish, but it is not necessary to even use all the steps. If you already have a clearly defined problem, the process can begin at Idea Finding.

What distinguishes the Osborn-Parnes CPS process from other "creative problem solving" methods is the use of both divergent and convergent thinking during each process step, and not just when generating possible solutions. Each step begins with divergent thinking, a broad search for many alternatives, followed by convergent thinking, the process of evaluating and selecting.

This process sifts through the nonessentials and gets to the core of the issue quickly without emotion that can obscure the picture and sidetrack the engine. The beauty of this model is that everyone is honored, listened to and respected. Teamwork brings it together.[2]

Teamwork and Collaboration

Once a direction to achieve the goal is identified, a sense of teamwork fuels enthusiasm to complete the project. Teamwork is essential. Multifaceted projects demand division of responsibilities to achieve the desired result. The idea that there is more than one way to achieve an outcome is reflected in the list of potentials.

Whether in government, business or families, many hands make light work. As development proceeds, input from colleagues expands understanding and widens the portfolio of experience, diversifying efforts while maintaining focus. Every business environment depends upon cooperation to be successful. As team building is strengthened, life and its multiplicity of expressions improve, especially when an attitude of gratitude pervades the environment.

Treating co-workers with respect generally elicits a favorable response and encourages greater teamwork so that it becomes trained behavior. Leadership by example is key to high performance and depends upon the perception of those involved. Leadership can also be self-designated, which implies cooperation and self-motivated enthusiasm.

When communications are open, there is less confusion. Dialoguing about plans put on the table assures understanding and agreement on how to proceed at every step along the path, assuring everyone concerned that the path is clearly cut. Each step is delineated. All that is needed is to carry the plan forward.

A very good example of the effectiveness of this method is the success story of how Dee Hock, founder of Visa, implemented an efficient and effective system for processing credit cards. The cumbersome BankAmericard model already in place reserved the card as proprietary to each bank, which turned out to be a mess. Unsecured loans, upon which the concept was conceived, were lagging behind in sectors unable to organize effectively. Hock shifted the perspective: as we've already seen, he treated the process as biological in nature and built collaborative business relationships worldwide. It was his ability to create a dialogue with partners on the project that helped define the shift to global card acceptance and more effective and efficient billing processes.

Top-down organization is the prevailing model in small business firms where employees implement the ideas of the owners who founded the company, and rightly so. Founders hold a vision of what their product will do in the marketplace, what need it fills, and push forward inspired by potential success. Corporations and larger companies may also employ the top-down management style. However, there is growing acceptance of the bottom-up style that invites feedback and often engages Action-Learning Teams to strategize direction and responsibilities based on team members' skills.

To explore perspectives for decision-making is the human's gift of a thinking brain and its ability to communicate thoughts and ideas in meaningful ways. To engage in dialogue, to problem-solve and expand awareness, requires at least two people attentively listening and sharing perspectives. When interested parties gather with the intention to identify difficulties, propose solutions and engage in meaningful discourse to resolve, redirect or impel a new direction, understanding is more easily achieved when all concerned participate.

Recall it took the single-cell amoeba millennia to wake up to a change in environment and to solve the crisis by joining with others as a cooperative multicellular organism. While the circumstances that threaten companies may be dissimilar, the same urgency to survive requires shifting perspectives and modifying behavior. When conditions are stagnant, lethargy sets in, and then the nudge to re-invent yourself, your company, your project or your relationship invites new beginnings.

Effective problem solving resides in inquiry, simple beginnings with basic questions emerging from fundamental observations: what do you want and what will it take for you to get there? Timelines and goalposts measure your progress. Openly sharing ideas in dialogue, bending a listening ear, going inside to analyze and massage possible solutions and outcomes is an exciting part of the process. It can be something as pleasant as teasing your senses with a barbecue or a fresh batch of chocolate-chip cookies. The aroma of possibility anticipates a pleasurable experience, leaving the memory to be shared with others. These delights are no different than when a captivating idea stimulates a fresh approach. The enlightened moment thrills the senses and excites resolve.

The idea of increasing awareness adds depth and richness to every aspect of life and that includes relationships and business. Piercing self-protective ideologies and practices with targeted focus can threaten the status quo, which can be a good thing; otherwise to continue as you always have with the same limitations and expectations allows problems to flounder on repetitive themes in the revolving door of no resolve. This keeps firms and individuals going in circles, like a dog chasing its tail.

It's easy to see how decisions are based on past experiences of a similar event or a person fitting the parameters of a given situation. That's where memory comes into play. You roll the known around in your mind, justifying and negating episodic details appearing on your mental movie screen. Your brain with its creative mind has all the art supplies necessary to mentally massage ideas until they are ready to bloom on the canvas of your imagination. Discussing possible outcomes in a forum where everyone's ideas are heard is critical for effective decision-making. Rather than cling tenaciously to faltering concepts held close on your pedestal of preference, let loose and allow them to fall away, opening the door to expanded awareness and alternatives that actually stimulate resolve.

There is so much to appreciate about life, and we have it all: the fragrance and beauty in every bloom and climbing morning glory, the magnificent dawn announcing a new day, as well as the warmth and peacefulness of a summer sunset. Its richness is met with gratitude, for we have only to shift awareness to appreciate the beauty.

Socratic Feedback

We have heard for years that life is a bowl of cherries, sweetness with pits. While we spit out the pits after ingesting the best part, seeds are valued for their ability to continue the pleasure when planted in a nourishing environment. The same is true in relationships and business. Channels are blocked for further discussion when the pits are thrown away—when contributions on subjects of common interest are ignored rather than cultivated.

Discussing how better to do things can reinvigorate a company and speed the process of change, once reasonable parameters are set for accomplishment. Some leaders are out of touch with their workforce and struggle to understand why things are not working very well. Most often, it is because they lack knowledge of what the down-liners are thinking behind the managers' backs and have no way to implement feedback.

In 2005, I had the good fortune to meet entrepreneur Dick Spady, owner of Dick's Drive-In, a successful fast-food chain in Seattle, Washington, and co-founder of the Forum Foundation, a nonprofit educational research organization. Spady, over a number of years, developed the Opinionnaire, a Socratic feedback system adaptable for business, government and organizations worldwide. Essential for gauging progress, this everyday problem-solving tool is based upon the concept that people learn best when asked questions. By self-inquiry, participants examine how they feel about various situations, define their understanding and come up with appropriate solutions.

According to the seminal work that Spady co-authored, *The Leadership of Civilization Building*[3], three key steps in the Socratic process of awareness are frustration, insight and verification. The first two take place at the personal level with no one else involved, an alone process of self-examination. You become aware of a problem and perhaps are frustrated because its resolution is not self-evident. Then, upon going deep into your mind where emotions are the wellspring of revitalization, the Aha! Moment lights your view of the situation. As if by magic, insight previously out of sight, reveals a solution.

The third step comes when you get "verification". We might call this bouncing our ideas off another person or group to test our hypothesis, otherwise known as feedback. This is where the Opinionnaire comes in.

To improve communications and capabilities of employees and leaders at all levels to solve common problems, sometimes across large geographic areas, is often challenging. Using the Socratic method of asking questions saves time by speeding the process in evaluating systemic problems, something everyone is interested in achieving. Often in large organizations, it is difficult to gather groups physically in person. In this case, it may be more appropriate to use an Opinionnaire, a non-threatening process that evokes a more accurate analysis of existing concerns and can be used in person or online.

This is how it works:

1. The event facilitator describes the issue at hand and possible solutions in a 20–30-minute audio or video presentation to all participants.
2. Participants then break up into groups of 4 to 12, choosing a group facilitator.
3. Groups agree to meet during a 15- to 45-day window.

4. Feedback session limits each participant initially to two minutes, followed by open discussion.
5. Small groups discuss issues and potentials.
6. The event facilitator distributes Opinionnaire Fast Forum machine-scannable "Councilor" Response Sheets, either on paper or in a web-based version, which allow participants to choose value alternatives as well as to "abstain" or "object" to questions.
7. The facilitator analyzes the Fast Forum reports and produces a Viewspaper of summary results and highlights to return to the participants.

The Opinionnaire itself consists of questions or statements, sometimes formulated by human resources personnel or organization-development practitioners, to seek input on such issues as pay, benefits satisfaction, leadership evaluations and strategies for direction. Spady suggests small group brainstorming sessions to generate user-friendly, non-threatening topical value statements and questions that appropriately narrow focus and refine the query. This helps arrive at an honest appraisal of issues. The questions—about ideas, policies, situations, events or just about anything else—are made as unbiased as possible so as not to unduly influence the respondent. Only in this way are results deemed of value. To torque the questions and statements to favor a position is not the way to get accuracy. In any event, participants can always abstain or object to a question if they wish to express their incomplete knowledge or their dissatisfaction.

Questions often take the form of general value statements like:

- I support the idea of…
- On balance, the annual… is good for the…
- Our city, company or organization should not host more…
- I believe the… plan is seriously flawed.
- I believe… is wrong.

For each statement, respondents are asked if they agree or disagree. They indicate their response using one or more of the following scales:

- Yes or no
- Multiple choice
- End anchors: for example, a scale of 1 to 5, with 1 as Not Appropriate, 5 as Highly Appropriate and 3 as Neutral

- Likert scale: Strongly Agree, Agree, Neutral, Disagree, Strongly Disagree

Each method includes "Abstain" and "Object" options to provide respondents a range of choices to reflect their opinions.

For more information on Dick Spady's work and using the Opinionnaire process, visit www.easycitizeninvolvement.com or www.forumfoundation. org.

Spady claims, "The world is on the verge of a major discovery in social science on the level of the printing press and the computer. Most of the knowledge in the world is in books and computer databanks, but most of the wisdom in the world is in the minds of people walking the earth and we have to learn how to reach it. And, we have; it is in the field of Zeitgeist communication."

Spady's model can be useful to hospitals, universities and other institutions as a way to evaluate procedures and their impact on the general public, especially where large numbers of people are involved. While corporate interests are one thing, the impact on the public is quite another. Using the bottom line as first order of defense may not be the best choice over time when it comes to human values.

All opinions are perceptions of the environment, based on past experiences or input generated through the media. How we perceive others and ourselves predetermines outcomes. We foresee future events that often play out just as we picture them in our head. Whether business, organization, institution, community, state, nation, political, economic or personal, opinions are based on past experience. What has happened before often happens again, almost as self-fulfilling prophecies, unless new ideas are purposely planted in our frontal lobe for delivery in free space.

Group Sharing

Getting together to share common concerns engages dialogue in a meaningful way. This may have been the impetus to form The National Coalition for Dialogue & Deliberation, a concept initiated by Andy Fluke and Sandy Heierbacher to build bridges between disciplines and to cross-pollinate interests.[4]

Jim Rough's Dynamic Facilitation workshop at the 2006 NCDD conference in San Francisco demonstrated how this works. The Wisdom Council Process, which he invented to assist in the expression of essential wisdom and virtue in all people, involves drawing diverse voices together to reach near-unanimous agreements and decisions to implement them in a spirit of community. It is based on the "We, the People" concept of the Declaration of Independence.

Rough suggests: "a true Wisdom Council should be chartered by a consensus of the people: on an ongoing basis, not by management or by just a vote of the people."[5]

Without preset goals that often bypass the impossible-seeming issues, the Wisdom Council is free to choose its own issues and float ideas in a natural way even if some in the group have emotional energy attached. They are allowed to speak naturally without fear of recrimination because the process is exploratory. The environment is structured to allow spontaneous comments on situations everyone cares about. This often defuses pent-up emotions that may lie beneath the surface to boil up and erupt if not allowed to vent in an appropriate way. Honoring everyone's points of view without judgment or rebuff can often relieve the pressure that builds when no one listens.

The beauty of giving everyone a hearing is that seemingly negative energy is released before becoming a time bomb. Differing views are accepted as part of the process. This collaborative think-tank environment provides safe harbor to address really big problems.

Ervin Laszlo, who founded the Club of Budapest, is co-chair of the World Wisdom Council. He is another thought-provoking individual who knows what it means to collaborate, to gather ideas from a consortium of interested parties, thus to gain consensus on important issues. Nation-building for the future will rely on a vision of the possible, where common ground for living in peace benefits everyone. For humanity to survive much seems dependent on respecting others' values, not on making people conform to a few individuals' ideas of how life should be lived.[6]

It is in discussion that shared thoughts expand points of view. Many times, we lack knowledge or experience on critical issues that affect us either on a personal level or on a global scale. In some ways, we are all affected as trickle-down theory pools in our laps.

This technique of open discussion prevents "top-down leadership" from bulldozing unpopular ideas considered necessary. Once there is consensus, implementation is more readily assured, thus allowing movement along a constructive path. You may also agree that opinions are more accurate than polls, because opinions involve emotional behavior and behavior is habitual. According to some experts, to change behavior takes up to 21 days of focused attention with repetitive reminders. Checking in with self when temptations arise is purposeful awareness, and awareness of self is the beginning of the insightful process. To know who you are changes everything for taking time to do the introspection into why you are as you are is growth-enhancing. It is asking the ultimate questions: Who am I? Why am I here? What is my purpose in life?

Such assessment of behavior as the Opinionnaire provides for business and government could as easily provide insight into Planet Earth's ecological system. One example of this approach is the Earth Charter Initiative (www.earthcharterinaction.org).

Insider information about how the group is doing can also be achieved by going down a checklist, asking such questions as is done in the World Café conversation process, where groups at small tables write ideas on butcher paper without talking, reserving discussion until later. Participants then address concerns using a talking stick, a legendary tool used by the American Indians where only the holder has the right to speak. In this way, no one is stepping on another as they share their understanding. There is honoring in this method, allowing each to share his or her thoughts. As each table reports to the whole, ideas are listed on a flip chart or white board, where they are easily kept in the brain's frontal lobe for further consideration. Inclusion is key. As team participants, everyone has a vested interest in reaching agreement.[7]

Since the Socratic method provides a feedback system to ascertain conditions and progress on many fronts, even states and countries can use it to advantage. In 2008 Oregon became the first state to use the Opinionnaire ballot as an assessment tool for conditions in health care. Seen as a launch pad for other states to more accurately portray the impact of services on citizens, the findings indicate future directions. These are posted on the Internet for all to see. To expand this concept to other interests will help leaders lead better based on how the populace feels. Without feedback, leaders lead from a limited perspective, which may not be in the best interests of the company, the people or the country. With the new frontier of citizen involvement in politics and health care, for instance, as well as other issues important to the human condition, business and governments will certainly have a better feel for what works and what does not. Ignoring public opinion is not healthy for business or government.

Whenever I think about a roundtable discussion, the vision of King Arthur comes to mind. Hearing everyone express concerns clears the path for amicable agreement that leads to fruitful liaisons. Everyone has different learning experiences, trials and errors to help us through life. This is why listening to others share their life story is healthy as we learn how better to handle our own life choices in the future. Success is far more likely to be realized when cooperation underlies the process. This management style is leadership from the bottom-up, rather than the top-down style so often refuted as unreasonable by those who must do the work.

It's teamwork that really gets the job done. As my mother often said, "Many hands make light work." She knew how to effectively utilize all involved to achieve a desired end. Those who participate share the appreciation, much as do shipbuilders when the symbolic bottle of champagne is smashed against a new ocean liner's seaworthy hull. Everyone's involvement is valued. This is the reward for successfully solving problems as they come up. Group effort respects everyone's input as valuable to the process. It is through discussion that flaws in thinking are revealed, making the outcome a collaborative effort that benefits everyone.

The Good of the Whole

Who, then, is the individual responsible for feeling the pulse of the marketplace? Acting in a similar capacity to the cell membrane reading signals from the environment as information to be acted upon, executives and department managers must be aware of how incoming signals translate to a company's internal operations; for their interpretations will dictate whether to increase production, improve employee-based efficiency or delivery of goods and services, or shield themselves from bad press. The very lifeblood of business depends upon perception being accurate.

In a small business, the owner/manager is the one tuned to market forces and their effect on everyone's livelihood, including his or her own. In some cases, he or she is also responsible for production. But in a larger company where ownership is shared by stockholders, they are much more interested in their stock dividends than in running the company.

Certainly, owners may not always be involved on a daily basis. More than likely, it will be the staff or managers who run the operation. Rarely is the board of directors involved, for they may not be as sensitive to the full operations either. So, who is accountable? Not the treasurer or the CFO, for their efforts depend upon distribution of the monies that flow in and go out, not the interpretation of environmental influences. Only when the company spends too much money or misappropriates funds are their watchdog talents questioned. The internal and external environments work together for the good of the whole, because survival of business depends upon all factions working harmoniously.

The buffer zone in any business is the interface between the top re-sponder and those who make sure the information coming in is important enough to take action, to act as the guardian preventing dangerous signals from infecting the core and stalling production. Access to the inside is the lock and key to the executive washroom, so to speak. At all costs, there must be guardians to prevent contamination by ill-suited parts. After all, a proprietary formula for the manufacturing process is equivalent to the body's DNA. This formula repairs and replicates processes, if need be, ac-cording to external conditions with the approval of the boss. However, let someone or something detrimental to the business come through the front door that can ultimately change the formula and alter the system, then you've got trouble.

The membrane of business, like the membrane of a human cell, is the sensitive exterior interface with the outside environment that has intimate connections to the inside. How well the product is accepted is only part of the process. There is the reporting of damaged goods on arrival, misdirection of advertising, lack of careful inspection, faulty performance endangering the customer, impractical applications and manufacturing defects. There are also shipping problems, inaccurate record-keeping, news analysis, government rules and regulations, inspections under scrutiny, inappropriate pricing, packaging difficulties, competition, insider trading, boardroom arguments, trade secrets leaked, and the list goes on and on. Almost anything can signal a demand for attention, and the watchful eyes of those in charge are critical to each business and its success.

Government is no different, though it produces nothing. Its existence depends upon taxes, money produced by the country's workers who are also consumers, purchasing goods and services. The government depends on a constant supply of money, even if it has to beg or borrow from other countries. Problem is that the government is inefficient, full of bureaucracy. If governments were run like a successful business, they would clearly be handled differently. With deficit spending, the government is depending upon future generations to pay for goods purchased today. That sounds like irresponsible spending, poor management and a huge credit-card debt that will never be paid off. Like the human body when it is overspent, it dies. There is no more energy. Money is energy, and without that kind of energy, business cannot stay afloat. The man on the street begs, borrows and steals to survive, and so do some businesses and governments.

What if there were no credit cards, no unsecured loans? What if we had to pay cash for all we bought as we go? It used to be that way before BankAmericard and Visa. The body of business lives off assets, relying on more to come through the door as muscle and talents are exercised.

Consider present-day conditions and the mountain of debt accumulated through the use of credit cards. What would happen if our world operated without money, but on the bartering system? What would it look like then?

Again, leadership is key. Without conscious capitalism to guide the focused mind to the best choice for all concerned, business will endure a painful relationship with the people of the world. It is the purpose of this book to inspire greatness with honesty and purpose, ever seeking beneficial outcomes for all of humanity. Leadership with a heart is critical to maintain balance the same as right thinking and intelligent decision-making is for the human body. The challenge is to live as one unified consortium of interested parties on a planet worthy of love and caring for all species and the environment. Let us work together for the good of the whole.

CHAPTER EIGHTEEN

ENERGETIC FIELDS OF INFLUENCE
The Body and the Machine

Energy is the force that drives all Creation: sex, biology, business and relationships. The human body is itself an energy generator with its own operating system that keeps the living machine alive: a world unto itself. Who and what we are today as the biped species *Homo sapiens* evolved over millions of years. As living, breathing entities, humans are vulnerable to the full range of energies: all seven levels of the electromagnetic field. For example, infrared waves have the ability to contort the framework of living tissues, given direct exposure, as in a laser beam. Infrared goggles can reveal living forms at night, unseen by the naked eye, while X-rays penetrate soft tissues to reveal bones and their structure. Gamma waves are energetically more powerful, vibrating at a higher frequency: in radiosurgery procedures a doctor can use a gamma knife to cut tiny paths through tissues. Cosmic energy waves, found in outer space, make up the rotating planetary bodies, the stars and the Milky Way, the domain of astronomers and NASA, while the seven levels of energy fields in the visible-light spectrum exhibit themselves in prismatic colorful rainbows, the familiar stuff of everyday life on Earth. Slow Hertzian waves are used to power telephones and transmitter stations on the ground, while off-planet satellite systems depend upon nearly instantaneous communication in the ultraviolet range, also the domain of telepathy. Different energy fields power them.

Energy in one form or another is in every thing and every non-thing. Since energy is ubiquitous, it is companies' proprietary rights that keep technology from being harnessed for the common good. Most agree the energy "crisis" that began in 2004 was all about oil, and that it is corporate greed driving Scrooge to the counting house.

As a result, resistance by some energy suppliers to modernize their operations, combined with a strange interlacing of special interests, keeps the U.S. in a regressive mode, despite talks about progress and explorations to the outer reaches of space. Why companies in the energy business are not eager to move to the next step, retooling when there is a better way to do things, is little understood by the general public and remains a matter of grave concern. Sad that we are not already using free energy technology, not monetarily free, but drawing energy from the vacuum as discovered around the turn of the 20th century: forms like scalar interferometry, which draws on the subtle energy of scalar waves embedded in common electromagnetic transverse waves, waves that run diagonally or crosswise in the direction of the flow.[1]

We already know that electricity does not travel along the wire, as we have been led to believe for more than a hundred years, but travels *around* the wire, using the wire merely as a directional focus. Thought is energy; your thoughts and mine are both electric and magnetic, traveling through the air, permeating every thing and every non-thing: human bodies, plants and animals, all things living and non-living, including crystals and metals. Thoughts as energy affect the food supply, the raising of our children, self-healing, and the desire for a satisfying career. Thoughts lead us to adventures that add wisdom to our evolving nature. We cannot remove ourselves from the electromagnetic energy fields, EMF. We live in cosmic soup.

The remarkable human body itself is composed of molecules and atoms held together by energy in the electromagnetic fields. In fact, the solidity of the human body is measured by the weight you see on your bathroom scales, while the invisible forces in and around your body keeping you alive weigh in the range of 11 ounces. There is healing energy and there are aberrant energies; no matter the name, energy is energy. Energy is what you are, a living, breathing electromagnetic light that glows in the darkness of creation.

You are a marvelous living machine that functions without conscious control, and as a creator, an entrepreneur, businesswoman or businessman, you use your body as a vehicle for transportation and your thinking brain to guide your actions. Experiences are necessary for personal growth, for the accumulation of knowledge of what works and what does not: we make mistakes to avoid them in the future.

You are an encyclopedia of experience, carrying with you the sum total of your thoughts and actions. Your body reveals how you think, what you eat, how well you digest your food and care about your body: what you become as a living, breathing being.

Lacking the passion to learn how better to live your life with a healthy curiosity about the unknown leaves you without answers to questions that pierce your solitude. In a lifetime there are plenty of opportunities to build a repertoire of experiences that enrich your life and increase your self-esteem. Your personal mission is to grow in awareness, to make known the unknown; to expand conscious awareness and become all you can be on the grander scale of the possible.

Consider for a moment the possibility of incarnating on Planet Earth again, knowing that what you learn this lifetime will be retained for the next go-around. What kind of decisions would you make about this life? Would your choices be different?

With energy everywhere and never lost, it is possible to access the sum total of human experience held in the energetic fields, in what mystics call the Akashic record; to draw on accumulated knowledge from earlier lifetimes to solve problems in your sleep that seem unsolvable in your waking.

With self-examination and deep thinking, through discussion and research, we eventually tap into the energetic fields where all knowledge is known. Through the intelligence of our brain as a transmitter of energies, we can download information in our sleep to solve problems. It is absolutely fascinating to consider. Think about how many times you've awakened in the morning with solutions to problems you've been struggling to resolve. Perhaps now you may agree that being scrupulous in your search for knowledge and expanding awareness is far more important than first imagined.

Uncanny Intelligence

In the 1970s, on a visit to Peru and the Lima Museum of Art, I was amazed to see small clay pots decorated with painted images of spaceships and hooded, space-suited travelers. Since mankind draws on what it knows and sees, this art is evidence of the existence of extraterrestrial life in Earth's history, confirming that we have been, and probably still are, not alone. Perhaps we were seeded here after all, as some historians have claimed: most notably author Zecharia Sitchin, a scholar of ancient Sumeria. Cave paintings have also been found that show spaceships traveling the heavens, star travelers in another incarnation. I certainly had to consider such when I saw the colorful ceramic pots decorated with those painted images sitting in the glass case on the second floor of the Lima museum.

We know about the Nazca Lines, geoglyphs of birds, fish and plants, some of them 12 miles long, spanning 800 miles in the Nazca Desert from Peru to northern Chile. Dated between 200 BC and 600 AD, the images are visible only from the air. It has been theorized that they are landmarks for spaceships traversing the skies. Who, exactly, were the extraterrestrial beings marking their spaceports in this way? What kind of capabilities did they have? Were they psychic? Where did they come from? Mars? Pluto? The Moon? What kind of knowledge did they have? How was the culture at Nazca destroyed—and will our culture meet its demise in the same way? Perhaps we come here for a little while before moving on to another incarnation. It gives cause for contemplation. It's been said that we are destined to repeat the future, if we do not learn from the past. There seem to be so many questions and too few answers.

How *do* we know what we know? Precognition can warn us of impending events. Your dog knows when you are en route home and can be found sitting by the door awaiting your arrival when you walk in. Birds fly across the sky in formations based on aerodynamics without going to school. Homing pigeons know where home is; yet science knows not why. We are fascinated by the owl delivering messages to Harry Potter, seeming to know a lot about showing up at just the right time in the right place. It may be more than fantasy.

Most of us have had an experience that sparks insight. You get an urge to call on a client, only to learn they are in decision-making mode and your timing couldn't be better. Because you showed up, you get the business. Parents have inklings when their child is in trouble. A dog barks when danger lurks, knows when an odor of smoke signals a fire and drags a child to safety without anyone telling it to do so. It is the innate intelligence to know without knowing how; to smell danger, to sense a friend in need or to have one just show up when least expected. These subtle events are the quantum exercising the principle.

Structural Integrity

The beauty of biology is that you can depend upon it to be truthful. It has integrity. If there is a pain somewhere in your body, it is nature's way to get your attention. Something is awry. By listening to your body talk, you develop insight and understanding, and at the same time in the same way, you can talk to your body and comfort it with kindness. The body does not lie, cheat or purposely harm itself. Our cellular body is one big family looking out for every cell and its well-being. When there is damage to the body, the cellular community sends in the rescue squad, differentiated cells trained in more than one capacity, like mast cells that rush in to heal a wound. There is a cooperative agreement in play. After all, when the body lives, so do all the cells. When one part of the body aches, there is sympathy as cells adjust to accommodate. There is instant communication, with no secrets withheld. It is honest all the way. The body plays no games to appease anyone. Nature is the great leveler of reality.

I am sure you are aware that feelings are more reliable than words, though we are trained to doubt them. To be with certain people can be exhausting. They may be low energy producers sucking energy from your field to revitalize or power their own. They are actually getting high at your expense. When you feel your vitality wane, excuse yourself from that environment and move into one that matches your own. When your guard is compromised, remaining in a negative orbit is not in your best interests and will surely end up making you sick.

When you are able to discern differences in frequencies, it is much easier to walk through life with confidence. You will recognize when you are on the right path, in the right place, and when it is time to veer in another direction. You will attract personalities, companies and products that match your frequency, because they will just *feel* right. It is really important to be knowledgeable about vibrations, for they reveal when situations are harmonious and when they are not. These clues are worth your attention for they could save you, your life and a ton of money should you err in judgment.

Everything, as you will see, communicates energetically, and each individual vibrates at his or her own frequency. Low-frequency vibrations of 10 Hz are not strong enough to match those of anyone with 50 to 60 Hz, a frequency that is high enough to create relationships of a long and lasting nature. Your heartbeat matches your frequency: if your heart rate is too low, you are listless and need to rest. Exercising or being with people you like and feel compatible with makes you feel really good about yourself, that's synchrony. Sometimes, you'll even feel the buzz.

I discovered some years ago that I am sensitive to color in a demonstrable way. I can walk into a clothing shop, scan the inventory and instantly know whether there is anything in the store for me color-wise. If not, I turn and walk out the door without wasting my time looking for possibilities. I save a lot of time by assessing the value to myself before making a commitment. I know when I am in the right place and when I am better off moving on. If you want to do this too, start paying attention to energy vibrations: notice how you feel where you are, what attracts your attention and what seems to push you away.

Energy shapes matter, so you can infer that energy shapes your body. If that is so, some frequencies can make you sick and some can make you well. It is all in the vibratory frequency of your cellular body that adapts to the environment. Remember that your thoughts are frequencies too, and they enjoy the same attunement. That is why I suggest people find happiness within themselves, for in happiness there is a love of life. Where there is a love for life, there is a healthy mind and a healthy body.

Russian scientists have made significant discoveries in this area, validating the human DNA as an extremely competent communicator in a biological network akin to the Internet. Alternative practitioners can validate the positive effects on the physical body when encouraging words are part of the treatment. Louise Hay, author of the landmark book *You Can Heal Your Life*, demonstrated how she healed her body of cancer by identifying the emotion she felt was responsible for it. By repeating a mantra of sorts, reinforced with emotional frequencies of healing, she proved it works and continues to live her life with that wisdom.

DNA is a smart catalog of potential patterns, but its actual expression is shaped by information coming across the cell membrane, the interface between incoming signals and outgoing behaviors interpreting information for future action. Cell receptors on the periphery of the membrane are very smart. They understand and respond to frequencies traversing the system. The body is programmable by thought, word and language, something the mystics, esoteric and spiritual teachers have known for ages. This knowledge is the base discipline used by hypnotists, psychotherapists and hypnotherapists, who know how to reframe a reference to reach the core of limiting beliefs. You can do the same thing through autosuggestion by reinforcing the desired outcome over and over and over again in consciousness.

Wisdom Waning

So, why is there so much stress? Why is there so much aggravation, so much aggression? According to the American Automobile Association, gas prices hit record highs of $4.086 a gallon on June 30, 2008. It's easy to see this as simply gouging the driver behind the wheel to benefit the big oil companies. Yet the issue is greater than that.

There has been no adaptation to evolve out of fossil fuels into more efficient, economical energy sources. Despite discoveries by dedicated inventors who seek better ways to do things, self-interests have thwarted their acceptance. Nikola Tesla, who discovered alternating current in the early 1900s, is a good example. Tesla's work demonstrated that energy is everywhere in the universe to be tapped for efficient use, as earlier discussed, but J. P. Morgan withdrew funding rather than support inventions that would have elevated this culture to near space-age living. More than likely, Morgan felt threatened by the potential for lost revenue because of it. Certainly, were Tesla's technology in use today our world would be very different. We'd be off of oil as a fuel for our wheeled vehicles, and life would be far more efficient. What a shame that the consciousness of one man thwarted progress that would surely have brought a different world to our doorstep.

As it is, energy from the vacuum is available now, but withheld by those who benefit from existing technologies. Some entrepreneurs with the courage and wherewithal to remove the chains and free us from outdated practices could be seen as saviors from the struggles of advancing cultures ready for better technology.

Perhaps the cell phone will lead us into the revolutionary use of free energy, traversing obstacles that for a hundred years have kept us captive. There is hope. Just as the human body is self-contained, carrying its bladder along for convenience and efficiency instead of being bound to a urinal, so business must be free to seek sustainable modalities. The power of money and influence continues to have a strong effect on the future of the world and on the daily lifestyle it encumbers.

The human body and all creatures in nature demonstrate that intelligence is built into the system. Only man with his thinking brain figures out how to keep some segments of society dumb and inefficient.

The Power of Thought

So, what is reality? Most of us think we know, but do we, really? Reality is experienced through our senses as structures of the universe, creations of our mind based on our brains' perceptions of incoming information. Traveling at almost infinite speed beyond visible light are tachyons, invisible units of perception that are read and processed by the rapidity of our brain's computer, which gives them meaning and gives us the quality of omniscience, of knowing.

The human body's cellular community is the perfect embodiment of holistic thinking. When a virus or a pathogen attacks the body it affects the whole body in the same ways, as does a worker with a bad attitude in business.

Manipulating the consumer's mind, planting seeds of insecurity about why they need an advertised remedy or procedure, is a double-edged sword. Not only does business apply this technique expertly, so do governments when they want to have their way with us. Is it possible to be in integrity with your body and with what you do in business at the same time? Of course! When an internal command is given by your conscious mind, there need be no words spoken. Only the feeling is necessary to complete the internal action. It is a cascade effect, from thought to behavior. One thing leads to another. And it is so in the body of business. A late appointment presses everyone: shortened time for a doctor's appointment could lead to a misdiagnosis, which could alter a human life. How do you ensure the desired outcome of some of your actions? You may never know, unless it is in treating yourself.

Awareness of how the power of thought can program the mind to manifest has grown exponentially, especially since the release of the video production of *The Secret*, starring Jack Canfield, Michael Beckwith, John Assaraf, Lisa Nichols, James Ray, John Demartini, Esther Hicks and Bob Proctor. Oprah devoted two shows to *The Secret* film, so important was its message. For many in her audience, previously unaware of how thoughts create reality, it has been an awakening experience. The power of human potential to bring joy and happiness into your life is achieved by making better choices. This works for personal issues, as well as for business and politics, in exactly the same way. The power of repetition on a theme is what advertising is all about, so we must be ever vigilant to mass-media hysteria that grips people's lives.

This seems to fit Albert Einstein's observation that when "the observer observes the observed," the mind/body connection becomes coherent. You will follow your perception, whatever it is that you perceive as the truth for you. It is true that what you think you see, you see, according to your perceptions of the environment. Observations are not separate from the observer's perception. True, as well, for business.

It may not be too far-fetched to consider that reality is created through our thoughts, and that we "know" things without consciously knowing. Freedom to be what we are as a gift of spirit is expressed through our self-confidence. Encouraged by those who respect the uniqueness in each individual, we can grow without limitation. Yet some of us might not fit in if we change. You might outgrow your job. Then you will be at a crossroads as to your next step. Since we are always trying to "fit in" to groups, organizations, society in general, there is often consternation about capabilities entering a new job: are we really up to meeting the challenge of something new, or fearful of tough competition? With more knowledge, you may be threatened by what you might or might not do or by who you might become. Relationships sometimes outgrow themselves. Limited expectations may thwart your progress, unless you stick to your goal of personal satisfaction.

If you care enough about who you are as a person in this lifetime, what could prevent you from reaching the next rung on the ladder? Direct your energy toward your life goal, be it business, creative expression or traveling the world. Escaping in television sitcoms, hiding behind boredom and a lack of initiative to test your prowess and creativity, deprives everyone of your contribution. Business depends upon inventive minds to dream of improving conditions on Planet Earth and to do the problem solving that goes hand in hand with growth. Entrepreneurs think outside the box. Without them, we could still be cavemen, ignorant of an expanding world of possibilities.

In some ways, we are not all that different from each other in the desire to satisfy urges and to earn our way in life. For myself, the excitement is in thinking beyond the ordinary, gaining wisdom from new dimensions that stretch my understanding beyond the conventional forms with their familiar tools. Some folks put off learning a new set of tools—say, working on a computer—because they think it is too hard and they're afraid they cannot succeed. But computer language is based on 0 and 1, elements of language and numbers. Their hesitancy is more in how it all works, because it doesn't function like a machine with movable parts that can be seen and manipulated.

When these folks finally do join the computer-user ranks, their vocabulary is expanded with new tools, new definitions and a key to the world of ideas through the Internet. It is learning a new language, a bit foreign at first, but on usage, becoming familiar. As a result, new neuronal pathways expand consciousness, causing the brain to wake up to the fact that school is back in session.

How did Nikola Tesla know what he knew about the electromagnetic energy fields when he came to the United States to test his theories? He didn't have some teacher in school teaching him what he knew. He was an inventor. Where did that knowledge come from?

His mind was connected to the invisible electromagnetic energy fields where memories are kept, and knowledge is available to minds that are open to receive. Perhaps his knowledge came from the Akashic records in a dream. Whatever the source, it's pretty certain that Tesla tapped into another level of consciousness where all is known, and captured the "light" of understanding in the doing.

Clearly, Tesla listened to thoughts that ran through his head then acted upon them. He questioned every nuance, keenly aware that his ability to connect the dots of information would create something meaningful.

Since the narrow visible-light spectrum of which the physical body is a part sits in the vast darkness of the electromagnetic fields of energy between infrared and ultraviolet light, the brain is strongly influenced by its connection to universal energies. To access the library of knowledge in the seven levels of the electromagnetic energy fields, sit quietly with closed eyes. Open your mind to possibilities without consciously attempting to control your thoughts. You may be surprised.

CHAPTER NINETEEN

TURNING GREEN WITH PRIDE
Reclaiming the Land

In a 2003 special property report for Canada's *Globe and Mail*, "Planners see gold in brownfields: New tax revenue can make cleanup effort worthwhile", Albert Warson wrote that Canadian business and principalities see a prosperous future in cleaning up polluted industrial sites.[1] With an estimated 30,000 contaminated "brownfields" across Canada, government officials in Quebec could see potential benefits in urban renewal, collaborating with cities like Shawinigan and major paint and chemical manufacturing company ICI Canada, to revitalize toxic land laid waste for half a century.

All over Canada there's fascination to revive communities by cleaning up contaminated sites. For example, a venture considered the largest master-planned mixed-use development in North America is in the city of Vancouver, just north of the U.S./Canada border. This thriving city enjoys its mixed culture and fewer of the regulatory limitations that seem to burden other cities of its size. One example of its progressive stance is the mixed-use development of Concord Place, built on remediated land formerly known as a "brownfield".

Perhaps because of potential awards for excellence, which bring acclaim, more brownfields are getting attention. For the sake of explanation, and for award judging purposes, "brownfields" are designated as "abandoned, idled, or under-used industrial and commercial facilities complicated by real or perceived environmental contamination." This description applies to a wide variety of sites including, though not limited to, industrial properties, old gas stations, vacant warehouses, former dry-cleaning establishments and abandoned residential buildings, which potentially could contain lead paint or asbestos. Under the new law, sites that contain petroleum products, as well as mine-scarred lands, are also included. According to the United States Conference of Mayors, brownfields are located in almost every community in the United States.[2]

The Shawinigan chlor-alkali plant manufactured mercury cells for 40 years, overlapped by a chlorinated solvent plant in the same general period, and proved to be a challenged property. The problem with the manufacturing of chlorine as a purifying agent for swimming pools is that, while benign in that usage, chlorine is toxic in sedimentary earth as it combines with minerals and living organisms. Disposal of 650,000 liters of solvents extracted from below the water table and the contaminated soil above it, amounting to multiple thousands of tons, took patience and conviction that it would eventually be worth the effort and expense.

Despite huge amounts of solvent already removed from below the chlor-alkali manufacturing plant, more remains to be excavated. To their credit, ICI, Imperial Chemical Industries of Canada Ltd., accelerated cleanup to avoid extending the process an estimated 60 years. As a result, ICI earned one of nine annual Canadian Urban Institute "Brownie Awards" in the technological solutions/green design category.

Happily, the $24.8-million land remediation program initiated in Shawinigan, Canada, was successful and everyone celebrated when Wal-Mart and a Canadian Tire "gas bar" found the site free from contaminants and worthy to build and develop. Quebec is the only Canadian province providing grants, under its Revi-Sols program, as a contribution to the cost of cleaning up contaminated sites. This joint venture encouraged revitalization of the 7.9-hectare site with urban renewal revenue streams to continue for years to come. This is a great example of community partnerships working together for mutual benefit.

Company investments in this land remediation project amounted to $20 million. When added to the provincial government's expected total of $8.1 million, everyone involved was assured a substantial return on investment. With only so much land, it is wise to reflect on future trends and follow the lead of conservation and remediation for sustainability. In this way, everyone benefits from forethought.

Creative Planning and Civic Challenges

The healing occurs as planners focus on green fields and an environmentally light footprint. Jeff Westeinde, co-founder and CEO of Windmill Development Group Ltd. in Ottawa, spoke wisely at the Brownfields Conference in 2004: "The concept of implementing environmentally sustainable initiatives that aren't useable is no good." He also likened green building on remediated brownfields to a "part gas, part electric hybrid car," emphasizing that his company specializes in brownfield remediation and green buildings that include water and energy conservation and waste management, using, of course, smart building technologies. This means that all sites they are involved with must be free of contaminants. In projects like these, there needs to be a strong community buy-in, which could mean a lot to future developments. In some cases, former contaminated sites now remediated will become apartment or condo complexes, emphasizing the improved conditions.

The Windmill Development Group has the goal of achieving "Canada's most environmentally sustainable building," which would use:

- 50 percent less energy and water
- A geothermal ground source heat pump
- 60 percent natural lighting to most floors
- Recycle kitchen and bathroom water
- Renewable building materials
- Energy efficient appliances
- Smart building technologies
- Green roofs plus other features

In lieu of a garage, the development proposes an innovative feature: a fleet of five cars that the board would own and rent by the hour to residents. Westeinde stressed that more creative solutions is the answer rather than depending on more money from government to right the wrongs of past generations. We have only now begun to be conscious of the impact humans have on the environment, and there are still contaminated lands that continue to make people sick. Sometimes, it depends upon whistle-blowers to alert an environmental agency.

The U.S. has also been making strides in redevelopment of previously contaminated lands, as pointed out by the U.S. Conference of Mayors, a nonprofit organization composed of cities with populations of 30,000 or more. Mayor J. Christian Bollwage of Elizabeth, New Jersey, co-chair of the Conference's Brownfields Task Force, comments on the benefits of brownfields development: "In Elizabeth, we have been able to convert older, contaminated properties into new and thriving developments within the heart of our community. With property values rising and available land disappearing, it is important for cities to revitalize communities and neighborhoods that have fallen into disrepair."[3]

Christopher De Sousa, a professor at the University of Wisconsin–Milwaukee and co-director of the Brownfields Research Consortium, said in a presentation to the U.S. Conference of Mayors in 2004 that:

- 153 U.S. cities have already redeveloped 900 brownfields representing over 10,000 acres, with another 700 sites in the works.
- 74 cities have already created over 83,000 new jobs, thereby adding $90 million to local tax revenues.
- 113 of the U.S. cities surveyed could support an additional 4.3 million people without placing an additional burden on existing infrastructure.

De Sousa also cited a study he conducted for Milwaukee County, which revealed that seven projects undertaken from 1995 to 2000 averaged about $5.6 million in redevelopment per project and created an average of 80 jobs each, and that $57 in private investment was leveraged for every $1 the city spent.

By 2006, more than one-half of the cities surveyed reported offering incentives to encourage brownfields redevelopment through tax credits, low-interest loans and infrastructure upgrades. Additionally, the Conference's survey found that many states are working with cities on brownfield issues, but that few city-state partnerships deal with the issue of sprawl that could result from broad redevelopment.

Other highlights of a survey include:

- 62 cities generated actual tax revenue from redeveloped brownfield sites totaling over $233 million.
- 52 percent of the 201 cities surveyed estimated that redevelopment of local brownfields sites would produce additional tax revenues between $958 million and $2.2 billion annually.
- More than 83,171 jobs were created on former brownfields sites

(21,977 jobs during redevelopment and 61,194 jobs created post-development).

- More than 75 percent of the cities surveyed called for additional assistance to redevelop brownfields sites, including tax incentives, low-interest loans and infrastructure upgrade funds to demolish obsolete buildings.

American policymakers lack appreciation for the value of open public space, more so than Canadian cities that view brownfields as a perfect place for green space. Either way, profitable ventures must exist for brownfield reclamation programs to be successful. De Sousa cites projects in the Canadian Don River valley, including a planned community built on a former racetrack that was once a munitions factory, as some of the most successful examples in North America of enhancing ecological functioning and environmental sustainability.

However terrific this idea of reclaiming polluted land, the question of who pays for what can turn into a boondoggle, as it did in New York State. Complaints arose in the 2008 legislature about a "retail city" complex in Syracuse whose builder, Destiny USA, expected to recoup much of the $2 billion to $6 billion in cleanup costs under the 2003 Brownfields Cleanup Program through tax credits that would cost New York taxpayers more than $1 billion. Based on a cleanup projection of 11 sites a year, the program was functioning no better than the voluntary system in place prior to the 2003 law. The tax incentives amount to up to 22 percent of the project's entire cost. In 2008, a few developments benefited disproportionately by "hauling in supersized tax benefits that, in many cases, vastly exceed the cost of cleaning up the brownfields," reported *The New York Times*.[4]

Still, Glynn County, Georgia, had to sue the owners of Allied Signal Inc., Honeywell International and Allied Chemical Corp to clean up their toxic pool of caustic brine that leaked into the groundwater. Like so many other sites, the belief that contaminants posed no threat to environmental safety became a horror story. Together, the plant's owners and the EPA worked to clean up a caustic plume thought to contain mercury and polychlorinated biphenyls, or PCBs, that was potent enough to dissolve the layer of sandstone beneath the Allied Chemical Company plant.

The settlement of $25 million is minor when you consider the costs to Allied Signal and former owners Arco and Georgia Power, who declared bankruptcy in the mid-1990s and who spent $60 million to remove the contaminants from the sensitive environment under EPA guidance.

It didn't end there. Convicted of conspiracy in U.S. District Court in 1999 for discharging pollutants into the water, Christian A. Hansen Jr., former CEO of the Hanlin Group, which owned the plant, was fined $20,000 and sentenced to nine years in federal prison. He was not alone: Alfred R. Taylor, former plant manager, was sentenced to six years, while Hansen's son, Robert W. Hansen, also a top executive in the Hanlin Group, was sentenced to three years and 10 months and fined $20,000.[5]

According to the U.S. EPA, the Brownfields remediation program is "designed to empower states, communities, and other stakeholders in economic redevelopment to work together in a timely manner to prevent, assess, safely clean up and sustainably reuse brownfields." They estimate that the EPA's grants program leverages more than $6.5 billion in brownfields cleanup and redevelopment from private and public sectors, as well as creating some 25,000 new jobs. If your city or company is interested in a brownfields remediation program, check with the EPA for a list of the 450,000 available sites.[6]

Clearly, these are quantum issues, moving from thought forms to reality. Conscious awareness of environmental concerns for health reasons, coupled with investment for the future based on solution-based creativity, is a constructive and responsible method of improving the quality of life on Planet Earth. The mayors' intention to make land livable, reducing illness and resultant dependency on health care, is to their credit. Acting as responsible entities is a good sign of progress. No longer is it cut-and-run, but living with Mother Nature in a compatible environment. Again, we see that conscious awareness of the interconnectivity of thought, action and sustainability is essential to survive the future.

Strides in the Right Direction

The USDA Agriculture Research Service is involved in phytoremediation, using green plants to remove pollutants from the environment or render them harmless, thus helping rid soils of toxic heavy metals and chemical pollution usually left by companies when they closed their operation. Since remediation of soils is a very expensive venture, vacuuming heavy metals from the soil through their roots is more economical and more efficient by far. The beauty of this system is that plant tissues can be collected and stored, and the metal recovered.

However, it's a two-sided coin. While this process is good for living plants that serve as ground cover, it is a major concern when the plants are part of the food chain. For instance, wheat plants of various genotypes are being studied for aluminum tolerance by plant physiologist Leon Kochian, who is an authority on mechanisms used by certain plants to take up essential mineral nutrients and toxic heavy metals from soils.

Kochian says, "A typical plant may accumulate about 100 parts per million (ppm) zinc and 1 ppm cadmium. *Thlaspi caerulescens*, a small weedy member of the cabbage family, can accumulate up to 30,000 ppm zinc and 1,500 ppm cadmium in its shoots, while exhibiting few or no toxicity symptoms." He adds: "A normal plant can be poisoned with as little as 1,000 ppm of zinc or 20 to 50 ppm of cadmium in its shoots."

The research also suggests an approach for economically recovering these metals. "Zinc and cadmium are metals that can be removed from contaminated soil by harvesting the plant's shoots and extracting the metals from them," says Kochian.[7]

North Carolina State University's College of Natural Resources is also engaged in pollution control, particularly regarding phytoremediation as an alternative to costly excavation and the burning of contaminated soil. Dr. Elizabeth Nichols, an assistant professor of environmental technology at the college, feels certain that "while it's a slow-moving process that can't be used everywhere...it could be an effective, affordable approach for many small sites...left unattended while more critical sites were cleaned."[8]

Bio-Retention

Three years ago, the parking lot of a strip mall in Lacey, Washington, not far from where I live, became the scene of major renovation that included repaving to accommodate the heavy use by U.S. Post Office customers. Along with an improved, more efficient drainage system to absorb runoff, the project involved the installation of eco-sustainable plantings. The repaving, however, was not ordinary. The porous asphalt was graded to gently lean toward the medians to allow rainwater to seep into the gravel bed below, where it would be purified through a sophisticated drainage system before reaching the water table.

With the attractive plantings water-resistant and capable of sustaining the variable weather without tending, meaning low maintenance, it was also a definite cost-saving measure. The assorted plant varieties were not planted just in earth, as would be done in a typical garden, but in dirt over layers of sand and graded gravel to control runoff. With the Pacific Northwest known for above-average rainfall, the efficient system acts as a filter, stripping the water of toxins as it flows. When the Lacey city planner approved the site, landscape architect Butch Haase of the firm Rock Star was charged with doing the work and admitted that project was the largest he had done so far.

At first I could not appreciate the aesthetics of the scrawny plants that looked more like they belonged in Arizona than in Washington State. However, after two years' growth I could see the beauty of the center as an environmental success story reaping huge benefits for sustainability in its contribution to the Green revolution.

Another entrant into the arena of sustainability is Pelindaba Lavender Farm in Friday Harbor on San Juan Island, Washington, which takes its name from a Zulu word meaning "place of great gatherings". Pelindaba is the inspiration of South African Stephen Robins, M.D., who moved to the San Juan Islands in 1998 after practicing internal and family medicine in London and then founding a medical video production company, Communicore, in Laguna Beach, California. Originally planning to settle on ten acres of land on the island's east side purchased in 1990, he and his partner decided to sell that land and buy 20 acres on the west. The potential economic benefit of more sun exposure and rich soil with minimal need for water and fertilizer influenced their decision.

Today, Pelindaba is a premier grower of lavender plants, distiller of lavender essential oils and handcrafter of lavender-based products. The beauty of the lavender plant is its self-sustaining winning nature: from pretty flowers to preparing essential oils to having a cup of tea at Pelindaba's shop on the main street of Friday Harbor, just up the hill from the ferry. To give back to the community, Robins makes the retail shop open to groups for meetings at no charge. That's being a good neighbor and builds a great community spirit.

When Robins moved north in 1998, he said that he was not sure where this venture would lead him, but it has been one of the most fascinating he could have imagined. He has literally been led from one step to another to discover the secrets in the beautiful lavender plant, both fragrant and versatile, requiring little care. Pelindaba has turned into one of the island's most encouraging business opportunities and is spreading its influence to other communities off-island. Each step has grown organically, without a plan of action, and each step has proven to be instrumental in the expansion of the original concept.

It is being open to possibility, flexible enough to explore new opportunities hitherto uninspired, that brings new products and uses to the marketplace. At the University of North Carolina at Chapel Hill, a joint program with NC State and a $49 million grant from the National Science Foundation is exploring the use of high-pressure carbon dioxide as a solvent. CO_2 pressurized to 1,000 pounds per square inch at room temperature approaches the density of a liquid and makes it possible for a number of molecules of small polymers to dissolve.

The beauty in exploring possibilities for use of the high-pressurized CO_2 is as diverse as pharmaceuticals, dry cleaning and microelectronics. One characteristic of this pressurized gas is that products no longer need to be rinsed and dried after a chemical bath, thereby conserving water and energy. It is a win-win for efficiency. The pressurized CO_2 not only cleans, but also has the ability to etch circuit patterns on semiconductors. Because the liquid can penetrate infinitely smaller spaces, chips can hold many more circuits.

In 2000, GreenEarth entered into a joint venture with General Electric Silicones as GreenEarth Solutions to change the way dry cleaning is done, all in answer to dry cleaners' dilemma over perchloroethylene, a polluting chemical that contaminates the environment.

The GreenEarth dry cleaning process uses an odorless, gentle, water-based solvent, environmentally friendly, and exhibits no adverse health effects when used properly. Customers can expect "better than ever results" when picking up their dry-cleaned clothing using this process, with no damaged trim or dye bleeding. Since its inception, Procter & Gamble has become a partner of GreenEarth Cleaning along with General Electric.

Since the introduction of the GreenEarth nonpolluting process, cleaners using the process have earned numerous environmental awards, including citations from the U.S. EPA and the states of Colorado, Connecticut, Oregon, Pennsylvania and Wisconsin. Receiving the EPA's Environmental Achievement Award in 2006, Colorado Mountain Cleaners in Silverthorne, Colorado, was cited for "outstanding contributions to environmental protection for operating an innovative and environmentally friendly dry cleaning business which complies with the spirit and intent of the

Pollution Prevention Act."

Green is the conscious path for evolving a more sustainable future, and great strides are being taken in that direction. More and more companies are waking to the benefits going green derives.

CHAPTER TWENTY

FORGING A NEW PATH
Harmony and Conscious Awareness

Throughout history, families worked side by side to grow their food and in some cases, sold or bartered their surplus. Teamwork was a family code. Just like the community of cells that function in the human body, the family is a business with communal responsibilities. In our biology, there are parallels to how the physical universe works that are closely aligned to the workings of business.

The physical body is a family of 50 to 70 trillion cells, more employees than any corporation in the universe. There are cells that differentiate, which means they morph temporarily to carry on body functions, often without interruption, because they know very well how to multitask. If damage control is of major importance, the body has the intelligence to go to the genes, responsible for repair and replication, and engage the process of rebuilding damaged cells to wholeness again.

We have only to look to biology as the mentor of common sense and as a sustainable model for business. Judging life by the color of the skin is only seeing the obvious. Dissecting a seed does not reveal how it knows to grow. In the space around everything and every non-thing is quantum energy. Biology is intelligent, efficient and economically conservative, with no unnecessary functions. Everything is recyclable. There is a harmonious rhythm when nature is in balance. There is also a hum to business when operations flow without a flaw. This symbiotic relationship is the new frontier of business, with the quantum world of potential a major player.

There is also the issue of accepting responsibility for creating the mess we're in, both physically and psychologically, with the expectation that corporations act responsibly. Acting unwisely has brought overpopulation, destruction of nature, pollution, and climate change, among other problems. Since a seared landscape sucked of its resources leaves a bruise on the land and a void felt by neighboring communities and beyond, the question that has plagued humankind from the beginning—whenever that was—is how to live in harmony with each other and with Mother Nature. We have been given the model and the tools, however greed makes it all insolvent. It's even been suggested that if our bodies behaved like some corporations, we'd all be dead.

The New Paradigm We Need

Greed and lack of consciousness have taken a toll much greater than humanity can afford. Old management styles no longer work. The "I-want-what–you-have-and-I-don't-care-how-I-get-it" attitude is on its way out. That is bullying, not negotiating. Intelligent management styles consistent with the new paradigm draw on cooperation.

As Alvin Toffler writes in *The Third Wave*, the commanding presence of behemoth corporations bears little relevance to the challenges top managers face in the changing landscape of a world economy.[1] The current corporate identity crisis, with top-down management styles on one side and individual responsibility on the other, is not unlike the 1980s with their fundamental ecological problems and expanding computer influence, of which Toffler also wrote: "The upheaval in the world economy threatens the survival of the corporation as we know it, throwing its managers into a wholly unfamiliar environment."[2]

More governments are in debt, including the United States, which has sold the company store, tollbooths and national parks to foreign investors, including China, and who knows what else? Consumers struggle with the lures to possess more, eat more and travel more, to invest more and more and more. How many corporations can you have at the top of the food chain in a race to consume the consumer? Insanity in this department seems to be the norm.

Insurrection, suicide bombers and civil unrest exacerbate struggles between governments whose ideologies differ, thwarting corporate handmaidens' efforts to exploit potential markets. Instability threatens the ease of management in industries involved in material assets in affected zones.

When speaking in Seattle at the Forum Foundation's 2006 Social Theology, Education & Citizenship Conference, Efiong Etuk, Nigerian founder of the Global Creativity Network and a Senior Scholar with the nonprofit organization Unity Scholars, and his colleague Niyi Laniyan, Coordinating Consultant to the Nigerian National Assembly, said that Africa is about to join together as a unified whole to drive change across the continent of 800 tribes. Etuk said Africa's dehumanization of life is a tragic disconnect from the rest of creation: rather than liberating the people, what they are experiencing is constraint of human capacities and possibilities. "Poverty in Africa is as much an existential and spiritual deprivation as it is material hardship," he said, "perhaps even more so."

In the case of Iraq, the cost financially and in human terms is equally high. Corruption seems to have no end as the profit-pot boils with advantages too numerous to pass up. It may be years before we know the true extent and cost of this entrenched conflict for oil.

In 2010, the catastrophic explosion of the BP *Deepwater Horizon* oil rig brought a sudden-death debacle to Mother Nature, erupting more than 116 million gallons of oil into the Gulf of Mexico. Much more than an "oil spill" off the coast of Louisiana, this event was compared to Alaska's *Exxon Valdez* disaster as attempts to repair the burst header failed miserably. With little to stop the escalating extent, disrupting hundreds of thousands of lives, oil-covered whales, dolphins, pelicans and other endangered species caught in the thick of it died.

Static-killing the well with cement and mud seems to have done the job, or so it appeared in August 2010, according to an article by Jaquetta White in *The Times-Picayune*. The cleanup could take years. One proven method to extract oil from the water is using straw, which soaks up the oil and returns the water clean, but whether there's enough straw or hay in the world is another question. Hair trimmings provide an abundant resource, recycled into mats that naturally collect oil spills from the oceans, and they are free and sustainable. They are also "waterproof, nonconductive, corrosion free, fire resistant, tough, strong, durable," with amazing strength that can support 8,750 times its own weight, up to 13 tons.[3]

Phil McCrory, a hairstylist from Alabama, came up with this idea when he watched television coverage of the *Exxon Valdez* aftermath and noticed how well Alaskan otters' fur soaked up the oil. He started experimenting with hair cuttings stuffed into his wife's nylon pantyhose. Today, the renewable-resources organization Matter of Trust is collaborating with thousands of salons both in the U.S. and abroad to donate collected hair clippings. According to its Hair for Oil Spills program, salons, animal groomers, fleece farmers, hairy individuals and pet owners can sign up to recycle hair, fur, fleece, feathers and nylons.

Any solution worth its salt is worth trying. When actor Kevin Costner, co-founder of Ocean Therapy Solutions, approached BP with his centrifugal machines, patented as long ago as 1968, to separate the denser water from the oil, BP placed an order for 32 based on his claim that the water coming out would be 99 percent pure.[4]

For the Gulf coastal area's fishing and tourism industries to recover and flourish again will take years. Meanwhile, lives and livelihoods are torn to shreds as bills pile up and funds die. This is a test for lenders whose own livelihoods depend upon the money that can be made, especially with the housing industry debacle still unsettling. The world banking and lending industry depends on money constantly flowing into their coffers. It's worth remembering the vision of Jacque Fresco, who offers another way to develop the world that profits the people rather than soulless institutions.

Frequency of the Future

While new tools are available to bring the world closer, there are also challenges impacting civilization, such as Alaskan icebergs melting in response to Earth's warming, a sure sign that humans have fouled Mother Nature's world. Then there is the eventuality of a pole shift, which will certainly affect the climate. As if that is not enough, an uncertain future is forecast should human folly continue thinking Mother Nature has no limits to her patience. Predictors are threatening that the world could have another great flood, or the Ice Age could return. Who is to say? Clearly, Earth is changing, and some postulate that humans and their activities are partially responsible. Since life is composed of living systems, it's no surprise that Mother Nature is listening to the vibes.

As I mentioned earlier in the book, the High Frequency Active Auroral Research Program (HAARP) at Gakona, Alaska, is a major Arctic facility for upper atmospheric and solar-terrestrial research, jointly owned by the U.S. Navy and Air Force, according to the Office of Public Affairs of the Air Force Research Laboratory at Kirtland AFB in New Mexico.[5] Principal instruments of the research station include a high power, high-frequency (HF) phased array radio transmitter known as the Ionospheric Research Instrument (IRI), which is used to stimulate small well-defined volumes of the ionosphere. There is also an ultra-high frequency (UHF) incoherent scatter radar (ISR) used to measure electron densities, electron and ion temperatures, and Doppler velocities in the stimulated region and in the natural ionosphere. To further the scientific capabilities and usefulness of the IRI and ISR, HAARP is supporting the design and installation of the latest in modern geophysical research instruments. This includes an HF ionosonde, ELF and VLF receivers, magnetometers, riometers, a LIDAR (Light Detection And Ranging), optical and infrared spectrometers and cameras used to observe the complex natural variations of Alaska's ionosphere, as well as to detect artificial effects produced by the IRI.

The disturbing effects of HAARP are addressed in *Angels Don't Play This Haarp* (Earthpulse Press, 1995), a book authored by Jeane Manning and Nick Begich, Ph.D. They say this new system "manipulates the environment in a way which can disrupt human mental processes, jam all global communications systems, change weather condition patterns over large areas, interfere with wildlife migration patterns, negatively affect your health and unnaturally impact the Earth's upper atmosphere."

Then there's scalar interferometry—longitudinal EM energy that fills the vacuum of space, the time domain of "space-time", time as compressed energy, $E=tc^2$, waves of time, phase conjugate wave pairs, energy from the vacuum that can be used for healing or weaponry. This subject is much too deep for the scope of this book, and for anyone interested, I refer you to cheniere.org. However, this is quantum energy, a powerful force that in day-to-day operations of business and healing can improve relationships and confirm the power of thought to manifest according to the law of attraction.

"Electric power is everywhere present in unlimited quantities and can drive the world's machinery without the need of coal, oil, gas, or any other of the common fuels," writes Nikola Tesla.

"At any point and at any time, one can freely and inexpensively extract enormous EM energy flows directly from the active vacuum itself," confirms physicist Tom Bearden, Ph.D.[6]

The surge to find water on other planets may be a way to make sure there is an escape plan when this planet is no longer habitable. All the money expended will assure a spot when Earth's resources have been fully exploited and there is no place else to go. It feels like we have been through this before. Noah and the Ark immediately come to mind. What about Atlantis now buried beneath the sea? How can we save Mother Earth this time? Will old-time religion save us, or condemn us to the hell we are experiencing in the cradle of civilization? Only time will tell.

With the current corporate model, it seems unlikely that we will see the light of peaceful coexistence any time soon, given the level of Alexandrian-style nation-conquering for resources. That is an old management style that no longer works. It is going to take intelligent management drawing upon wisdom and love for all of mankind to give us the ideal model for growth. Humanity is in this together. We either sink or swim in the coming tidal wave triggered by irresponsibility and the urge to control world markets to increase profits. Some corporations may be on the verge of choking on their own gluttony.

Looking to link progress with intelligent leadership means that change is inevitable if we are to continue in any sensible direction. Given right thinking, everyone will be able to breathe clean air, drink clean water and live with a clear conscience. How about you—is your life and business on the right track to make the world a better place in which to live?

We acknowledge that growth is essential, though not necessarily equated with the acquisition of money as a pure goal. Growth is the act of increasing awareness of the environment, local and global, doing the right thing for the right reason. It is seeing benefits and rewards that might otherwise be missed. Growth in awareness is about an increased understanding that lends itself well to a sense of community. Most everyone agrees it is not a good thing to step all over your competition, or to emotionally dismantle egos to get ahead, as some people have been doing.

INNOVATION RULES

China has a critical need to house its people and must depend upon architects' analysis. As one architect states, if conventional building materials were used in China, all the natural resources in the world would be depleted, so expansive is the need. With this heightened awareness of environmental impact, innovative architects are including green roofs in their plans, even recycling demolished building materials to strengthen structures. They are also using recycled bottles as insulation for glass walls, as well as recycling gray water for new air circulation systems, a sign of designing responsibly. To see progress focused on concern for humanity and environmental sustainability in fresh statements of creativity is gratifying, evidence that definitely points the world in an enlightened direction.

I still get excited when I think about the inspiring e^2 *design* PBS series sponsored by Autodesk that I saw in 2006. The four-part series focused on architectural innovations that incorporate green principles, featuring architects from Chicago to New York to China and Singapore thoughtfully recycling usable scrap materials from building debris to use where needed in new construction, such as ground support for new cement. This has additional benefits in reducing the impact of waste on transfer stations while cleaning up the air, as well as enhancing the landscape with new building design. The idea is rapidly emerging as an accepted model for future design considerations. Like McDonough, Braungart and Fresco inventing the future through design with a vision of the possible, this series brought architectural innovations incorporating green principles front and center.

The driver of innovation is the experiential directive for personal satisfaction. Firing enthusiasm is the sense of fulfillment in seeing projects such as these through to completion. Teamwork's division of responsibilities expands awareness of the possible, and is essential for multifaceted projects to succeed. In government, business or families, many hands make light work for all are structured teams and function best when sharing a common vision.

Whether it is community service or exercising compassion in the workplace, it is experience after experience building confidence and a great repertoire from which all can continue to draw. If you are an executive or entrepreneurial risk-taker, you qualify because of your experience. You are valued for what you bring to the company, your knowledge, enthusiasm and charisma. It is what you learn along the way and can bring to the table that makes you valuable.

No one person has all the answers. Every one of us is a composite of unique experiences and acquired knowledge useful to creative problem solving. We come together to share our gifts and a common goal, whether in resolving conflict, meeting a new challenge or creating new products.

True, technology is bringing the world closer together. What we perceive as a large world has suddenly grown smaller. We are learning how to get along with people whose vision of the world differs from our own developed model. We are fast realizing that we share humanity's common needs and goals. Life experience differs and so do beliefs. As we reach out across the globe, gaps in education narrow. Yet business and the business of the body remain the same. No matter the culture, conscious awareness is key to life and business sustainability, growth and each venture's success.

CHAPTER TWENTY-ONE

EVOLUTION AT RISK
A Challenge for the Future

Most will agree that the Earth and its inhabitants are in serious trouble. Every living entity is in decline. Once unlimited natural resources are being depleted. With abuse and man-made pollution, the entire biosphere and ecosystem are endangered. It has been called "generational tyranny": poor stewardship and inhuman manipulation of the food supply, as seen in terminator seeds, by corporate entities with their headstrong desire to control life for a price. Perhaps terminator seeds will be responsible for the end times that the Hopi prophesied. Perhaps that is the intended consequence. As big business deals inhuman cards of fate for species they exploit, they deal a blow to nature and her evolving spirit, leaving a terrible legacy of proportional destruction that may take millions of years to undo. It is the age-old battle between good and evil, played out on the real-life stage instead of at the big-screen movie house.

If mankind's survival is dependent upon the greenhouse for food production, with winds blowing genetically manipulated pollen and seeds into farmers' fields, will Mother Nature use her own methods to thwart the inevitable consequences? Without environmental vision, myopic corporations are destroying the Earth's living systems, taking from nature without giving back. That is greed at its worst, with devastating consequences. Unless we save the legacy of natural abundance, the future of mankind living on this beautiful planet is questionable. It is obvious some products should not be produced, because they are not in the best interests of living systems' survival. Plundering the planet for monetary profit, power and influence is misdirected energy and some say that motive is maniacal. Others call it irresponsibility as a human being.

Environmental activist Bill McKibben has written a number of books on living well as a conscious human being responsible for our planet's health and well-being. Having heart for nature and each other is critical for an evolving spirit. As poet Robert Bly said on Bill Moyers's PBS television show, "Only a greedy spirit would go to war."

Taking Back Our Power

The age-old nurture/nature viewpoints remain at the center of the debate. Even in U.S. political parties, as George Lakoff writes in the best-seller *Don't Think of an Elephant!*, the conservative view of the world is seen through the colored glasses of a "strict father" prototype, disciplinarian, self-reliant and forceful in defense. Contrast that with the progressive view of a supportive "nurturant parent", emphasizing mutual responsibility. It is the same right-brain/left-brain thinking, the male-female dichotomy that continues to fill the pages of psychology books.

Studies show that you cannot be in growth and protection at the same time, because they are polar opposites. Growth is regenerative, part of the evolutionary process. Protection is hiding and fighting, fueled by fear.[1]

As Frances Moore Lappé, author of *You Have the Power: Choosing Courage in a Culture of Fear* (Tarcher/Penguin, 2004), suggests, what is needed is a model beyond the hierarchy of the nuclear family, taking the best of both and adding some new dimensions. She says the big shift underway bests the strict-father/soft-mother approach and breaks it into three areas.

First is the advancement of communication technologies: the world is as close to us as our living-room television set and computer screen. We are now aware of the devastation of cultures whose beliefs differ from our own by those who view opposing viewpoints as a threat to their perceived power. Through the miracle of computers, cell phones and satellites, information is transmitted instantly. The world is an open book laying bare the devastation of natural forces as well as man's inhumanity to man. It gets harder and harder to conceal the truth of injustice in starving countries like Darfur and the Sudan, and the inhumane mutilation of women's genitals after the men have their way with them. In Eastern Congo, hundreds of thousands, from children as young as 3 years to women of 75, are gang-raped.[2]

Surely, it would be a different story and a different world if it were the men whose genitals were mutilated? There is not a man born who didn't come through a woman. How dare they behave this way?

The World Trade Center attack on 9/11/2001 and the uncomfortable war in Iraq are stark reminders of the ignorance and injustice that still exist in the world. No one is immune to the emotional grief gripping families embroiled in combat. The stark reality of war portrayed by images on the evening news shocks our senses. Crumbled lives, starvation and primitive living conditions amid destruction act as warnings that this could become a greater threat if differences in perspectives and perceptions are not soon resolved.

Second, the ecological revolution awakens awareness of misspent energies in wasteful polluting of land and waters, and invites humane consciousness to the table for a discussion of what to do about it.

Third is the "revolution in human dignity". All of us are responsible for our construct of reality, how we see the world through our mind's eye, often formulated by tradition, family training and news whose views we depend upon. Humans can usually manage themselves better than might be expected. As communities speak out against the top-down management style of nation, city or state rule through active participation in planning, they join together in efforts that work for everyone, not just the privileged few with a bigger house and more money in the bank. As Lappé points out, "'regular' citizens have the capacity for self-governance, but...without their engagement our huge global crises cannot be addressed."

There is more than personal survival at stake. It is whether humans will participate as a society, owning up to the problem-solving challenges as stakeholders to enact changes that benefit everyone. More people are stepping up to the plate and batting the ball on the field of negotiation, protesting the insanity of GMOs, the privatization of water and chemical pollution by greedy consortiums whose only cares in the world are money, power and influence.

The revolution in open-source software that anyone can use without violating any proprietary Microsoft rights, with the blessing of its pioneer, Richard Stallman, creator of the GNU/Linux system, is an example of the mutual help and mutual learning inherent in cooperative communities.

Other examples are the farmers' markets springing up all over the U.S. in answer to the public's cries for organic food, spawned by outrage over

GMO companies' attempt to control our food supply. Restaurants now feature local produce and homegrown varieties through alliances with farmers. The family garden is flourishing. Some schools have vegetable gardens to teach students how to grow food so that they can feed themselves. Even on a small scale, these actions have a profound effect on reducing the total consumption of bio-engineered foods that corrupt the human gene pool.

The public is responding favorably by assuming responsibility and control over their lives, speaking loudly through their actions. In the 1976 film *Network*, the emotional explosion of a New York news anchor expressing his frustration over network policies—"I'm mad as hell, and I'm not going to take this anymore"—was a demonstration of what happens when people hit the wall of unfair compliance standards in the corporate world. Even today, mainstream television and radio commercials continue hammering away to convince viewers that their products are the best on the market and to live without them is impossible. Repetitious ads act as mantras, lulling the senses into believing their latest product will cure your ailments, real or imagined. Advertising agencies are smart about what ad works, because it is their business. Programming the audience to believe one drug is better than another is simply competitive practice. One must be alert to these gimmicks and mute the sound or turn off the station to preserve sanity. Relating to the same frustration as the news anchor in *Network*, we too can open our minds and echo his cry of protestation.

When humanity gets the message, they will come to the fore. They will embrace the role of responsible citizenry willing to take charge of their lives. They will take an active part in effecting necessary change, heightening environmental awareness and promoting responsible community governance.

In my own community, property owners protested the top-down management style of county government and the Growth Management board when land use and development controls became an issue. The community was outraged when only one meeting was planned for discussion. The county building's meeting room was much too small for the turnout, as people swarmed in droves to line the walls five deep once all the chairs were filled. Protest after protest brought the commissioners' decision to break it up into multiple meetings to involve more citizens taking to heart unfair rules made by those who did not live in the area. Everyone had a chance to voice their protestations and all were recorded for review.

The end result was that the county sued the Growth Management board and a moratorium was called until the matter was resolved. Meanwhile, development stalled.

New Leadership Models

Moving from one-to-many directives to the many-to-many mutuality of personal investiture is the hallmark of new leadership models that embrace involvement through active participation. We see the success of this idea in the U.S. Army's implementation of Action-Learning Teams and Dick Spady's Opinionnaire that fairly reports how people feel about things, more reliable than taking a vote.

We see progress in what Ari Cowan is doing with his reframing program for offenders whose increasing numbers are staggering commentary on the inequities existing in America and the sickness of our country's prisons. Like Cowan's model for civility and healing the mixed-up minds of offenders, corporations might also use his technique to deal with greed. Rehabilitate the corporate body by instilling life as a viable value, especially since the corporation operates as a living entity.

With consumption and the ease of credit, many people are living on borrowed time while the stock market plays cat-and-mouse with corporate profits. Never has the buying drive been so pervasive. For many, days are spent wanting more and more that's bigger and better to assuage a sense of not being enough. Measured against the wealthy, we think we will be wealthy too when we have enough of what they have—as if that measure of wealth in the broad sense is truth. When the last bell rings, we will be assessed, not by the amount of money we made in a lifetime, but by our character as individuals and the good that we did. Brooke Astor died at 105 to leave a legacy of good works that made her a giant in society. She used her money to build a better city, a better environment. She loved being a benefactor to the arts, and she is an example of the right use of wealth. What will be your legacy?

The times in which we are living demand a lot from all of us. Increasing uncertainty about the future seems to make many people edgy. And with good reason, as we watch the news. How do we maintain a stable presence in the midst of perceived chaos hammered each day into our psyche? Even the U.S. government is off course in directing the country. Leadership is misguided and a course correction is in order. Perhaps in the course of history there has never been more chaos. The chessboard is in disarray and confusion reigns. There are no winners. Desperate for the game to end, people clamor for sanity and order.

We see effects in the physical body, with all manner of disease emanating around us, and perceive the environment as threatening. Advertisers' continual bombardment implying we need their products to be whole is an attempt to unseat the inner wise counsel that has the right answer for each of us. Living systems are intelligent. We may comfort ourselves by knowing that out of chaos order does come, but right now, the world is desperate for leaders who can lead, as Lee Iacocca asserts.

The tug-of-war in the automobile industry to maximize profits and performance while being good environmentalists is best explained by Bill Ford in the new direction Ford Motor Company is taking. Inspired design by architect William McDonough and Michael Braungart to make "cradle to cradle" products that turn waste into food is a huge step forward in aligning with Mother Nature. Taking control of your health is another giant step forward. Tending to your mind and your body, as would a good gardener, removes dependency on a health-care system gone awry. You can help by aligning priorities with healthy choices, refusing to buy genetically modified foods, being a good steward of the land and loving all people for the best that is within them.

Every human being and every corporation worth their salt has an obligation to do the right thing for the right reason. Accountability is essential, especially when it comes to the survival of Mother Earth and her creations. Since perception is key to growth and sustainability, without conscious awareness and accountability of the impact corporations and its people play in the creative drama, there can be no future. So, what will be your legacy? Will it be that you followed a false prophet for personal gain or that you did the right thing for the right reason, adhering to the principles of regeneration authentically to preserve the beauty and sustainability of all life?

As you accept responsibility for your actions, you grow into the kind of self-responsible human being you are meant to be. Pay attention to the signals. Develop keen awareness of your actions and their consequences. Be conscious that you are doing the right thing for the right reason. With this in mind, you'll be led to take the high road and be glad that you did.

Notes

Chapter One: Planetary Crisis

1. Jane Perlez and Raymond Bonner, "Below a Mountain of Wealth, a River of Waste," *New York Times*, December 27, 2005.
2. ibid.
3. Bob Herbert, "In America; Sweatshop Beneficiaries," *New York Times*, July 24, 1995.

Chapter Two: Pay-Ups and Payoffs

1. LawBuzz, http://www.lawbuzz.com/.
2. MesoLink.org, http://www.mesolink.org/.
3. "EPA, DuPont Settle Teflon Lawsuit," CBS News, November 29, 2005.

Chapter Four: Creativism

1. *The Hindustan Times*, March 7, 2006.
2. Bill & Melinda Gates Foundation, "Education Strategy," http://www.gatesfoundation.org/united-states/Pages/education-strategy.aspx.
3. Tiger Woods Foundation, http://web.tigerwoodsfoundation.org/programs/twlc/index.
4. William McCall, "Sleep essential for creative thinking, survey says," Associated Press Archive, January 21, 2004.
5. Christopher Ketcham, "Snooze, You Win," *Men's Journal*, January 2006.
6. McCall, "Sleep essential for creative thinking, survey says".
7. John Schwartz, "Always on the Job, Employees Pay with Health," *New York Times*, September 5, 2004.
8. Yoko Kubota and Chang-Ran Kim, "Court rules employee worked to death," Reuters, November 30, 2007.
9. Hugo Westerlund et al., "Workplace Expansion and Cardiovascular Disease." Paper presented at the International Congress of Health Fourth Annual Conference on Work Environment and Cardiovascular Diseases, Newport Beach, CA, March 9–11, 2005.
10. Janice K. Kiecolt-Glaser, Ph.D., et al., "Hostile Marital Interactions, Proinflammatory Cytokine Production, and Wound Healing," *Archives of General Psychiatry* 62 (December 2005):1377–1384.

11. "Happy marriage 'helps fight flu,'" BBC News, November 8, 2005, http://news.bbc.co.uk/2/hi/health/4417428.stm.

12. Patricia Aburdene, *Megatrends 2010* (Charlottesville, VA: Hampton Roads, 2007), 24.

13. Milton Friedman, "The Social Responsibility of Business Is to Increase Its Profits," *New York Times Magazine*, September 13, 1970.

14. "Rethinking the Social Responsibility of Business: A *Reason* debate featuring Milton Friedman, Whole Foods' John Mackey, and Cypress Semiconductor's T. J. Rodgers," *Reason*, October 2005, http://reason.com/archives/2005/10/01/rethinking-the-social-responsi.

15. Ceres, "Ceres Network Companies," http://www.ceres.org//Page.aspx?pid=426.

Chapter Five: Progress on the Move

1. Larry Lipman, "Many workers lack health coverage," *Atlanta Journal-Constitution*, May 6, 2004.

2. Institute of Medicine (IOM), "To Err Is Human: Building a Safer Health System," November 1, 1999.

3. Massachusetts State Board of Registration in Pharmacy.

4. Jonathan V. Wright, "Are errors along the medical 'assembly line' costing you your health?" Health Sciences Institute, June 29, 2004.

5. *Minneapolis/St. Paul Business Journal*, February 16, 2006.

6. "Medical Errors: The Scope of the Problem," Fact sheet, Publication No. AHRQ 00-PO37, Agency for Healthcare Research and Quality, Rockville, MD.

7. "Not that leg! New rules to fight surgery errors," Associated Press, June 29, 2004; http://www.news.com.au/story/0,23599,22968749-13762,00.html.

8. ibid.

9. Jim Giles, "Scientists behaving badly," *Nature*, March 4, 2004.

10. Editorial, "Disclosure at the Medical Journals," *New York Times*, September 30, 2003.

11. Linda A. Johnson, "Conflicts of interest taint drug guidelines, groups say," *Seattle Times*, July 17, 2004.

12. Chris Gupta, "The spooky reality behind drug-related 'news,'" http://www.newmediaexplorer.org/chris/2003/10/09/the_spooky_reality_behind_drugrelated_news.htm.

13. Kevin P. Casey, "When Trust in Doctors Erodes, Other Treatments Fill the Void," *New York Times*, February 3, 2006.

14. Editorial, "When Drug Companies Hide Data," *New York Times*, June 6, 2004.

15. Barry Meier, "Glaxo Plans Public Listing of Drug Trials on Web Site," *New York Times*, June 19, 2004.

16. Bernard Meunier, "Catalytic Degradation of Chlorinated Phenols," *Science* 296, no. 5566 (April 12, 2002), 270–271, DOI: 10/1126/science/1070976.

Chapter Six: Collaboration

1. Elaine Smitha, *If You Make the Rules, How Come You're Not Boss?* (Charlottesville, VA: Hampton Roads, 2004), 85–86.
2. Smitha, *If You Make the Rules, How Come You're Not Boss?*, 87.
3. Rupert Sheldrake, *Seven Experiments That Could Change the World* (London: Fourth Estate Limited, 1994), 35.
4. ibid.
5. Julius Fast, *Body Language* (New York: Pocket Books, 1970), 21–25.
6. Lewis Thomas, *The Lives of a Cell*, (New York: Viking, 1974).
7. Amit Goswami, Ph.D., *Physics of the Soul* (Charlottesville, VA: Hampton Roads, 2001), footnote p. 220.

Chapter Seven: Green Is the New Frontier

1. E. J. Dionne, "Paging Walter Reuther," *Seattle Times*, November 3, 2005.
2. Reed Abelson and Jonathan D. Glater, "Suit Challenges Hospital Bills of Uninsured," *New York Times*, June 17, 2004.
3. Clifford Krauss, "Canada Looks for Ways to Fix Its Health Care System," *New York Times*, September 12, 2004.
4. Micheline Maynard, "Ford Seeking a Future by Going Backward," *New York Times*, July 17, 2007.
5. Dionne, "Paging Walter Reuther."
6. Steve Lohr, "Outsourcing Is Climbing Skills Ladder," *New York Times*, February 16, 2004.
7. Anne Underwood, "Designing the Future," interview with William McDonough, *Newsweek*, May 15, 2005, www.newsweek.com/id/52058.
8. William McDonough website, http://www.mcdonough.com/.
9. Steven Barrie-Anthony, "A natural, inside and out," *Los Angeles Times*, January 6, 2005.
10. Judy Newman, "Zapping waste for a profit," *Wisconsin State Journal*, November 22, 2006.
11. Keiko Morris, "Selling a kinder touch of clean," *Newsday*, July 30, 2006.
12. Interface, Inc., press release, "2008 Ford Escape Hybrid Features InterfaceFABRIC Interior," http://www.csrwire.com/press/press_release/25533-2008-Ford-Escape-Hybrid-Features-InterfaceFABRIC-Interior.
13. Dennis Nishi, "A Builder of Castles Made of Trash," *Wall Street Journal*, June 16, 2009.
14. International Energy Agency, *Renewables in Global Energy Supply: An IEA Fact Sheet*, January 2007.

15. Mark Z. Jacobson, "Review of solutions to global warming, air pollution and energy security," *Energy & Environmental Science*, 2009, issue 2, 148–173.

Chapter Eight: The Nature of Leadership

1. Peter Drucker, "Trusting the teacher in the grey-flannel suit," *Economist*, November 17, 2005, http://www.economist.com/node/5165460.
2. Bruce LaRue, *Leading Organizations from the Inside Out* (Hoboken, NJ: Wiley, 2004).
3. Bill Witherspoon, as told to Leigh Buchanan, "How to Build a Beautiful Company," *Inc.*, June 8, 2010, http://www.inc.com/top-workplaces/2010/how-to-build-a-beautiful-company.html.
4. Dee Hock, *Birth of the Chaordic Age* (San Francisco: Berrett-Koehler, 2000).
5. Lee Iacocca with Catherine Whitney, *Where Have All the Leaders Gone?* (New York: Scribner, 2007).
6. William New, "Collapse of WTO Talks Washes Away Hope for TRIPS Changes," *Intellectual Property Watch*, July 29, 2008, http://www.ip-watch.org/weblog/index.php?p=1181.
7. David Korten, *The Great Turning: From Empire to Earth Community* (San Francisco: Berrett-Koehler, 2006), 59.

Chapter Nine: Invention and Performance

1. Lemelson-MIT Program, Inventor of the Week, "Art Fry & Spencer Silver," http://web.mit.edu/invent/iow/frysilver.html.
2. Jui Chakravorty, "Toyota joined the 'Big Three' in 2006," Reuters, January 3, 2007, http://www.reuters.com/article/2007/01/04/us-autos-sales-idUSN0339857020070104.
3. Bill Vlasic, "The Road Ahead for Ford Is Full of Smaller Cars," *New York Times*, July 24, 2008, http://www.nytimes.com/2008/07/24/business/24ford.html.
4. Sony Pictures Classics, http://www.sonyclassics.com/whokilledtheelectriccar/.
5. Soyoung Kim, "Ford, Microsoft align to recharge cars," Reuters, March 31, 2010, http://www.reuters.com/article/2010/03/31/us-autoshow-ford-microsoft-idUSTRE62U3EX20100331.
6. Jerry Hirsch, "GM to recall about 1.5 million vehicles because of fire hazard," *Los Angeles Times*, June 9, 2010.
7. Altshuller Institute for TRIZ Studies, http://www.aitriz.org/.
8. "Inside the Google Empire," *Time*, February 12, 2006.
9. Emily Eakin, "How to Save the World? Treat It Like a Business," *New York Times*, December 20, 2003.

Chapter Ten: The Business of DNA

1. "Breaking the Four Minute Mile," interview with Sir Roger Bannister, Academy of Achievement, June 7, 2002.
2. Michael Hopkin, "Man breaks world records with Antarctic swim," *Nature*, December 19, 2005.
3. "Swimming," About.com, http://swimming.about.com/od/swimhistoryandstars/a/antarctic_swim.htm.
4. NewsFeedResearcher.com, June 29, 2007.
5. "Singapore plans audacious new twisting bridge," Reuters, March 6, 2006.
6. Mark Dowie, "Biotech critics at risk: Economics calls the shots in the debate," *San Francisco Chronicle*, January 11, 2004.
7. Smitha, *If You Make the Rules, How Come You're Not Boss?*
8. Peter Tyson, "The Hippocratic Oath Today," *NOVA*, http://www.pbs.org/wgbh/nova/doctors/oath.html.
9. Vandana Shiva, *Stolen Harvest* (Cambridge, MA: South End Press, 2000), 10.
10. Leora Broydo, "A Seedy Business," *Mother Jones Online*, April 6, 1998, http://motherjones.com/politics/1998/04/seedy-business
11. Shiva, *Stolen Harvest*, 82.
12. Shiva, *Stolen Harvest*, 63.
13. ibid.
14. Beverly Bell, "Haitian Farmers Commit to Burning Monsanto Hybrid Seeds," *Truthout*, May 18, 2010, http://www.truth-out.org/.
15. Wangari Maathai, "The Linkage between Patenting of Life Forms, Genetic Engineering and Food Insecurity," November 20, 2004.
16. Colin Tudge, "Why we don't need GM foods," *New Statesman*, February 19, 1999.
17. Jeffrey Smith, *Seeds of Deception: Exposing Industry and Government Lies about the Safety of the Genetically Engineered Foods You're Eating* (Fairfield, IA: Yes! Books, 2003) and *Genetic Roulette: The Documented Health Risks of Genetically Engineered Foods* (Chelsea, VT: Chelsea Green, 2007).

Chapter Eleven: Innovation and Intention

1. Online Encyclopedia, article on Howard Schultz, http://encyclopedia.jrank.org/articles/pages/6337/Schultz-Howard.html.
2. "Forbidden City Starbucks closes," BBC News, July 14, 2007, http://news.bbc.co.uk/2/hi/asia-pacific/6898629.stm.
3. Starbucks Coffee Company, "Working at Starbucks," http://www.starbucks.com/career-center/working-at-starbucks.
4. Changing World Technologies, Inc., http://www.changingworldtech.com/press_room/.

5. Mississippi State University, "Scientist Seeks Ways to Squeeze More Oil out of Existing Wells," *ScienceDaily*, April 11, 2008, http://www.sciencedaily.com/releases/2008/04/080409204618.htm.

6. Bob Herbert, "An Unnatural Disaster," *New York Times*, May 29, 2010.

7. Matthew L. Wald, "The Energy Challenge; Gassing Up with Garbage," *New York Times*, July 24, 2008.

8. Millennium Park website, http://www.millenniumpark.net/.

9. Arcosanti, "Arcology Theory," http://www.arcosanti.org/theory/arcology/main.html.

10. "Review: SimCity 3000," Classic Gaming, http://classicgaming.gamespy.com/View.php?view=Articles.Detail&id=305.

11. Erica Gies, "Sustainable living through one man's architecture," Environmental News Network, January 4, 2002.

12. Anna Salleh, "Nanotech windows to conduct electricity," ABC News Online, August 19, 2005, http://www.abc.net.au/science/articles/2005/08/19/1440828.htm.

13. Julie Steenhuysen, "Scientists make advances on 'nano' electronics," Reuters, February 18, 2009.

14. ibid.

15. Michelle R. Smith, "Fears grow that tiny particles may pose major health risks," *Seattle Times*, December 12, 2005.

16. Yale University, "Nanomaterials May Have Large Environmental Footprint," *ScienceDaily*, October 23, 2008, http://www.sciencedaily.com/releases/2008/10/081022135805.htm.

17. Intention Experiment website, http://www.theintentionexperiment.com/.

Chapter Twelve: Serving Mankind's Needs

1. Hock, *Birth of the Chaordic Age*.

2. Ari Cowan website, http://www.aricowan.net/.

3. Jenna Goudreau, "Dispatches from the War on Stress: Business begins to reckon with the enormous costs of workplace angst," *BusinessWeek*, August 6, 2007, http://www.businessweek.com/magazine/content/07_32/b4045061.htm.

4. Jonathan Standing, "Hon Hai to raise China wages after spate of suicides," Reuters, May 28, 2010.

5. "Survey: Performance evaluations more frequent," *Business Examiner Daily*, August 22, 2007.

6. Goudreau, "Dispatches from the War on Stress."

7. ibid.

8. Steve Lohr, "The Crowd Is Wise (When It's Focused)," *New York Times*, July 19, 2009.

Chapter Thirteen: Global Awareness

1. T. E. Bearden, Ph.D, *Energy from the Vacuum* (Santa Barbara, CA: Cheniere Press, 2002).
2. Ohio State University, "How Water 'Lubricates' Proteins," *ScienceDaily*, November 17, 2007, http://www.sciencedaily.com/releases/2007/11/071114130440.htm.
3. Jonathan Fildes, "Physics promises wireless power," BBC News, November 15, 2006, http://news.bbc.co.uk/2/hi/6129460.stm.
4. "Avure's high pressure system speeds up process," *Food Production Daily*, July 22, 2005, http://www.foodproductiondaily.com/Processing/Avure-s-high-pressure-system-speeds-up-process.
5. Janet Adamy, "High-Pressure Process Helps Keep Food Bacteria-Free," *Wall Street Journal*, February 17, 2005.
6. Read Right Systems website, http://www.readright.com/.
7. Heiner Wesemann, *Papua-Neuguinea: Steinzeit-Kulturen auf dem Weg ins 20. Jahrhundert* [Papua New Guinea: Stone-Age Cultures on Their Way into the 20th Century] (Köln: DuMont Buchverlag, 1985), 264, quoted in Ton Otto and Robert J. Verloop, "The Asaro Mudmen," *The Contemporary Pacific* 8, no. 2 (Fall 1996): 349–386.
8. Simon Harrison, "Ritual as Intellectual Property," *Man (NS)* 27:235, quoted in Otto and Verloop, "The Asaro Mudmen."

Chapter Fourteen: Bottom-Line Trends

1. Bethany McLean and Peter Elkin, "Partners in Crime," *Fortune*, October 27, 2003, 78.
2. Jyoti Thottam, "Wal-Mart's Bank Shot," *Time*, April 24, 2006.
3. Editorial, "The Truth about Coal," *New York Times*, February 25, 2007.
4. WRAP website, http://www.wrap.org.uk/.
5. Sharon Pian Chan, "Seattle approves bag fee and foam ban," *Seattle Times*, July 28, 2008; Phuong Le, "Seattle voters reject 20-cent grocery bag fee," *Seattle Times*, August 18, 2009.
6. Clint Witchalls, "Plastic carriers: Nasty old bags," *Independent (UK)*, September 26, 2005.
7. Kristine Owram, "Teen's recycling recipe bags award," *Record (Kitchener, ON)*, July 2, 2008.
8. Abid Aslam, "Bottled Water: Nectar of the Frauds?" *OneWorld*, February 5, 2006, http://us.oneworld.net/.
9. Vandana Shiva, *Water Wars: Privatization, Pollution, and Profit* (Cambridge, MA: South End Press, 2000), 10.
10. Katie Scott, "Irrigation system can grow crops with salt water," *Wired UK*, May 1, 2009, http://www.wired.co.uk/news/archive/2009-05/01/irrigation-system-can-grow-crops-with-salt-water.

11. Jamilla El-Shafei, "Another town says no to Nestlé," *Socialist Worker,* March 18, 2009, http://socialistworker.org/2009/03/18/another-town-says-no-to-nestle.

Chapter Fifteen: Quantum Mind and Business

1. Max Planck Institute, "First Quantum Teleportation Between Light and Matter," *SpaceRef,* October 5, 2006, http://www.spaceref.com/news/viewpr.html?pid=20993.
2. Hiroko Tabuchi, "Hitachi: Move the train with your brain," Associated Press, June 22, 2007.
3. "Magnetic Control: Tongue Drive System Allows Individuals with Disabilities to Operate Powered Wheelchairs and Computers," Georgia Tech Research News, June 30, 2008, http://gtresearchnews.gatech.edu/newsrelease/tongue-drive.htm.
4. ICT Results, "Virtual Smart Home Controlled by Your Thoughts," *ScienceDaily,* May 26, 2009, http://www.sciencedaily.com/releases/2009/05/090511091733.htm.
5. F. David Peat, *Superstrings and the Search for the Theory of Everything* (New York: McGraw-Hill, 1989), 7.
6. David Hawkins, M.D., Ph.D., *Power vs. Force: The Hidden Determinants of Human Behavior,* (Carlsbad, CA: Hay House, 2002), 125.
7. Robert O. Becker, M.D., *The Body Electric: Electromagnetism and the Foundation of Life* (New York: Morrow, 1985), 204.
8. Privacy International, "Radio-Frequency Identification (RFID)," http://www.privacyinternational.org/article.shtml?cmd[347]=x-347-559094
9. Smitha, *If You Make the Rules, How Come You're Not Boss?*
10. Sora Song, "Mind over Medicine," *Time,* March 27, 2006, http://www.time.com/time/magazine/article/0,9171,1174707,00.html.
11. Laurie Tarkan, "Brain Surgery, Without Knife or Blood, Gains Favor," *New York Times,* April 29, 2003.
12. Sidney B. Lang et al., "Piezoelectricity in the human pineal gland," *Bioelectrochemistry and Bioenergetics* 41, no. 2 (December 1996): 191–195.
13. David Klenerman et al., "Direct and sensitive detection of a human virus by rupture event scanning," *Nature Biotechnology* 19, no. 9 (September 2001): 823-824, 833-837
14. Sharon Begley, "The Unconscious 'You' May Be the Wiser Half," *Wall Street Journal,* August 30, 2002, http://online.wsj.com/article/SB1030644674233767915.html.
15. ibid.
16. Gareth Cook, "'Follow your gut,' study advises on big decisions," *Boston Globe,* February 17, 2006. See also http://www.medrants.com/index.php/archives/2723.

17. Tania Singer et al., "Empathy for pain involves the affective but not the sensory components of pain," *Science* 303, no. 5661 (February 20, 2004): 1157–1162, and Tor D. Wager et al., "Placebo-induced changes in fMRI in the anticipation and experience of pain," *Science* 303 (2004): 1162–1167.
18. "Delusions of Feeling Better," *New York Times*, March 19, 2003.

Chapter Sixteen: Brain Power and Connections

1. Daniel Golden, "Building a Better Brain," *Life*, July 1994.
2. "Age, exercise may boost memory," CNN.com, November 25, 2003, http://articles.cnn.com/2003-10-17/health/improve.memory_1_memory-function-intelligent-memory-brain?_s=PM:HEALTH.
3. Laura L. Colgin and Edvard I. Moser, "Neuroscience: Rewinding the Memory Record," *Nature*, March 30, 2006, 615–617; David J. Foster and Matthew A. Wilson, "Reverse replay of behavioural sequences in hippocampal place cells during the awake state," *Nature*, March 30, 2006, 680–683.
4. John Gatto, *Dumbing Us Down: The Hidden Curriculum of Compulsory Schooling* (Gabriola Island, BC: New Society Publishers, 1992).

Chapter Seventeen: Socratic Method

1. Win Wenger, Ph.D., "Effective Problem-Solving: Using What We Know," *Winsights* no. 72, January 2004, http://www.winwenger.com/part72.htm.
2. Creative Problem Solving Institute website, http://www.cpsiconference.com/home.cfm.
3. Richard J. Spady and Richard S. Kirby in collaboration with Cecil H. Bell, Jr., *The Leadership of Civilization Building* (Seattle: Forum Foundation, 2002).
4. National Coalition for Dialogue & Deliberation website, http://www.ncdd.org/.
5. Dynamic Facilitation Associates website, http://dynamicfacilitation.com/.
6. "The World Wisdom Council," Wisdom Page, http://wisdompage.com/worldwisdomcouncil.html.
7. World Café website, http://www.theworldcafe.com/.

Chapter Eighteen: Energetic Fields of Influence

1. Bearden, *Energy from the Vacuum*. See also http://www.cheniere.org/.

Chapter Nineteen: Turning Green with Pride

1. "Planners see gold in brownfields," *Globe and Mail*, November 25, 2003.

2. U.S. Conference of Mayors, "Brownfields," http://www.mayors.org/brownfields/.

3. U.S. Conference of Mayors, press release, "Brownfields Report Shows Untapped Potential for Redevelopment in the Nation's Cities," www.usmayors.org/74thAnnualMeeting/brownfields_060506.pdf.

4. Editorial, "From Brownfields to Greenbacks," *New York Times*, June 21, 2008.

5. Terry Dickson, "Glynn will receive $25 million from LCP suit settlement," *Florida Times-Union*, November 23, 2006, http://jacksonville.com/tu-online/stories/112306/geo_6413224.shtml.

6. U.S. Environmental Protection Agency, "About Brownfields," http://epa.gov/brownfields/about.htm.

7. "Phytoremediation: Using Plants to Clean Up Soils," *Agricultural Research*, June 2000, http://www.ars.usda.gov/is/ar/archive/jun00/soil0600.htm.

8. NC State University, "Planting Seeds for Soil Cleanup," *Results* VI, no. 1 (Winter 2006), http://www.ncsu.edu/research/results/vol11/2.html.

Chapter Twenty: Forging a New Path

1. Alvin Toffler, *The Third Wave* (New York: Bantam, 1984), 212.

2. Toffler, *The Third Wave*, 213.

3. Jennifer Viegas, "Chair Made from Recycled Hair," Discovery News, December 14, 2006, http://dsc.discovery.com/news/2006/12/14/hairchair_hum.html?category=human.

4. "BP Agrees to Purchase 32 of Actor Kevin Costner's Centrifugal Oil and Water Separating Machines," Timelines.com, June 12, 2010, http://timelines.com/2010/6/12/bp-agrees-to-purchase-32-of-actor-kevin-costners-centrifugal-oil-and-water-separating-machines.

5. HAARP website, http://www.haarp.alaska.edu/.

6. Bearden, *Energy from the Vacuum*.

Chapter Twenty-One: Evolution at Risk

1. Bruce H. Lipton, Ph.D., *The Biology of Belief* (Carlsbad, CA: Hay House, 2011).

2. "War Against Women," *60 Minutes*, August 17, 2008, http://www.cbsnews.com/stories/2008/01/11/60minutes/main3701249.shtml.